Evil and the Hiddenness of God

MICHAEL REA
University of Notre Dame

CENGAGE
Learning®

Australia • Brazil • Mexico • Singapore • United Kingdom • United States

CENGAGE
Learning

Evil and the Hiddenness of God
Michael Rea

Product Director: Suzanne Jeans

Product Manager: Debra Matteson

Content Developer: Ian Lague

Content Coordinator: Joshua Duncan

Media Developer: Phil Lanza

Associate Marketing Manager: Shanna Shelton

Content Project Manager: Alison Eigel Zade

Art Director: Kristina Mose-Libon, PMG

Manufacturing Planner: Sandee Milewski

Rights Acquisition Specialist: Roberta Broyer

Production Service & Compositor: Cenveo® Publisher Services

Cover Designer: PreMediaGlobal

Cover Image: © Danita Delimont/Gallo Images/Getty Images

For product information and technology assistance, contact us at **Cengage Learning Customer & Sales Support, 1-800-354-9706**

For permission to use material from this text or product, submit all requests online at **www.cengage.com/permissions**.
Further permissions questions can be emailed to **permissionrequest@cengage.com**.

Library of Congress Control Number: 2013952677

ISBN-13: 978-1-285-19735-7

ISBN-10: 1-285-19735-6

Cengage Learning
200 First Stamford Place, 4th Floor
Stamford, CT 06902
USA

Cengage Learning is a leading provider of customized learning solutions with office locations around the globe, including Singapore, the United Kingdom, Australia, Mexico, Brazil and Japan. Locate your local office at **international.cengage.com/region**.

Cengage Learning products are represented in Canada by Nelson Education, Ltd.

For your course and learning solutions, visit **www.cengage.com**.

Purchase any of our products at your local college store or at our preferred online store **www.cengagebrain.com**.

Instructors: Please visit **login.cengage.com** and log in to access instructor-specific resources.

Printed in the United States of America
1 2 3 4 5 6 7 17 16 15 14 13

Contents

PREFACE   v
GENERAL INTRODUCTION   1

Historical and Literary Perspectives   4

1   *The Argument from Evil*   5
    David Hume

2   *Theodicy: A Defense of Theism*   10
    Gottfried Leibniz

3   *Rebellion*   16
    Fyodor Dostoevsky

4   *The Ones Who Walk Away from Omelas*   23
    Ursula K. LeGuin

The Problems of Evil and Divine Hiddenness   27

5   *Evil and Omnipotence*   29
    J. L. Mackie

6   *The Inductive Argument from Evil against the Existence of God*   37
    William Rowe

7   *Evolution and the Problem of Evil*   44
    Paul Draper

8   *Whose Problem Is the "Problem of Evil"?*   56
    Grace M. Jantzen

9   *Divine Hiddenness Justifies Atheism*   61
    J. L. Schellenberg

Responses   71

10   *The Free Will Defense*   73
Alvin Plantinga

11   *Evil and Soul-Making*   92
John Hick

12   *Epistemic Humility, Arguments from Evil, and Moral Skepticism*   97
Daniel Howard-Snyder

13   *The Problem of Evil and the Desires of the Heart*   111
Eleonore Stump

14   *Horrendous Evils and the Goodness of God*   124
Marilyn McCord Adams

15   *Suffering as Religious Experience*   133
Laura Waddell Ekstrom

16   *Deus Absconditus*   142
Michael J. Murray

17   *Divine Hiddenness, Divine Silence*   156
Michael Rea

INDEX   166

Preface

The book of Job, from the collection of writings that comprise the Hebrew Bible and the Christian Old Testament, is probably the most well-known text in Western religion and literature dealing with the problem of evil—the manifest tension between the claim that the world is governed by a perfectly powerful and loving creator and the all too unavoidable fact that our world is filled with pain and suffering. In the form in which we have it, the book of Job looks to be the perfect vehicle for providing a response to this problem. The prologue in heaven tells us that Job is blameless. But Job is afflicted anyway—and horribly so. His friends tell him that his afflictions must be due to his own sins. Job insists not, and ultimately demands a hearing before God. And then . . . God speaks from the whirlwind.

Far from answering the problem of evil, the divine speeches in Job only seem to make it more vexing. "Brace yourself like a man," says God from the whirlwind. "I will question you, and you will answer me." Following this stern imperative, God recounts for Job a tale of divine power and care for creation. Job sees God in a way in which no one has ever seen God. But he gets no explanation for his afflictions. Job's response, furthermore, is ambiguous. "Before, I had only heard of you. Now I have seen you. Therefore . . ." What? The word that follows means, literally, "I reject."[1] Reject what? Most commentators think that Job rejects something about himself. He repents. He recants. He despises himself. Standard translations reflect these lines of interpretation. But some commentators think that Job rejects God—indeed, they think that what is conveyed here is Job's utter loathing toward God.[2] Job questioned the justice of God; God responded with a display of power. Job's conclusion (on this way of interpreting the passage) is that God is unjust and not to be worshipped; indeed, "God" is no *true* God at all.

Only a minority of commentators attribute to Job the impious response just described. But however impious it may be—and however crazy it might seem to rebel openly against a supernatural being speaking to you from a whirlwind—the response is understandable. For religious believers who have no explanations of their own to offer as to why a perfectly powerful and loving God might be justified in permitting the manifold sufferings we find in this world, a hard question looms. Why *not* take the impious response? What entitles us to persist in the belief that the universe is superintended by a *just and loving* God in the face of what many take to be overwhelming evidence to the contrary? Even if we are convinced for other reasons that

---

[1] Samuel E. Balentine, *Job* (Macon, GA: Smyth & Helwys, 2006), 694–5. (Thanks to C. L. Brinks for the reference.)
[2] J. B. Curtis, "On Job's Response to Yahweh," *Journal of Biblical Literature* 98 (1979): 503–4; cited in Balentine, *op. cit.*, 695.

the universe must have a very powerful supernatural creator, shouldn't we stand against the evils of this world—even if it means denouncing God in the process? Doesn't our moral integrity demand this of us?

It is now fashionable in some quarters simply to dismiss the philosophical problem of evil as a mere philosophers' conundrum. The *real* problem of evil, some insist, is simply that evil is *bad* and needs to be dealt with. Philosophers' puzzles about how evil can coexist with a perfect being are quite beside the point. Indeed, some go so far as to say that philosophical efforts to address the problem of evil are crass, trivializing evil by treating it as a mere puzzle for religious belief. The tacit accusation is that those spending their time reflecting on the philosophical problem of evil are not behaving with moral integrity; they should be reflecting instead on what God has done about evil and what God expects *us* to do about evil. But the rhetorical questions in the previous paragraph suggest that moral integrity makes other demands upon us. Ignoring the philosophical problem may call our integrity into question as well. Indeed, not just our moral integrity, but also our intellectual integrity; for we face a further problem that Job ultimately did not face: the problem of the hiddenness of God.

When philosophers talk about divine hiddenness, they usually have in mind the fact that neither direct and unambiguous experience of God nor conclusive evidence of God's existence is widely available. The problem of hiddenness raises many of the same concerns raised by the problem of evil: questions about God's love for human beings, questions about God's goodness, and questions about God's very existence. Indeed, the two problems exacerbate one another. Evil and suffering would be far more endurable if experience of God's love and comforting presence were available in the midst of it; the hiddenness of God would seem less problematic if we were not constantly confronted by evils that make us wonder why God does not *show up* more often to intervene.

As one might expect, historical and contemporary discussions of both problems have produced a wide range of responses to the question of how religious believers can rationally and morally maintain belief in and devotion to God in the face of evils of the sort that we find in our world and in the face of persistent divine hiddenness. Many, of course, think that these responses fail and have sought to sharpen their formulation of the problems in light of them; others, however, think that the theistic responses ultimately succeed and have sought to give them the most rigorous defense possible. In selecting readings for this volume, I have made every effort to do justice to both sides of these discussions.

Although I am listed as the sole editor of this present volume, the contents herein (apart from this preface) are extracted from a larger volume, now in its 7th edition, of which the late Louis Pojman is the co-editor. That volume, *Philosophy of Religion: An Anthology*, has been in print for over two decades and has become a standard text for use in introductory courses in the philosophy of religion. My own involvement with that volume began with the 5th edition, and I am grateful for the opportunities I have had to shape its development.

In preparing this reader, I have received help from a number of people. In particular, I would like to thank Joann Kozyrev and Ian Lague at Cengage Learning for encouraging the project and for their helpful advice and support along the way, Kathryn Pogin and Meg Schmitt for valuable assistance in finding some of the readings that have been incorporated here, and Stacey Dong and Meg Schmitt for help in clearing the permissions. Thanks are also due various friends and family members who have, in one way or another influenced my thinking about the issues treated in this book and inspired me to want to learn how to make those issues more accessible to others: Darci (Cadis) Bradbury, Megan (Cadis) Hudzinski, Robert Timm, Tracy Peck, Kevin McClure, Mark Rodriguez, and Marc Bellaart; my sister, Cheryl Marzano; my children, Aaron, Kristina, Gretchen, Matthias, and Penelope Rea; and my wife, Chris.

Michael C. Rea
University of Notre Dame
South Bend, Indiana

General Introduction

Is he willing to prevent evil, but not able? then is he impotent.
Is he able, but not willing? then is he malevolent. Is he both
able and willing? whence then is evil?

EPICURUS (341–270 B.C.E.)

Lord my God, who am I that You should forsake me? . . . I call,
I cling, I want—and there is no One to answer—no One on
Whom I can cling—no, No One.—Alone. . . . What are You
doing my God to one so small?

MOTHER TERESA (1910–1997)

The problem of evil arises from the apparent tension between the divine attributes of omnipotence, omniscience, and omnibenevolence on the one hand and the existence of evil on the other. The Judeo-Christian tradition has affirmed each of the following propositions:

1. God is all-powerful.
2. God is all-knowing.
3. God is perfectly good.
4. Evil exists.

Generally, Western thought has distinguished between two types of evil: moral and natural. *Moral evil* covers all those bad things for which creatures are morally responsible. *Natural evil* includes those terrible events that occur in nature of their own accord, such as hurricanes, tornadoes, earthquakes, volcanic eruptions, natural diseases, and so on, that cause suffering to humans and animals. Evil of both kinds, obviously, is prevalent in our world. But if God is perfectly good, it seems that God would not want evil to exist. Being omniscient, God must surely know what potentials for evil lurk in the world and what evils will arise apart from divine intervention. Being omnipotent, God could prevent any evil that God knows about and wants to prevent. So, then, why does our world contain so much evil? Indeed, why does it contain any evil at all? It seems that the existence of God logically precludes the existence of evil, and vice versa.

The problem of divine hiddenness is related to the problem of evil in that it focuses on what seems to be a particular and prevalent instance of evil—the hiddenness of God—and mounts an argument for the nonexistence of God on the basis of that. When people talk about the hiddenness of God, they usually have in mind at least this phenomenon: the evidence for God's existence and its distribution among human beings is such that it is possible for a reasonable person *not* to believe in God. The problem, in short, is as follows. In the theistic traditions God is understood to be perfectly loving, perfectly powerful, and perfectly knowledgeable. Now, if God exists, a relationship with God is a great good—indeed, the highest good—for human beings; and if God is perfectly knowledgeable, God will know this fact. Furthermore, if God is perfectly loving, God will do whatever God can do to ensure that human beings can attain their highest good. But having a relationship with God requires believing in God. Thus, if God loves us, God will (if God is able) see to it that there is enough evidence for God's existence distributed widely enough throughout the world that *nobody* can reasonably fail to believe in God at any time. And, of course, if God is perfectly powerful, God is able to do this. But God has *not* done this—reasonable nonbelief occurs. Therefore, God does not exist.

Theists sometimes respond to these problems with what are known in the literature as defenses; other times they respond with an attempt at theodicy. A *theodicy* is a theory whose aim is to explain why God in fact permits evil; a *defense* is simply a demonstration of consistency—an effort to show that there is no formal contradiction between the existence of God on the one hand and the existence of evil or the phenomenon of divine hiddenness on the other. The difference is that one can offer a defense without affirming the details, and so without really offering a theory about why God permits evil. For example: You are told that the defendant's fingerprints were found on the gun, and security cameras in an outside room place him at the scene of the crime within five minutes of when the crime took place. If (as is unlikely) your goal is simply to show that the evidence is logically consistent with the defendant's innocence, you might say, "Well, for all we know, he walked in, saw the crime being committed, went over and handled the gun right afterward, and then departed without calling the police." You probably won't believe this story, and you might even go on to qualify it by saying something like, "Of course, I really doubt that that's what happened; but my point is just that it's *possible*." But that does not matter if your goal is simply to demonstrate consistency. This is analogous to a defense. If, on the other hand, you tried to offer a theory explaining the evidence in a way consistent with the defendant's innocence—perhaps, say, a story, complete with suspects, motives and opportunities, according to which the defendant was framed, and which you were proposing for us actually to believe—you would be giving something analogous to a theodicy.

One important defense of theism in response to the problem of evil is the free will defense, going back as far as St. Augustine (354–430 C.E.) and receiving modern treatment in the work of John Hick, Alvin Plantinga, and Richard Swinburne. The free will defense maintains that the existence of evil is consistent with the existence of an all powerful, perfectly loving, and knowledgeable God because (a) it is impossible even for an omnipotent being to create free creatures and *guarantee* that they will never do evil, and (b) for all we know, freedom might be a great enough good that God is justified in permitting evil in order to make room for freedom. A similar defense has been mounted in response to the problem of divine hiddenness.

Another response to both problems—sometimes set forth as a theodicy, other times set forth as a mere defense—cites the value of evil and divine hiddenness for "soul-making." This response trades on the familiar idea that character is built through suffering of various kinds. Indeed, suffering and other forms of evil appear to be necessary conditions for the manifestation of certain kinds of virtuous traits. One can manifest courage, for example, only in the face of danger; one can manifest compassion for the poor only if there are some poor to whom one can be compassionate; one can manifest perseverance in seeking after God only if God is to some extent difficult to find; and so on. Moreover, in human beings anyway, it appears that having opportunities to manifest such virtues is an important means of cultivating and developing them—so that one could not even *become* courageous or compassionate or persistent in seeking God unless there were danger, poverty, and divine hiddenness in the world. Then again, one might note that *God* managed to be good and virtuous before there was ever evil and suffering in the world; and so one might well wonder why God could not have created human beings with the same sort of goodness and virtue while at the same time locating us in a world free from evil.

Both of the responses just given argue, in effect, that there are *goods we know of*—freedom, or soul-making, for example—that might well justify God in permitting evil and divine hiddenness in our world. Atheists, however, often press the point that *no good we know of* seems adequate to justify horrendous evils like the holocaust, or the brutal mistreatment of innocent children. Given this, say the atheists, the existence of such evils counts as strong evidence against the existence of God. Even if the existence of evil or divine hiddenness is not absolutely inconsistent with God's existence, the fact that there are so many evils that seemingly cannot be justified by any known good at least renders very probable the hypothesis that God does not exist.

In response, many theists have adopted a strategy known as "skeptical theism"—skeptical because it expresses skepticism about the extent of our grasp of possible goods and evils and relations among them. According to the skeptical theist, it simply does not matter that no good we know of seems to be sufficient to justify permitting the evils that plague our world. For our understanding of good and evil and of the ways in which evils might lead to goods is miniscule in comparison with the understanding that would be possessed by an *omniscient* and *morally perfect* being. So, says the skeptical theist, our inability to see how any good might possibly justify God in permitting horrendous evil or widespread divine hiddenness is only to be expected given the small, self-centered brains with which we have to work.

There are, of course, other strategies and perspectives to be considered as well, many of which are captured in the readings that follow. We begin our treatment of the problems of evil and divine hiddenness in the first section with four important and widely discussed historical and literary treatments of the problem of evil. In the second section, we examine several contemporary formulations. Finally, in the third section, we look at responses.

HISTORICAL AND LITERARY PERSPECTIVES

Introduction

IN THE FIRST READING, "The Argument from Evil," David Hume argues through his persona Philo that the existence of God is called into doubt not just by the mere existence of evil, but by the enormous amount of evil in the world. It is arguable that there is actually more evil than good in the world, and it is hard to reconcile this fact with the existence of an all-powerful, omnibenevolent deity.

In the second reading, "Theodicy: A Defense of Theism," Gottfried Leibniz (1646–1716) argues that the fact of evil in no way refutes theism, and he answers the kinds of objections raised by Hume. He contends that God permitted evil to exist in order to bring about greater goods and that Adam's fall was a *felix culpa* ("blessed fault") because it led to the incarnation of the Son of God, raising humanity to an ultimately higher destiny. Leibniz's response to the problem of evil also includes the idea that, as the creation of a perfectly good God, our world must be the best of all possible worlds.

In the third reading—the famous "Rebellion" chapter from Dostoevsky's *The Brothers Karamazov*—we find a poignant response to the Leibnizian idea that God is justified in permitting evil in order to bring about greater goods. The troubled Ivan Karamazov angrily describes cases of horrendous suffering on the part of children and then challenges his religious brother Alyosha to say whether, if *he* were the architect of the universe, he could bring himself to permit such suffering in order to bring about global happiness. The expected answer is "No"; and that is precisely the answer that Alyosha sadly gives.

Finally, in the fourth selection, Ursula LeGuin, one of the most important fantasy and science-fiction writers of the twentieth century, tells the story of a fictional utopia, Omelas, where happiness is centrally founded upon the suffering of one small child. All in Omelas are aware of the child's suffering; some come to behold it. What happens when they do? Some come to terms with it. Others—following the path of Ivan Karamazov—become the ones who walk away from Omelas.

1

The Argument from Evil

DAVID HUME

The Scottish empiricist and skeptic David Hume (1771–1776) is one of the most important philosophers who ever lived. Among his most important works are A Treatise on Human Nature, An Enquiry Concerning Human Understanding, *and* Dialogues Concerning Natural Religion *(published posthumously in 1779). In the present selection, Hume argues through his persona Philo that not merely the fact of evil, but the enormous amount of evil, makes it dubious that a deity exists. It is arguable that there is actually more evil than good in the world, so it is hard to see how one can reconcile the existence of evil with the existence of an all-powerful, omnibenevolent deity.*

PART X

It is my opinion, I own, replied Demea, that each man feels, in a manner, the truth of religion within his own breast, and, from a consciousness of his imbecility and misery rather than from any reasoning, is led to seek protection from that Being on whom he and all nature is dependent. So anxious or so tedious are even the best scenes of life that futurity is still the object of all our hopes and fears. We incessantly look forward and endeavour, by prayers, adoration, and sacrifice, to appease those unknown powers whom we find, by experience, so able to afflict and oppress us. Wretched creatures that we are! What resource for us amidst the innumerable ills of life did not religion suggest some methods of atonement, and appease those terrors with which we are incessantly agitated and tormented?

I am indeed persuaded, said Philo, that the best and indeed the only method of bringing everyone to a due sense of religion is by just representations of the misery and wickedness of men. And for that purpose a talent of eloquence and strong imagery is more requisite than that of reasoning and argument. For is it necessary to prove what everyone

feels within himself? It is only necessary to make us feel it, if possible, more intimately and sensibly.

The people, indeed, replied Demea, are sufficiently convinced of this great and melancholy truth. The miseries of life, the unhappiness of man, the general corruptions of our nature, the unsatisfactory enjoyment of pleasures, riches, honours—these phrases have become almost proverbial in all languages. And who can doubt of what all men declare from their own immediate feeling and experience?

In this point, said Philo, the learned are perfectly agreed with the vulgar; and in all letters, *sacred* and *profane*, the topic of human miscry has been insisted on with the most pathetic eloquence that sorrow and melancholy could inspire. The poets, who speak from sentiment, without a system, and whose testimony has therefore the more authority, abound in images of this nature. From Homer down to Dr. Young, the whole inspired tribe have ever been sensible that no other representation of things would suit the feeling and observation of each individual.

As to authorities, replied Demea, you need not seek them. Look round this library of Cleanthes. I shall venture to affirm that, except authors of

Reprinted from David Hume, *Dialogues Concerning Natural Religion* (1979); London: Longmans Green, 1878.

particular sciences, such as chemistry or botany, who have no occasion to treat of human life, there is scarce one of those innumerable writers from whom the sense of human misery has not, in some passage or other, extorted a complaint and confession of it. At least, the chance is entirely on that side; and no one author has ever, so far as I can recollect, been so extravagant as to deny it.

There you must excuse me, said Philo: Leibniz has denied it, and is perhaps the first[1] who ventured upon so bold and paradoxical an opinion; at least, the first who made it essential to his philosophical system.

And by being the first, replied Demea, might he not have been sensible of his error? For is this a subject in which philosophers can propose to make discoveries especially in so late an age? And can any man hope by a simple denial (for the subject scarcely admits of reasoning) to bear down the united testimony of mankind, founded on sense and consciousness?

And why should man, added he, pretend to an exemption from the lot of all other animals? The whole earth, believe me, Philo, is cursed and polluted. A perpetual war is kindled amongst all living creatures. Necessity, hunger, want stimulate the strong and courageous; fear, anxiety, terror agitate the weak and infirm. The first entrance into life gives anguish to the new-born infant and to its wretched parent; weakness, impotence, distress attend each stage of that life, and it is, at last, finished in agony and horror.

Observe, too, says Philo, the curious artifices of nature in order to embitter the life of every living being. The stronger prey upon the weaker and keep them in perpetual terror and anxiety. The weaker, too, in their turn, often prey upon the stronger, and vex and molest them without relaxation. Consider that innumerable race of insects, which either are bred on the body of each animal or, flying about, infix their stings in him. These insects have others still less than themselves which torment them. And thus on each hand, before and behind, above and below, every animal is surrounded with enemies which incessantly seek his misery and destruction.

Man alone, said Demea, seems to be, in part, an exception to this rule. For by combination in society he can easily master lions, tigers, and bears, whose greater strength and agility naturally enable them to prey upon him.

On the contrary, it is here chiefly, cried Philo, that the uniform and equal maxims of nature are most apparent. Man, it is true, can, by combination, surmount all his real enemies and become master of the whole animal creation; but does he not immediately raise up to himself *imaginary* enemies, the demons of his fancy, who haunt him with superstitious terrors and blast every enjoyment of life? His pleasure, as he imagines, becomes in their eyes a crime; his food and repose give them umbrage and offence; his very sleep and dreams furnish new materials to anxious fear; and even death, his refuge from every other ill, presents only the dread of endless and innumerable woes. Nor does the wolf molest more the timid flock than superstition does the anxious breast of wretched mortals.

Besides, consider, Demea: This very society by which we surmount those wild beasts, our natural enemies, what new enemies does it not raise to us? What woe and misery does it not occasion? Man is the greatest enemy of man. Oppression, injustice, contempt, contumely, violence, sedition, war, calumny, treachery, fraud—by these they mutually torment each other, and they would soon dissolve that society which they had formed were it not for the dread of still greater ills which must attend their separation.

But though these external insults, said Demea, from animals, from men, from all the elements, which assault us form a frightful catalogue of woes, they are nothing in comparison of those which arise within ourselves, from the distempered condition of our mind and body. How many lie under the lingering torment of diseases? Hear the pathetic enumeration of the great poet.

> *Intestine stone and ulcer, colic-pangs,*
> *Demoniac frenzy, moping melancholy,*
> *And moon-struck madness, pining atrophy,*
> *Marasmus, and wide-wasting pestilence.*
> *Dire was the tossing, deep the groans: Despair*

Tended the sick, busiest from couch to couch.
And over them triumphant Death his dart
Shook: but delay'd to strike, though oft invok'd
With vows, as their chief good and final hope.[2]

The disorders of the mind, continued Demea, though more secret, are not perhaps less dismal and vexatious. Remorse, shame, anguish, rage, disappointment, anxiety, fear, dejection, despair—who has ever passed through life without cruel inroads from these tormentors? How many have scarcely ever felt any better sensations? Labour and poverty, so abhorred by everyone, are the certain lot of the far greater number; and those few privileged persons who enjoy ease and opulence never reach contentment or true felicity. All the goods of life united would not make a very happy man, but all the ills united would make a wretch indeed; and any one of them almost (and who can be free from every one?), nay, often the absence of one good (and who can possess all?) is sufficient to render life ineligible.

Were a stranger to drop on a sudden into this world, I would show him, as a specimen of its ills, an hospital full of diseases, a prison crowded with malefactors and debtors, a field of battle strewed with carcases, a fleet foundering in the ocean, a nation languishing under tyranny, famine, or pestilence. To turn the gay side of life to him and give him a notion of its pleasures—whither should I conduct him? To a ball, to an opera, to court? He might justly think that I was only showing him a diversity of distress and sorrow.

There is no evading such striking instances, said Philo, but by apologies which still further aggravate the charge. Why have all men, I ask, in all ages, complained incessantly of the miseries of life? ... They have no just reason, says one: these complaints proceed only from their discontented, repining, anxious disposition.... And can there possibly, I reply, be a more certain foundation of misery than such a wretched temper?

But if they were really as unhappy as they pretend, says my antagonist, why do they remain in life? ...

Not satisfied with life, afraid of death—

this is the secret chain, say I, that holds us. We are terrified, not bribed to the continuance of our existence.

It is only a false delicacy, he may insist, which a few refined spirits indulge, and which has spread these complaints among the whole race of mankind.... And what is this delicacy, I ask, which you blame? Is it anything but a greater sensibility to all the pleasures and pains of life? And if the man of a delicate, refined temper, by being so much more alive than the rest of the world, is only so much more unhappy, what judgment must we form in general of human life?

Let men remain at rest, says our adversary, and they will be easy. They are willing artificers of their own misery.... No! reply I: an anxious langour follows their repose; disappointment, vexation, trouble, their activity and ambition.

I can observe something like what you mention in some others, replied Cleanthes, but I confess I feel little or nothing of it in myself, and hope that it is not so common as you represent it.

If you feel not human misery yourself, cried Demea, I congratulate you on so happy a singularity. Others, seemingly the most prosperous, have not been ashamed to vent their complaints in the most melancholy strains. Let us attend to the great, the fortunate emperor, Charles V, when, tired with human grandeur, he resigned all his extensive dominions into the hands of his son. In the last harangue which he made on that memorable occasion, he publicly avowed *that the greatest prosperities which he had ever enjoyed had been mixed with so many adversities that he might truly say he had never enjoyed any satisfaction or contentment.* But did the retired life in which he sought for shelter afford him any greater happiness? If we may credit his son's account, his repentance commenced the very day of his resignation.

Cicero's fortune, from small beginnings, rose to the greatest lustre and renown; yet what pathetic complaints of the ills of life do his familiar letters, as well as philosophical discourses, contain? And suitably to his own experience, he introduces Cato, the great, the fortunate Cato protesting in his old age that had he a new life in his offer he would reject the present.

Ask yourself, ask any of your acquaintance, whether they would live over again the last ten or twenty years of their life. No! but the next twenty, they say, will be better:

And from the dregs of life, hope to receive
What the first sprightly running could not give.[3]

Thus, at last, they find (such is the greatness of human misery, it reconciles even contradictions) that they complain at once of the shortness of life and of its vanity and sorrow.

And is it possible, Cleanthes, said Philo, that after all these reflections, and infinitely more which might be suggested, you can still persevere in your anthropomorphism, and assert the moral attributes of the Deity, his justice, benevolence, mercy, and rectitude, to be of the same nature with these virtues in human creatures? His power, we allow, is infinite; whatever he wills is executed; but neither man nor any other animal is happy; therefore, he does not will their happiness. His wisdom is infinite; he is never mistaken in choosing the means to any end; but the course of nature tends not to human or animal felicity; therefore, it is not established for that purpose. Through the whole compass of human knowledge there are no inferences more certain and infallible than these. In what respect, then, do his benevolence and mercy resemble the benevolence and mercy of men?

Epicurus' old questions are yet unanswered.

Is he willing to prevent evil, but not able? then is he impotent. Is he able, but not willing? then is he malevolent. Is he both able and willing? whence then is evil?

You ascribe, Cleanthes, (and I believe justly) a purpose and intention to nature. But what, I beseech you, is the object of that curious artifice and machinery which she has displayed in all animals—the preservation alone of individuals, and propagation of the species? It seems enough for her purpose, if such a rank be barely upheld in the universe, without any care or concern for the happiness of the members that compose it. No resource for this purpose: no machinery in order merely to give pleasure or ease; no fund of pure joy and contentment; no indulgence without some want or

necessity accompanying it. At least, the few phenomena of this nature are overbalanced by opposite phenomena of still greater importance.

Our sense of music, harmony, and indeed beauty of all kinds, gives satisfaction, without being absolutely necessary to the preservation and propagation of the species. But what racking pains, on the other hand, arise from gouts, gravels, megrims, toothaches, rheumatisms, where the injury to the animal machinery is either small or incurable? Mirth, laughter, play, frolic seem gratuitous satisfactions which have no further tendency; spleen, melancholy, discontent, superstition are pains of the same nature. How then does the Divine benevolence display itself, in the sense of you anthropomorphites? None but we mystics, as you were pleased to call us, can account for this strange mixture of phenomena, by deriving it from attributes infinitely perfect but incomprehensible.

And have you, at last, said Cleanthes smiling, betrayed your intentions, Philo? Your long agreement with Demea did indeed a little surprise me, but I find you were all the while erecting a concealed battery against me. And I must confess that you have now fallen upon a subject worthy of your noble spirit of opposition and controversy. If you can make out the present point, and prove mankind to be unhappy or corrupted, there is an end at once of all religion. For to what purpose establish the natural attributes of the Deity, while the moral are still doubtful and uncertain?

You take umbrage very easily, replied Demea, at opinions the most innocent and the most generally received, even amongst the religious and devout themselves; and nothing can be more surprising than to find a topic like this—concerning the wickedness and misery of man—charged with no less than atheism and profaneness. Have not all pious divines and preachers who have indulged their rhetoric on so fertile a subject, have they not easily, I say, given a solution of any difficulties which may attend it? This world is but a point in comparison of the universe; this life but a moment in comparison of eternity. The present evil phenomena, therefore, are rectified in other regions, and in some future period of existence. And the eyes of men, being then opened to larger views of things, see the whole connection of general laws, and trace, with adoration, the benevolence and rectitude of the Deity through all the mazes and intricacies of his providence.

No! replied Cleanthes, no! These arbitrary suppositions can never be admitted, contrary to matter of fact, visible and uncontroverted. Whence can any cause be known but from its known effects? Whence can any hypothesis be proved but from the apparent phenomena? To establish one hypothesis upon another is building entirely in the air; and the utmost we ever attain by these conjectures and fictions is to ascertain the bare possibility of our opinion, but never can we, upon such terms, establish its reality.

The only method of supporting Divine benevolence—and it is what I willingly embrace—is to deny absolutely the misery and wickedness of man. Your representations are exaggerated; your melancholy views mostly fictitious; your inferences contrary to fact and experience. Health is more common than sickness; pleasure than pain; happiness than misery. And for one vexation which we meet with, we attain, upon computation, a hundred enjoyments.

Admitting your position, replied Philo, which yet is extremely doubtful, you must at the same time allow that, if pain be less frequent than pleasure, it is infinitely more violent and durable. One hour of it is often able to outweigh a day, a week, a month of our common insipid enjoyments; and how many days, weeks, and months are passed by several in the most acute torments? Pleasure, scarcely in one instance, is ever able to reach ecstasy and rapture; and in no one instance can it continue for any time at its highest pitch and altitude. The spirits evaporate, the nerves relax, the fabric is disordered, and the enjoyment quickly degenerates into fatigue and uneasiness. But pain often, good God, how often! rises to torture and agony; and the longer it continues, it becomes still more genuine agony and torture. Patience is exhausted, courage languishes, melancholy seizes us, and nothing terminates our misery but the removal of its cause or another event which is the sole cure of all evil, but which, from our natural folly, we regard with still greater horror and consternation.

But not to insist upon these topics, continued Philo, though most obvious, certain, and important, I must use the freedom to admonish you, Cleanthes, that you have put the controversy upon a most dangerous issue, and are unawares introducing a total scepticism into the most essential articles of natural and revealed theology. What! no method of fixing a just foundation for religion unless we allow the happiness of human life, and maintain a continued existence even in this world, with all our present pains, infirmities, vexations, and follies, to be eligible and desirable! But this is contrary to everyone's feeling and experience; it is contrary to an authority so established as nothing can subvert. No decisive proofs can ever be produced against this authority; nor is it possible for you to compute, estimate, and compare all the pains and all the pleasures in the lives of all men and of all animals; and thus, by your resting the whole system of religion on a point which, from its very nature, must forever be uncertain, you tacitly confess that that system is equally uncertain.

But allowing you what never will be believed, at least, what you never possibly can prove, that animal or, at least, human happiness in this life exceeds its misery, you have yet done nothing; for this is not, by any means, what we expect from infinite power, infinite wisdom, and infinite goodness. Why is there any misery at all in the world? Not by chance, surely. From some cause then. Is it from the intention of the Deity? But he is perfectly benevolent. Is it contrary to his intention? But he is almighty. Nothing can shake the solidity of this reasoning, so short, so clear, so decisive, except we assert that these subjects exceed all human capacity, and that our common measures of truth and falsehood are not applicable to them—a topic which I have all along insisted on, but which you have, from the beginning, rejected with scorn and indignation.

But I will be contented to retire still from this intrenchment, for I deny that you can ever force me in it. I will allow that pain or misery in man is *compatible* with infinite power and goodness in the Deity, even in your sense of these attributes: what are you advanced by all these concessions? A mere possible compatibility is not sufficient. You must prove these pure, unmixed, and uncontrollable attributes from the present mixed and confused phenomena, and from these alone. A hopeful undertaking! Were the phenomena ever so pure and unmixed, yet, being finite, they would be insufficient for that purpose. How much more, where they are also so jarring and discordant!

Here, Cleanthes, I find myself at ease in my argument. Here I triumph. Formerly, when we argued concerning the natural attributes of intelligence and design, I needed all my sceptical and metaphysical subtilty to elude your grasp. In many views of the universe and of its parts, particularly

the latter, the beauty and fitness of final causes strike us with such irresistible force that all objections appear (what I believe they really are) mere cavils and sophisms; nor can we then imagine how it was ever possible for us to repose any weight on them. But there is no view of human life or of the condition of mankind from which, without the greatest violence, we can infer the moral attributes or learn that infinite benevolence, conjoined with infinite power and infinite wisdom, which we must discover by the eyes of faith alone. It is your turn now to tug the labouring oar, and to support your philosophical subtilties against the dictates of plain reason and experience.

NOTES

1. That sentiment had been maintained by Dr. King and some few others before Leibniz, though by none of so great fame as that German philosopher.

2. Milton: *Paradise Lost,* Bk. XI.

3. John Dryden, *Aureng-Zebe*, Act IV, sc. 1.

2

Theodicy: A Defense of Theism

GOTTFRIED LEIBNIZ

Gottfried Wilhelm Leibniz (1646–1716) was a German idealist who tried to set forth a thorough-going theodicy, a justification of the ways of God. In this selection he argues that the fact of evil in no way refutes theism, and he answers the kinds of objections raised by Hume. He contends that God permitted evil to exist in order to bring about greater good and that Adam's fall was a felix culpa (a "blessed fault") because it led to the incarnation of the Son of God, raising humanity to an ultimately higher destiny. He argues that although God can foresee the future, humans are still free in that they act voluntarily.

Reprinted from Gottfried Leibniz, *The Theodicy: Abridgement of the Argument Reduced to Syllogistic Form* (1710) in *The Philosophical Works of Leibniz*, ed. & trans. by G. M. Duncan (New Haven: Tuttle, Morehouse, & Taylor, 1890).

Some intelligent persons have desired that this supplement be made [to the Theodicy], and I have the more readily yielded to their wishes as in this way I have an opportunity again to remove certain difficulties and to make some observations which were not sufficiently emphasized in the work itself.

I. Objection.   Whoever does not choose the best is lacking in power, or in knowledge, or in goodness.

God did not choose the best in creating this world.

Therefore, God has been lacking in power, or in knowledge, or in goodness.

Answer. I deny the minor, that is, the second premise of this syllogism; and our opponent proves it by this.

Prosyllogism. Whoever makes things in which there is evil, which could have been made without any evil, or the making of which could have been omitted, does not choose the best.

God has made a world in which there is evil; a world, I say, which could have been made without any evil, or the making of which could have been omitted altogether.

Therefore, God has not chosen the best.

Answer. I grant the minor of this prosyllogism; for it must be confessed that there is evil in this world which God has made, and that it was possible to make a world without evil, or even not to create a world at all, for its creation has depended on the free will of God; but I deny the major, that is, the first of the two premises of the prosyllogism, and I might content myself with simply demanding its proof; but in order to make the matter clearer, I have wished to justify this denial by showing that the best plan is not always that which seeks to avoid evil, since it may happen that *the evil is accompanied by a greater good*. For example, a general of an army will prefer a great victory with a slight wound to a condition without wound and without victory. We have proved this more fully in the large work by making it clear, by instances taken from mathematics and elsewhere, that an imperfection in the part may be required for a greater perfection in the whole. In this I have followed the opinion of St. Augustine, who has said a hundred times, that God has permitted evil

in order to bring about good, that is, a greater good; and that of Thomas Aquinas (in libr. II. sent. dist. 32, qu. I, art. 1), that the permitting of evil tends to the good of the universe. I have shown that the ancients called Adam's fall *felix culpa*, a happy sin, because it had been retrieved with immense advantage by the incarnation of the Son of God, who has given to the universe something nobler than anything that ever would have been among creatures except for it. For the sake of a clearer understanding, I have added, following many good authors, that it was in accordance with order and the general good that God allowed to certain creatures the opportunity of exercising their liberty, even when he foresaw that they would turn to evil, but which he could so well rectify; because it was not fitting that, in order to hinder sin, God should always act in an extraordinary manner. To overthrow this objection, therefore, it is sufficient to show that a world with evil might be better than a world without evil; but I have gone even farther, in the work, and have even proved that this universe must be in reality better than every other possible universe.

II. Objection.   If there is more evil than good in intelligent creatures, then there is more evil than good in the whole work of God.

Now, there is more evil than good in intelligent creatures.

Therefore, there is more evil than good in the whole work of God.

Answer. I deny the major and the minor of this conditional syllogism. As to the major, I do not admit it at all, because this pretended deduction from a part to the whole, from intelligent creatures to all creatures, supposes tacitly and without proof that creatures destitute of reason cannot enter into comparison nor into account with those which possess it. But why may it not be that the surplus of good in the non-intelligent creatures which fill the world, compensates for, and even incomparably surpasses, the surplus of evil in the rational creatures? It is true that the value of the latter is greater; but, in compensation, the others are beyond comparison the more numerous, and it may be that the proportion of number and quantity surpasses that of value and of quality.

As to the minor, that is no more to be admitted; that is, it is not at all to be admitted that there is more evil than good in the intelligent creatures. There is no need even of granting that there is more evil than good in the human race, because it is possible, and in fact very probable, that the glory and the perfection of the blessed are incomparably greater than the misery and the imperfection of the damned, and that here the excellence of the total good in the smaller number exceeds the total evil in the greater number. The blessed approach the Divinity, by means of a Divine Mediator, as near as may suit these creatures, and make such progress in good as is impossible for the damned to make in evil, approach as nearly as they may to the nature of demons. God is infinite, and the devil is limited; the good may and does go to infinity, while evil has its bounds. It is therefore possible, and is credible, that in the comparison of the blessed and the damned, the contrary of that which I have said might happen in the comparison of intelligent and non-intelligent creatures, takes place; namely, it is possible that in the comparison of the happy and the unhappy, the proportion of degree exceeds that of number, and that in the comparison of intelligent and non-intelligent creatures, the proportion of number is greater than that of value. I have the right to suppose that a thing is possible so long as its impossibility is not proved; and indeed that which I have here advanced is more than a supposition.

But in the second place, if I should admit that there is more evil than good in the human race, I have still good grounds for not admitting that there is more evil than good in all intelligent creatures. For there is an inconceivable number of genii, and perhaps of other rational creatures. And an opponent could not prove that in all the City of God, composed as well of genii as of rational animals without number and of an infinity of kinds, evil exceeds good. And although in order to answer an objection, there is no need of proving that a thing is, when its mere possibility suffices; yet, in this work, I have not omitted to show that it is a consequence of the supreme perfection of the Sovereign of the universe, that the kingdom of God is the most perfect of all possible states or governments, and that consequently the little evil there is, is required for the consummation of the immense good which is found there.

III. Objection.   If it is always impossible not to sin, it is always unjust to punish.

Now, it is always impossible not to sin; or, in other words, every sin is necessary.

Therefore, it is always unjust to punish.

The minor of this is proved thus:

1. *Prosyllogism.* All that is predetermined is necessary.

   Every event is predetermined.

   Therefore, every event (and consequently sin also) is necessary.

   Again this second minor is proved thus:

2. *Prosyllogism.* That which is future, that which is foreseen, that which is involved in the causes, is predetermined.

   Every event is such.

   Therefore, every event is predetermined.

Answer. I admit in a certain sense the conclusion of the second prosyllogism, which is the minor of the first; but I shall deny the major of the first prosyllogism, namely, that every thing predetermined is necessary; understanding by the *necessity* of sinning, for example, or by the impossibility of not sinning, or of not performing any action, the necessity with which we are here concerned, that is, that which is essential and absolute, and which destroys the morality of an action and the justice of punishments. For if anyone understood another necessity or impossibility, namely, a necessity which should be only moral, or which was only hypothetical (as will be explained shortly); it is clear that I should deny the major of the objection itself. I might content myself with this answer and demand the proof of the proposition denied; but I have again desired to explain my procedure in this work, in order to better elucidate the matter and to throw more light on the whole subject, by explaining the necessity which ought to be rejected and the determination which must take place. That *necessity* which is contrary to morality and which ought to be rejected, and which would render punishment unjust, is an insurmountable necessity which would make all opposition useless, even if we should wish with all our heart to avoid the necessary action, and should make all possible efforts to that end. Now, it is manifest that this is not applicable to voluntary actions, because we would not perform them if we did not choose to. Also their prevision and predetermination are not absolute, but presuppose the will: if it is certain that we shall perform them, it is not less certain that we shall choose to perform them. These voluntary actions and their consequences will not take place no matter what we do or whether we wish them or not; but, *through* that which we shall do and through that which we shall wish to do, which leads to them. And this is involved in prevision and in predetermination, and even constitutes their ground. And the necessity of such an event is called conditional or hypothetical, or the necessity of consequence, because it supposes the will, and the other *requisites*; whereas the necessity which destroys morality and renders punishment unjust and reward useless, exists in things which will be whatever we may do or whatever we may wish to do, and, in a word, is in that which is essential; and this is what is called an absolute necessity. Thus it is to no purpose, as regards what is absolutely necessary, to make prohibitions or commands, to propose penalties or prizes, to praise or to blame; it will be none the less. On the other hand, in voluntary actions and in that which depends upon them, precepts armed with power to punish and to recompense are very often of use and are included in the order of causes which make an action exist. And it is for this reason that not only cares and labors but also prayers are useful; God having had these prayers in view before he regulated things and having had that consideration for them which was proper. This is why the precept which says *ora et labora* (pray and work), holds altogether good; and not only those who (under the vain pretext of the necessity of events) pretend that the care which business demands may be neglected, but also those who reason against prayer, fall into what the ancients even then called the *lazy sophism*. Thus the predetermination of events by causes is just what contributes to morality instead of destroying it, and causes incline the will, without compelling it. This is why the

determination in question is not a necessitation—it is certain (to him who knows all) that the effect will follow this inclination; but this effect does not follow by a necessary consequence, that is, one the contrary of which implies contradiction. It is also by an internal inclination such as this that the will is determined, without there being any necessity. Suppose that one has the greatest passion in the world (a great thirst, for example), you will admit to me that the soul can find some reason for resisting it, if it were only that of showing its power. Thus, although one may never be in a perfect indifference of equilibrium and there may be always a preponderance of inclination for the side taken, it, nevertheless, never renders the resolution taken absolutely necessary.

IV. *Objection.* Whoever can prevent the sin of another and does not do so, but rather contributes to it although he is well informed of it, is accessory to it.

God can prevent the sin of intelligent creatures; but he does not do so, and rather contributes to it by his concurrence and by the opportunities which he brings about, although he has a perfect knowledge of it.

Hence, etc.

Answer. I deny the major of this syllogism. For it is possible that one could prevent sin, but ought not, because he could not do it without himself committing a sin, or (when God is in question) without performing an unreasonable action. Examples have been given and the application to God himself has been made. It is possible also that we contribute to evil and that sometimes we even open the road to it, in doing things which we are obliged to do; and, when we do our duty or (in speaking of God) when, after thorough consideration, we do that which reason demands, we are not responsible for the results, even when we foresee them. We do not desire these evils; but we are willing to permit them for the sake of a greater good which we cannot reasonably help preferring to other considerations. And this is a *consequent* will, which results from *antecedent* wills by which we will the good. I know that some persons, in speaking of the antecedent and consequent will of God, have understood by the *antecedent* that which wills that all men should be saved; and by the consequent, that which wills, in consequence of persistent sin, that some should be damned. But these are merely illustrations of a more general idea, and it may be said for the same reason that God, by his antecedent will, wills that men should not sin; and by his consequent or final and decreeing will (that which is always followed by its effect), he wills to permit them to sin, this permission being the result of superior reasons. And we have the right to say in general that the antecedent will of God tends to the production of good and the prevention of evil, each taken in itself and as if alone (*particulariter et secundum quid*, Thom. I, qu. 19, art. 6), according to the measure of the degree of each good and each evil; but that the divine consequent or final or total will tends toward the production of as many goods as may be put together, the combination of which becomes in this way determined, and includes also the permission of some evils and the exclusion of some goods, as the best possible plan for the universe demands. Arminius, in his *Antiperkinsus*, has very well explained that the will of God may be called consequent, not only in relation to the action of the creature considered beforehand in the divine understanding, but also in relation to other anterior divine acts of will. But this consideration of the passage cited from Thomas Aquinas, and that from Scotus (I. dist. 46, qu. XI), is enough to show that they make this distinction as I have done here. Nevertheless, if anyone objects to this use of terms let him substitute *deliberating* will, in place of antecedent, and final or decreeing will, in place of consequent. For I do not wish to dispute over words.

V. Objection. Whoever produces all that is real in a thing, is its cause.

God produces all that is real in sin.

Hence, God is the cause of sin.

Answer. I might content myself with denying the major or the minor, since the term real admits of interpretations which would render these propositions false. But in order to explain more clearly, I will make a distinction. *Real* signifies either that which is positive only, or, it includes also privative beings: in the first case, I deny the major and admit

the minor; in the second case, I do the contrary. I might have limited myself to this, but I have chosen to proceed still farther and give the reason for this distinction. I have been very glad therefore to draw attention to the fact that every reality purely positive or absolute is a perfection; and that imperfection comes from limitation, that is, from the privative: for to limit is to refuse progress, or the greatest possible progress. Now God is the cause of all perfections and consequently of all realities considered as purely positive. But limitations or privations result from the original imperfection of creatures, which limits their receptivity. And it is with them as with a loaded vessel, which the river causes to move more or less slowly according to the weight which it carries: thus its speed depends upon the river, but the retardation which limits this speed comes from the load. Thus in the *Theodicy*, we have shown how the creature, in causing sin, is a defective cause; how errors and evil inclinations are born of privation; and how privation is accidentally efficient; and I have justified the opinion of St. Augustine (lib. I, ad Simpl. qu. 2) who explains, for example, how God makes the soul obdurate, not by giving it something evil, but because the effect of his good impression is limited by the soul's resistance and by the circumstances which contribute to this resistance, so that he does not give it all the good which would overcome its evil. *Nec (inquit) ab illo erogatur aliquid quo homo fit deterior, sed tantum quo fit melior non erogatur.* But if God had wished to do more, he would have had to make either other natures for creatures or other miracles to change their natures, things which the best plan could not admit. It is as if the current of the river must be more rapid than its fall admitted or that the boats should be loaded more lightly, if it were necessary to make them move more quickly. And the original limitation or imperfection of creatures requires that even the best plan of the universe could not receive more good, and could not be exempt from certain evils, which, however, are to result in a greater good. There are certain disorders in the parts which marvelously enhance the beauty of the whole; just as certain dissonances, when properly used, render harmony more beautiful. But this depends on what has already been said in answer to the first objection.

VI. Objection. Whoever punishes those who have done as well as it was in their power to do, is unjust.

God does so.

Hence, etc.

Answer. I deny the minor of this argument. And I believe that God always gives sufficient aid and grace to those who have a good will, that is, to those who do not reject this grace by new sin. Thus, I do not admit the damnation of infants who have died without baptism or outside of the church; nor the damnation of adults who have acted according to the light which God has given them. And I believe that if *any one has followed the light which has been given him*, he will undoubtedly receive greater light when he has need of it, as the late M. Hulseman, a profound and celebrated theologian at Leipzig, has somewhere remarked; and if such a man has failed to receive it during his lifetime he will at least receive it when at the point of death.

VII. Objection. Whoever gives only to some, and not to all, the means which produces in them effectively a good will and salutary final faith, has not sufficient goodness.

God does this.

Hence, etc.

Answer. I deny the major of this. It is true that God could overcome the greatest resistance of the human heart; and does it, too, sometimes, either by internal grace, or by external circumstances which have a great effect on souls; but he does not always do this. Whence comes this distinction? it may be asked, and why does his goodness seem limited? It is because, as I have already said in answering the first objection, it would not have been in order always to act in an extraordinary manner, and to reverse the connection of things. The reasons of this connection, by means of which one is placed in more favorable circumstances than another, are hidden in the depths of the wisdom of God; they depend upon the universal harmony. The best plan of the universe, which God could not fail to choose, made

it so. We judge from the event itself; since God has made it, it was not possible to do better. Far from being true that this conduct is contrary to goodness, it is supreme goodness which led him to it. This objection with its solution might have been drawn from what was said in regard to the first objection; but it seemed useful to touch upon it separately.

VIII. Objection. Whoever cannot fail to choose the best, is not free.

God cannot fail to choose the best.

Hence, God is not free.

Answer. I deny the major of this argument; it is rather true liberty, and the most perfect, to be able to use one's free will for the best, and to always exercise this power, without ever being turned aside either by external force or by internal passions, the first of which causes slavery of the body, the second, slavery of the soul. There is nothing less servile, and nothing more in accordance with the highest degree of freedom, than to be always led toward the good, and always by one's own inclination, without any constraint and without any displeasure. And to object therefore that God had need of external things, is only a sophism. He created them freely; but having proposed to himself an end, which is to exercise his goodness, wisdom has determined him to choose the means best fitted to attain this end. To call this a need, is to take that term in an unusual sense which frees it from all imperfection, just as when we speak of the wrath of God.

Seneca has somewhere said that God commanded but once but that he obeys always, because he obeys laws which he willed to prescribe to himself: *semel jussit, semper paret.* But he might better have said that God always commands and that he is always obeyed; for in willing, he always follows the inclination of his own nature, and all other things always follow his will. And as this will is always the same, it cannot be said that he obeys only that will which he formerly had. Nevertheless, although his will is always infallible and always tends toward the best, the evil, or the lesser good, which he rejects, does not cease to be possible in itself; otherwise the necessity of the good would be geometrical (so to speak), or metaphysical, and altogether absolute; the contingency of things would be destroyed, and there would be no choice. But this sort of necessity, which does not destroy the possibility of the contrary, has this name only by analogy; it becomes effective, not by the pure essence of things, but by that which is outside of them, above them, namely, by the will of God. This necessity is called moral, because, to the sage, *necessity* and *what ought to be* are equivalent things; and when it always has its effect, as it really has in the perfect sage, that is, in God, it may be said that it is a happy necessity. The nearer creatures approach to it, the nearer they approach to perfect happiness. Also this kind of necessity is not that which we try to avoid and which destroys morality, rewards and praise. For that which it brings, does not happen whatever we may do or will, but because we will it so. And a will to which it is natural to choose well, merits praise so much the more; also it carries its reward with it, which is sovereign happiness. And as this constitution of the divine nature gives entire satisfaction to him who possesses it, it is also the best and the most desirable for the creatures who are all dependent on God. If the will of God did not have for a rule the principle of the best, it would either tend toward evil, which would be the worst; or it would be in some way indifferent to good and to evil, and would be guided by chance: but a will which would allow itself always to act by chance, would not be worth more for the government of the universe than the fortuitous concourse of atoms, without there being any divinity therein. And even if God should abandon himself to chance only in some cases and in a certain way (as he would do, if he did not always work entirely for the best and if he were capable of preferring a lesser work to a greater, that is, an evil to a good, since that which prevents a greater good is an evil), he would be imperfect, as well as the object of his choice; he would not merit entire confidence; he would act without reason in such a case, and the government of the universe would be like certain games, equally divided between reason and chance. All this proves that this objection which is made against the choice of the best, perverts the notions of the free and of the necessary, and represents to us the best even as evil: which is either malicious or ridiculous.

3

Rebellion

FYODOR DOSTOEVSKY

Fyodor Dostoevsky (1821–1881) was one of the greatest and most influential Russian novelists. He is the author of Crime and Punishment, Notes from the Underground, The Gambler, *and* The Brothers Karamazov, *from which the present selection is taken. In this chapter, Ivan Karamazov challenges the idea that some greater good might justify the horrendous suffering of even one small child, much less the vast amounts of such suffering that our world has so far seen.*

"Rebellion," from *The Brothers Karamazov*, by Fyodor Dostoevsky. Trans. Constance Garnett. (New York: The MacMillan Company, 1922).

"I must make you one confession," Ivan began. "I could never understand how one can love one's neighbours. It's just one's neighbours, to my mind, that one can't love, though one might love those at a distance. I once read somewhere of John the Merciful, a saint, that when a hungry, frozen beggar came to him, he took him into his bed, held him in his arms, and began breathing into his mouth, which was putrid and loathsome from some awful disease. I am convinced that he did that from 'self-laceration,' from the self-laceration of falsity, for the sake of the charity imposed by duty, as a penance laid on him. For any one to love a man, he must be hidden, for as soon as he shows his face, love is gone."

"Father Zossima has talked of that more than once," observed Alyosha, "he, too, said that the face of a man often hinders many people not practised in love, from loving him. But yet there's a great deal of love in mankind, and almost Christ-like love. I know that myself, Ivan."

"Well, I know nothing of it so far, and can't understand it, and the innumerable mass of mankind are with me there. The question is, whether that's due to men's bad qualities or whether it's inherent in their nature. To my thinking, Christ-like love for men is a miracle impossible on earth. He was God. But we are not gods. Suppose I, for instance, suffer intensely. Another can never know how much I suffer, because he is another and not I. And what's more, a man is rarely ready to admit another's suffering (as though it were a distinction). Why won't he admit it, do you think? Because I smell unpleasant, because I have a stupid face, because I once trod on his foot. Besides there is suffering and suffering; degrading, humiliating suffering such as humbles me—hunger, for instance,—my benefactor will perhaps allow me; but when you come to higher suffering—for an idea, for instance—he will very rarely admit that, perhaps because my face strikes him as not at all what he fancies a man should have who suffers for an idea. And so he deprives me instantly of his favour, and not at all from badness of heart. Beggars, especially genteel beggars, ought never to show themselves, but to ask for charity through the newspapers. One can

love one's neighbours in the abstract, or even at a distance, but at close quarters it's almost impossible. If it were as on the stage, in the ballet, where if beggars come in, they wear silken rags and tattered lace and beg for alms dancing gracefully, then one might like looking at them. But even then we should not love them. But enough of that. I simply wanted to show you my point of view. I meant to speak of the suffering of mankind generally, but we had better confine ourselves to the sufferings of the children. That reduces the scope of my argument to a tenth of what it would be. Still we'd better keep to the children, though it does weaken my case. But, in the first place, children can be loved even at close quarters, even when they are dirty, even when they are ugly (I fancy, though, children never are ugly). The second reason why I won't speak of grown-up people is that, besides being disgusting and unworthy of love, they have a compensation—they've eaten the apple and know good and evil, and they have become 'like gods.' They go on eating it still. But the children haven't eaten anything, and are so far innocent. Are you fond of children, Alyosha? I know you are, and you will understand why I prefer to speak of them. If they, too, suffer horribly on earth, they must suffer for their fathers' sins, they must be punished for their fathers, who have eaten the apple; but that reasoning is of the other world and is incomprehensible for the heart of man here on earth. The innocent must not suffer for another's sins, and especially such innocents! You may be surprised at me, Alyosha, but I am awfully fond of children, too. And observe, cruel people, the violent, the rapacious, the Karamazovs are sometimes very fond of children. Children while they are quite little—up to seven, for instance—are so remote from grown-up people; they are different creatures, as it were, of a different species. I knew a criminal in prison who had, in the course of his career as a burglar, murdered whole families, including several children. But when he was in prison, he had a strange affection for them. He spent all his time at his window, watching the children playing in the prison yard. He trained one little boy to come up to his window and made great friends with him. . . .

You don't know why I am telling you all this, Alyosha? My head aches and I am sad."

"You speak with a strange air," observed Alyosha uneasily, "as though you were not quite yourself."

"By the way, a Bulgarian I met lately in Moscow," Ivan went on, seeming not to hear his brother's words, "told me about the crimes committed by Turks and Circassians in all parts of Bulgaria through fear of a general rising of the Slavs. They burn villages, murder, outrage women and children, they nail their prisoners by the ears to the fences, leave them so till morning, and in the morning they hang them—all sorts of things you can't imagine. People talk sometimes of bestial cruelty, but that's a great injustice and insult to the beasts; a beast can never be so cruel as a man, so artistically cruel. The tiger only tears and gnaws, that's all he can do. He would never think of nailing people by the ears, even if he were able to do it. These Turks took a pleasure in torturing children, too; cutting the unborn child from the mother's womb, and tossing babies up in the air and catching them on the points of their bayonets before their mother's eyes. Doing it before the mother's eyes was what gave zest to the amusement. Here is another scene that I thought very interesting. Imagine a trembling mother with her baby in her arms, a circle of invading Turks around her. They've planned a diversion; they pet the baby, laugh to make it laugh. They succeed, the baby laughs. At that moment a Turk points a pistol four inches from the baby's face. The baby laughs with glee, holds out its little hands to the pistol, and he pulls the trigger in the baby's face and blows out its brains. Artistic, wasn't it? By the way, Turks are particularly fond of sweet things, they say."

"Brother, what are you driving at?" asked Alyosha.

"I think if the devil doesn't exist, but man has created him, he has created him in his own image and likeness."

"Just as he did God, then?" observed Alyosha.

"'It's wonderful how you can turn words,' as Polonius says in *Hamlet*," laughed Ivan. "You turn my words against me. Well, I am glad. Yours must be a fine God, if man created Him in His image and likeness. You asked just now what I was driving at. You see, I am fond of collecting certain facts, and, would you believe, I even copy anecdotes of a certain sort from newspapers and books, and I've already got a fine collection. The Turks, of course, have gone into it, but they are foreigners. I have specimens from home that are even better than the Turks. You know we prefer beating—rods and scourges—that's our national institution. Nailing ears is unthinkable for us, for we are, after all, Europeans. But the rod and the scourge we have always with us and they cannot be taken from us. Abroad now they scarcely do any beating. Manners are more humane, or laws have been passed, so that they don't dare to flog men now. But they make up for it in another way just as national as ours. And so national that it would be practically impossible among us, though I believe we are being inoculated with it, since the religious movement began in our aristocracy. I have a charming pamphlet, translated from the French, describing how, quite recently, five years ago, a murderer, Richard, was executed—a young man, I believe, of three and twenty, who repented and was converted to the Christian faith at the very scaffold. This Richard was an illegitimate child who was given as a child of six by his parents to some shepherds on the Swiss mountains. They brought him up to work for them. He grew up like a little wild beast among them. The shepherds taught him nothing, and scarcely fed or clothed him, but sent him out at age seven to herd the flock in cold and wet, and no one hesitated or scrupled to treat him so. Quite the contrary, they thought they had every right, for Richard had been given to them as a chattel, and they did not even see the necessity of feeding him. Richard himself describes how in those years, like the Prodigal Son in the Gospel, he longed to eat of the mash given to the pigs, which were fattened for sale. But they wouldn't even give him that, and beat him when he stole from the pigs. And that was how he spent all his childhood and his youth, till he grew up and was strong enough to go away and be a thief. The savage began to earn his living as a day labourer in Geneva. He drank what he earned, he lived like a brute, and finished by killing and robbing an old man. He was caught, tried, and condemned to death. They are not sentimentalists there. And in prison he was immediately surrounded by pastors, members of Christian brotherhoods, philanthropic ladies, and the like. They taught him to read and write in prison, and expounded the Gospel to him. They exhorted him, worked upon him, drummed at him incessantly, till at last he solemnly confessed his crime. He was converted. He wrote to the court himself that he was a monster, but that in the end God had vouchsafed him light and shown grace. All Geneva was in excitement about him—all philanthropic and religious Geneva. All the aristocratic and well-bred society of the town rushed to the prison, kissed Richard and embraced him; 'You are our brother, you have found grace.' And Richard does nothing but weep with emotion, 'Yes, I've found grace! All my youth and childhood I was glad of pigs' food, but now even I have found grace. I am dying in the Lord.' 'Yes, Richard, die in the Lord; you have shed blood and must die. Though it's not your fault that you knew not the Lord, when you coveted the pig's food and were beaten for stealing it (which was very wrong of you, for stealing is forbidden); but you've shed blood and you must die.' And on the last day, Richard, perfectly limp, did nothing but cry and repeat every minute: 'This is my happiest day. I am going to the Lord.' 'Yes,' cry the pastors and the judges and philanthropic ladies. 'This is the happiest day of your life, for you are going to the Lord!' They all walk or drive to the scaffold in procession behind the prison van. At the scaffold they call to Richard: 'Die, brother, die in the Lord, for even thou hast found grace!' And so, covered with his brothers' kisses, Richard is dragged on to the scaffold, and led to the guillotine. And they chopped off his head in brotherly fashion, because he had found grace. Yes, that's characteristic. That pamphlet is translated into Russian by some Russian philanthropists of aristocratic rank and evangelical aspirations, and has been distributed gratis for the enlightenment of the people. The case of Richard is interesting because it's national. Though to us it's absurd to cut off a man's head, because he has become our brother and has found grace, yet we have our own speciality, which is all but worse. Our

historical pastime is the direct satisfaction of inflicting pain. There are lines in Nekrassov describing how a peasant lashes a horse on the eyes, 'on its meek eyes,' every one must have seen it. It's peculiarly Russian. He describes how a feeble little nag has foundered under too heavy a load and cannot move. The peasant beats it, beats it savagely, beats it at last not knowing what he is doing in the intoxication of cruelty, thrashes it mercilessly over and over again. 'However weak you are, you must pull, if you die for it.' The nag strains, and then he begins lashing the poor defenseless creature on its weeping, on its 'meek eyes.' The frantic beast tugs and draws the load, trembling all over, gasping for breath, moving sideways, with a sort of unnatural spasmodic action—it's awful in Nekrassov. But that's only a horse, and God has given horses to be beaten. So the Tatars have taught us, and they left us the knout as a remembrance of it. But men, too, can be beaten. A well-educated, cultured gentleman and his wife beat their own child with a birch rod, a girl of seven. I have an exact account of it. The papa was glad that the birch was covered with twigs. 'It stings more,' said he, and so he began stinging his daughter. I know for a fact there are people who at every blow are worked up to sensuality, to literal sensuality, which increases progressively at every blow they inflict. They beat for a minute, for five minutes, for ten minutes, more often and more savagely. The child screams. At last the child cannot scream, it gasps, 'Daddy! daddy!' By some diabolical unseemly chance the case was brought into court. A counsel is engaged. The Russian people have long called a barrister 'a conscience for hire.' The counsel protests in his client's defense. 'It's such a simple thing,' he says, 'an everyday domestic event. A father corrects his child. To our shame be it said, it is brought into court.' The jury, convinced by him, give a favourable verdict. The public roars with delight that the torturer is acquitted. Ah, pity I wasn't there! I would have proposed to raise a subscription in his honor! ... Charming pictures.

"But I've still better things about children. I've collected a great, great deal about Russian children, Alyosha. There was a little girl of five who was hated by her father and mother, 'most worthy and respectable people, of good education and breeding.' You see, I must repeat again, it is a peculiar characteristic of many people, this love of torturing children, and children only. To all other types of humanity these torturers behave mildly and benevolently, like cultivated and humane Europeans; but they are very fond of tormenting children, even fond of children themselves in that sense. It's just their defencelessness that tempts the tormentor, just the angelic confidence of the child who has no refuge and no appeal, that sets his vile blood on fire. In every man, of course, a demon lies hidden—the demon of rage, the demon of lustful heat at the screams of the tortured victim, the demon of lawlessness let off the chain, the demon of diseases that follow on vice, gout, kidney disease, and so on.

"This poor child of five was subjected to every possible torture by those cultivated parents. They beat her, thrashed her, kicked her for no reason till her body was one bruise. Then, they went to greater refinements of cruelty—shut her up all night in the cold and frost in a privy, and because she didn't ask to be taken up at night (as though a child of five sleeping its angelic, sound sleep could be trained to wake and ask), they smeared her face and filled her mouth with excrement, and it was her mother, her mother did this. And that mother could sleep, hearing the poor child's groans! Can you understand why a little creature, who can't even understand what's done to her, should beat her little aching heart with her tiny fist in the dark and the cold, and weep her meek unresentful tears to dear, kind God to protect her? Do you understand that, friend and brother, you pious and humble novice? Do you understand why this infamy must be and is permitted? Without it, I am told, man could not have existed on earth, for he could not have known good and evil. Why should he know that diabolical good and evil when it costs so much? Why, the whole world of knowledge is not worth that child's prayer to 'dear, kind God'! I say nothing of the sufferings of grown-up people, they have eaten the apple, damn them, and the devil take them all! But these little ones! I am making you suffer, Alyosha, you are not yourself. I'll leave off if you like."

"Never mind. I want to suffer too," muttered Alyosha.

"One picture, only one more, because it's so curious, so characteristic, and I have only just read it in some collection of Russian antiquities. I've forgotten the name. I must look it up. It was in the darkest days of serfdom at the beginning of the century, and long live the Liberator of the People! There was in those days a general of aristocratic connections, the owner of great estates, one of those men—somewhat exceptional, I believe, even then—who, retiring from the service into a life of leisure, are convinced that they've earned absolute power over the lives of their subjects. There were such men then. So our general, settled on his property of two thousand souls, lives in pomp, and domineers over his poor neighbors as though they were dependents and buffoons. He has kennels of hundreds of hounds and nearly a hundred dog-boys—all mounted, and in uniform. One day a serf boy, a little child of eight, threw a stone in play and hurt the paw of the general's favorite hound. 'Why is my favorite dog lame?' He is told that the boy threw a stone that hurt the dog's paw. 'So you did it.' The general looked the child up and down. 'Take him.' He was taken—taken from his mother and kept shut up all night. Early that morning the general comes out on horseback, with the hounds, his dependents, dog-boys, and huntsmen, all mounted around him in full hunting parade. The servants are summoned for their edification, and in front of them all stands the mother of the child. The child is brought from the lock-up. It's a gloomy cold, foggy autumn day, a capital day for hunting. The general orders the child to be undressed; the child is stripped naked. He shivers, numb with terror, not daring to cry.... 'Make him run,' commands the general. 'Run! run!' shout the dog-boys. The boy runs.... 'At him!' yells the general, and he sets the whole pack of hounds on the child. The hounds catch him, and tear him to pieces before his mother's eyes! ... I believe the general was afterwards declared incapable of administering his estates. Well—what did he deserve? To be shot? To be shot for the satisfaction of our moral feelings? Speak, Alyosha!"

"To be shot," murmured Alyosha, lifting his eyes to Ivan with a pale, twisted smile.

"Bravo!" cried Ivan delighted. "If even you say so ... You're a pretty monk! So there is a little devil sitting in your heart, Alyosha Karamazov!"

"What I said was absurd, but—"

"That's just the point that 'but'!" cried Ivan. "Let me tell you, novice, that the absurd is only too necessary on earth. The world stands on absurdities, and perhaps nothing would have come to pass in it without them. We know what we know!"

"What do you know?"

"I understand nothing," Ivan went on, as though in delirium. "I don't want to understand anything now. I want to stick to the fact. I made up my mind long ago not to understand. If I try to understand anything, I shall be false to the fact and I have determined to stick to the fact."

"Why are you trying me?" Alyosha cried, with sudden distress. "Will you say what you mean at last?"

"Of course, I will; that's what I've been leading up to. You are dear to me, I don't want to let you go, and I won't give you up to your Zossima."

Ivan for a minute was silent, his face became all at once very sad.

"Listen! I took the case of children only to make my case clearer. Of the other tears of humanity with which the earth is soaked from its crust to its centre, I will say nothing. I have narrowed my subject on purpose. I am a bug, and I recognize in all humility that I cannot understand why the world is arranged as it is. Men are themselves to blame, I suppose; they were given paradise, they wanted freedom, and stole fire from heaven, though they knew they would become unhappy, so there is no need to pity them. With my pitiful, earthly, Euclidean understanding, all I know is that there is suffering and that there are none guilty; that cause follows effect, simply and directly; that everything flows and finds its level—but that's only Euclidean nonsense, I know that, and I can't consent to live by it! What comfort is it to me that there are none guilty and that cause follows effect simply and directly, and that I know it—I must have

justice, or I will destroy myself. And not justice in some remote infinite time and space, but here on earth, and that I could see myself. I have believed in it. I want to see it, and if I am dead by then, let me rise again, for if it all happens without me, it will be too unfair. Surely I haven't suffered, simply that I, my crimes and my sufferings, may manure the soil of the future harmony for somebody else. I want to see with my own eyes the hind lie down with the lion and the victim rise up and embrace his murderer. I want to be there when every one suddenly understands what it has all been for. All the religions of the world are built on this longing, and I am a believer. But then there are the children, and what am I to do about them? That's a question I can't answer. For the hundredth time I repeat, there are numbers of questions, but I've only taken the children, because in their case what I mean is so unanswerably clear. Listen! If all must suffer to pay for the eternal harmony, what have children to do with it, tell me, please? It's beyond all comprehension why they should suffer, and why they should pay for the harmony. Why should they, too, furnish material to enrich the soil for the harmony of the future? I understand solidarity in sin among men. I understand solidarity in retribution, too; but there can be no such solidarity with children. And if it is really true that they must share responsibility for all their fathers' crimes, such a truth is not of this world and is beyond my comprehension. Some jester will say, perhaps, that the child would have grown up and have sinned, but you see he didn't grow up, he was torn to pieces by the dogs, at eight years old. Oh, Alyosha, I am not blaspheming! I understand, of course, what an upheaval of the universe it will be, when everything in heaven and earth blends in one hymn of praise and everything that lives and has lived cries aloud: 'Thou art just, O Lord, for Thy ways are revealed.' When the mother embraces the fiend who threw her child to the dogs, and all three cry aloud with tears, 'Thou art just, O Lord!' then, of course, the crown of knowledge will be reached and all will be made clear. But what pulls me up here is that I can't accept that harmony. And while I am on earth, I make haste to take my own measures. You see, Alyosha, perhaps it really may happen that if I live to that moment, or rise again to see it, I, too, perhaps, may cry aloud with the rest, looking at the mother embracing the child's torturer, 'Thou art just, O Lord!' but I don't want to cry aloud then. While there is still time, I hasten to protect myself and so I renounce the higher harmony altogether. It's not worth the tears of that one tortured child who beat itself on the breast with its little fist and prayed in its stinking outhouse, with its unexpiated tears to 'dear, kind God'! It's not worth it, because those tears are unatoned for. They must be atoned for, or there can be no harmony. But how? How are you going to atone for them? Is it possible? By their being avenged? But what do I care for avenging them? What do I care for a hell for oppressors? What good can hell do, since those children have already been tortured? And what becomes of harmony, if there is hell? I want to forgive. I want to embrace. I don't want more suffering. And if the sufferings of children go to swell the sum of sufferings which was necessary to pay for truth, then I protest that the truth is not worth such a price. I don't want the mother to embrace the oppressor who threw her son to the dogs! She dare not forgive him! Let her forgive him for herself, if she will, let her forgive the torturer for the immeasurable suffering of her mother's heart. But the sufferings of her tortured child she has no right to forgive; she dare not forgive the torturer, even if the child were to forgive him! And if that is so, if they dare not forgive, what becomes of harmony? Is there in the whole world a being who would have the right to forgive and could forgive? I don't want harmony. From love for humanity I don't want it. I would rather be left with the unavenged suffering. I would rather remain with my unavenged suffering and unsatisfied indignation, *even if I were wrong*. Besides, too high a price is asked for harmony; it's beyond our means to pay so much to enter on it. And so I hasten to give back my entrance ticket, and if I am an honest man I am bound to give it back as soon as possible. And that I am doing. It's not God that I don't accept, Alyosha, only I most respectfully return Him the ticket."

"That's rebellion," murmured Alyosha, looking down.

"Rebellion? I am sorry you call it that," said Ivan earnestly. "One can hardly live in rebellion, and I want to live. Tell me yourself, I challenge you—answer. Imagine that you are creating a fabric of human destiny with the object of making men happy in the end, giving them peace and rest at last, but that it was essential and inevitable to torture to death only one tiny creature—that little child beating its breast with its fist, for instance—and to found that edifice on its unavenged tears, would you consent to be the architect on those conditions? Tell me, and tell the truth."

"No, I wouldn't consent," said Alyosha softly.

"And can you admit the idea that men for whom you are building it would agree to accept their happiness on the foundation of the unexpiated blood of a little victim? And accepting it would remain happy forever?"

"No, I can't admit it. Brother," said Alyosha suddenly, with flashing eyes, "you said just now, is there a being in the whole world who would have the right to forgive and could forgive? But there is a Being and He can forgive everything, all and for all, because He gave His innocent blood for all and everything. You have forgotten Him, and on Him is built the edifice, and it is to Him they cry aloud, 'Thou art just, O Lord, for Thy ways are revealed!'"

"Ah! the One without sin and his blood! No, I have not forgotten Him; on the contrary I've been wondering all the time how it was you did not bring Him in before, for usually all arguments on your side put Him in the foreground. Do you know, Alyosha—don't laugh! I composed a poem about a year ago. If you can waste another ten minutes on me, I'll tell it to you."

"You wrote a poem?"

"Oh, no, I didn't write it," laughed Ivan, "and I've never written two lines of poetry in my life. But I composed up this poem in prose and I remembered it. I was carried away when I made it up. You will be my first reader—that is, listener. Why should an author forego even one listener?" smiled Ivan. "Shall I tell it to you?"

"I am all attention," said Alyosha. . . .

4

The Ones Who Walk Away from Omelas

URSULA K. LeGUIN

Ursula K. LeGuin (1929–) has written numerous works of poetry, realistic fiction, science fiction, fantasy, and children's fiction, many of which have been widely influential and have attained the status of contemporary classics. She is perhaps best known for her six Books of Earthsea *(1968–2001), as well as* The Left Hand of Darkness *(1969),* The Lathe of Heaven *(1971), and* The Dispossessed: An Ambiguous Utopia *(1974). In the present story, she tells the tale of a fictional utopia whose blessedness depends on the ongoing suffering of a lone child. We see the reactions of the inhabitants of Omelas as they discover the price of their happiness, and we are thus invited to reflect upon what goods, if any, might possibly justify the permission of suffering.*

With a clamor of bells that set the swallows soaring, the Festival of Summer came to the city Omelas, bright-towered by the sea. The rigging of the boats in harbor sparkled with flags. In the streets between houses with red roofs and painted walls, between old moss-grown gardens and under avenues of trees, past great parks and public buildings, processions moved. Some were decorous: old people in long stiff robes of mauve and grey, grave master workmen, quiet, merry women carrying their babies and chatting as they walked. In other streets the music beat faster, a shimmering of gong and tambourine, and the people went dancing, the procession was a dance. Children dodged in and out, their high calls rising like the swallows' crossing flights over the music and the singing. All the processions wound towards the north side of the city, where on the great water-meadow called the Green Fields boys and girls, naked in the bright air, with mud-stained feet and ankles and long, lithe arms, exercised their restive horses before the race. The horses wore no gear at all but a halter without bit.

Their manes were braided with streamers of silver, gold, and green. They flared their nostrils and pranced and boasted to one another; they were vastly excited, the horse being the only animal who has adopted our ceremonies as his own. Far off to the north and west the mountains stood up half encircling Omelas on her bay. The air of morning was so clear that the snow still crowning the Eighteen Peaks burned with white-gold fire across the miles of sunlit air, under the dark blue of the sky. There was just enough wind to make the banners that marked the racecourse snap and flutter now and then. In the silence of the broad green meadows one could hear the music winding through the city streets, farther and nearer and ever approaching, a cheerful faint sweetness of the air that from time to time trembled and gathered together and broke out into the great joyous clanging of the bells.

Joyous! How is one to tell about joy? How describe the citizens of Omelas?

They were not simple folk, you see, though they were happy. But we do not say the words of cheer much any more. All smiles have become archaic. Given a description such as this one tends to make certain assumptions. Given a description such as this one tends to look next for the King, mounted on a splendid stallion and surrounded by his noble knights, or perhaps in a golden litter borne by great-muscled slaves. But there was no king. They did not use swords, or keep slaves. They were not barbarians. I do not know the rules and laws of their society, but I suspect that they were singularly few. As they did without monarchy and slavery, so they also got on without the stock exchange, the advertisement, the secret police, and the bomb. Yet I repeat that these were not simple folk, not dulcet shepherds, noble savages, bland utopians. They were not less complex than us. The trouble is that we have a bad habit, encouraged by pedants and sophisticates, of considering happiness as something rather stupid. Only pain is intellectual, only evil interesting. This is the treason of the artist: a refusal to admit the banality of evil and the terrible boredom of pain. If you can't lick 'em, join 'em. If it hurts, repeat it. But to praise despair is to condemn delight, to embrace violence is to lose hold of everything else. We have almost lost hold; we can no longer describe a happy man, nor make any celebration of joy. How can I tell you about the people of Omelas? They were not naive and happy children—though their children were, in fact, happy. They were mature, intelligent, passionate adults whose lives were not wretched. O miracle! but I wish I could describe it better. I wish I could convince you. Omelas sounds in my words like a city in a fairy tale, long ago and far away, once upon a time. Perhaps it would be best if you imagined it as your own fancy bids, assuming it will rise to the occasion, for certainly I cannot suit you all. For instance, how about technology? I think that there would be no cars or helicopters in and above the streets; this follows from the fact that the people of Omelas are happy people. Happiness is based on a just discrimination of what is necessary, what is neither necessary nor destructive, and what is destructive. In the middle category, however—that of the unnecessary but undestructive, that of comfort, luxury, exuberance, etc.—they could perfectly well have central heating, subway trains, washing machines, and all kinds of marvelous devices not yet invented here, floating light-sources, fuelless power, a cure for the common cold. Or they could have none of that; it doesn't matter. As you like it. I incline to think that people from towns up and down the coast have been coming in to Omelas during the last days before the Festival on very fast little trains and double-decked trams, and that the train station of Omelas is actually the handsomest building in town, though plainer than the magnificent Farmers' Market. But even granted trains, I fear that Omelas so far strikes some of you as goody-goody. Smiles, bells, parades, horses, bleh. If so, please add an orgy. If an orgy would help, don't hesitate. Let us not, however, have temples from which issue beautiful nude priests and priestesses already half in ecstasy and ready to copulate with any man or woman, lover or stranger, who desires union with the deep godhead of the blood, although that was my first idea. But really it would be better not to have any temples in Omelas—at least, not manned temples. Religion yes, clergy no. Surely the beautiful nudes can just wander about, offering themselves like divine soufflés to the hunger of the needy and the rapture of the flesh. Let them join the processions. Let tambourines be struck above the copulations, and the glory of desire be proclaimed upon the gongs, and (a not unimportant point) let the offspring of these delightful rituals be beloved and looked after by all. One thing I know there is none of in Omelas is guilt. But what else should there be? I thought at first there were not drugs, but that is puritanical. For those who like it, the faint insistent sweetness of *drooz* may perfume the ways of the city, *drooz* which first brings a great lightness and brilliance to the mind and limbs, and then after some hours a dreamy languor, and wonderful visions at last of the very arcana and inmost secrets of the Universe, as well as exciting the pleasure of sex beyond belief; and it is not habit-forming. For more modest tastes I think there ought to be beer. What else, what else belongs in the joyous city? The sense of victory, surely, the celebration of courage. But as we did without clergy, let us do without soldiers. The joy built upon successful slaughter is not the right kind of joy; it will not do; it is fearful and it is trivial. A boundless and generous contentment, a magnanimous triumph felt not against some outer enemy but in communion with the finest and fairest in the souls of all men everywhere and the splendor of the world's summer: this is what swells the hearts of the people of Omelas, and the victory they celebrate is that of life. I really don't think many of them need to take *drooz*.

Most of the procession have reached the Green Fields by now. A marvelous smell of cooking goes forth from the red and blue tents of the provisioners. The faces of small children are amiably sticky; in the benign grey beard of a man a couple of crumbs of rich pastry are entangled. The youths and girls have mounted their horses and are beginning to group around the starting line of the course. An old women, small, fat, and laughing, is passing out flowers from a basket, and tall young men [wear] her flowers in their shining hair. A child of nine or ten sits at the edge of the crowd, alone, playing on a wooden flute. People pause to listen, and they smile, but they do not speak to him, for he never ceases playing and never sees them, his dark eyes wholly rapt in the sweet, thin magic of the tune.

He finishes, and slowly lowers his hands holding the wooden flute.

As if that little private silence were the signal, all at once a trumpet sounds from the pavilion near the starting line: imperious, melancholy, piercing. The horses rear on their slender legs, and some of them neigh in answer. Sober-faced, the young riders stroke the horses' necks and soothe them, whispering, "Quiet, quiet, there my beauty, my hope...." They begin to form in rank along the starting line. The crowds along the racecourse are like a field of grass and flowers in the wind. The Festival of Summer has begun.

Do you believe? Do you accept the festival, the city, the joy? No? Then let me describe one more thing.

In a basement under one of the beautiful public buildings of Omelas, or perhaps in the cellar of one of its spacious private homes, there is a room. It has one locked door, and no window. A little light seeps in dustily between cracks in the boards, secondhand from a cobwebbed window somewhere across the cellar. In one corner of the little room a couple of mops, with stiff, clotted, foul-smelling heads stand near a rusty bucket. The floor is dirt, a little damp to the touch, as cellar dirt usually is. The room is about three paces long and two wide: a mere broom closet or disused tool room. In the room a child is sitting. It could be a boy or a girl. It looks about six, but actually is nearly ten. It is feeble-minded. Perhaps it was born defective, or perhaps it has become imbecile through fear, malnutrition, and neglect. It picks its nose and occasionally fumbles vaguely with its toes or genitals, as it sits hunched in the corner farthest from the bucket and the two mops. It is afraid of the mops. It finds them horrible. It shuts its eyes, but it knows the mops are still standing there; and the door is locked; and nobody will come. The door is always locked; and nobody ever comes, except that sometimes—the child has no understanding of time or interval—sometimes the door rattles terribly and opens, and a person, or several people, are there. One of them may come in and kick the child to make it stand up. The others never come close, but peer in at it with frightened, disgusted eyes. The food bowl and the water jug are hastily filled, the door is locked, the eyes disappear. The people at the door never say anything, but the child, who has not always lived in the tool room, and can remember sunlight and its mother's voice, sometimes speaks. "I will be good," it says. "Please let me out. I will be good!" They never answer. The child used to scream for help at night, and cry a good deal, but now it only makes a kind of whining, "eh-haa, eh-haa," and it speaks less and less often. It is so thin there are no calves to its legs; its belly protrudes; it lives on a half-bowl of corn meal and grease a day. It is naked. Its buttocks and thighs are a mass of festered sores, as it sits in its own excrement continually.

They all know it is there, all the people of Omelas. Some of them have come to see it, others are content merely to know it is there. They all know that it has to be there. Some of them understand why, and some do not, but they all understand that their happiness, the beauty of their city, the tenderness of their friendships, the health of their children, the wisdom of their scholars, the skill of their makers, even the abundance of their harvest and the kindly weathers of their skies, depend wholly on this child's abominable misery.

This is usually explained to children when they are between eight and twelve, whenever they seem capable of understanding; and most of those who come to see the child are young people, though often enough an adult comes, or comes back, to see the child. No matter how well the matter has been explained to them, these young spectators are always shocked and sickened at the sight. They feel disgust, which they had thought themselves superior to. They feel anger, outrage, impotence, despite all the explanations. They would like to do something for the child. But there is nothing they can do. If the child were brought up into the sunlight out of that vile place, if it were cleaned and fed and comforted, that would be a good thing indeed; but if it were done, in that day and hour all the prosperity and beauty and delight of Omelas would wither and be destroyed. Those are the terms. To exchange all the goodness and grace of every life in Omelas for that single, small improvement: to throw away the happiness of thousands for the chance of the happiness of one: that would be to let guilt within the walls indeed.

The terms are strict and absolute; there may not even be a kind word spoken to the child.

Often the young people go home in tears, or in a tearless rage, when they have seen the child and faced this terrible paradox. They may brood over it for weeks or years. But as time goes on they begin to realize that even if the child could be released, it would not get much good of its freedom: a little vague pleasure of warmth and food, no doubt, but little more. It is too degraded and imbecile to know any real joy. It has been afraid too long ever to be free of fear. Its habits are too uncouth for it to respond to humane treatment. Indeed, after so long it would probably be wretched without walls about it to protect it, and

darkness for its eyes, and its own excrement to sit in. Their tears at the bitter injustice dry when they begin to perceive the terrible justice of reality, and to accept it. Yet it is their tears and anger, the trying of their generosity and the acceptance of their helplessness, which are perhaps the true source of the splendor of their lives. Theirs is no vapid, irresponsible happiness. They know that they, like the child, are not free. They know compassion. It is the existence of the child, and their knowledge of its existence, that makes possible the nobility of their architecture, the poignancy of their music, the profundity of their science. It is because of the child that they are so gentle with children. They know that if the wretched one were not there sniveling in the dark, the other one, the flute-player, could make no joyful music as the young riders line up in their beauty for the race in the sunlight of the first morning of summer.

Now do you believe in them? Are they not more credible? But there is one more thing to tell, and this is quite incredible.

At times one of the adolescent girls or boys who go to see the child does not go home to weep or rage, does not, in fact, go home at all. Sometimes also a man or woman much older falls silent for a day or two, and then leaves home. These people go out into the street, and walk down the street alone. They keep walking, and walk straight out of the city of Omelas, through the beautiful gates. They keep walking across the farmlands of Omelas. Each one goes alone, youth or girl, man or woman. Night falls; the traveler must pass down village streets, between the houses with yellow-lit windows, and on out into the darkness of the fields. Each alone, they go west or north, towards the mountains. They go on. They leave Omelas, they walk ahead into the darkness, and they do not come back. The place they go towards is a place even less imaginable to most of us than the city of happiness. I cannot describe it at all. It is possible that it does not exist. But they seem to know where they are going, the ones who walk away from Omelas.

THE PROBLEMS OF EVIL AND DIVINE HIDDENNESS

Introduction

THE PREVIOUS FOUR SELECTIONS presented three (rather different) historical and literary formulations of the problem of evil and one of the most well-known historical replies. In the present section, we turn to contemporary philosophical formulations of the problems of evil and divine hiddenness.

We begin with J. L. Mackie's classic statement of the "logical problem of evil"—an argument for the conclusion that the existence of the God of the Judeo-Christian tradition is logically inconsistent with the existence of evil. A perfectly good being, Mackie contends, always eliminates evil as far as it can; and an omnipotent and omniscient being, he argues, can eliminate evil entirely. He considers the response that the value of creating a world with free creatures might justify God in permitting the existence of evil. But he argues that since it is not *impossible* for there to be a world in which free creatures always do what is right, God must have been able to create such a world. And so, since a world in which free creatures always do what is right is clearly better than one in which free creatures sometimes do what is wrong, the appeal to freedom fails to solve the problem.

Despite the intuitive appeal of Mackie's argument, most philosophers nowadays agree that the argument fails. As William Rowe puts it in one of the notes to our next selection:

> Some philosophers have contended that the existence of evil is logically inconsistent with the existence of the theistic God. No one, I think, has succeeded in establishing such an extravagant claim.

Rowe goes on to credit Alvin Plantinga for showing in a clear and compelling way why Mackie's argument fails. (Plantinga's argument is given in selection 10.) Nevertheless, Rowe says,

> [t]here remains . . . what we may call the evidential form—as opposed to the logical form—of the problem of evil; the view that the variety and profusion of evil in our world although perhaps not logically inconsistent with the existence of the theistic God, provides, nevertheless, rational support for atheism.

It is the evidential form of the argument with which his article (selection 6) is concerned.

As it is typically presented, the "evidential problem of evil" relies on the premise that a good God would permit evil only if it contributed to some greater good, together with the claim that many of the evils we in fact observe seem not to contribute to any greater good. This is roughly the argument defended by Rowe; but Paul Draper, in the third reading of this section, takes a different tack. According to Draper, the "pattern of both pain and pleasure" in the world constitutes evidence against theism and in favor of naturalism. (As he defines it, naturalism is the hypothesis that the universe is a closed system, and it entails that there are no supernatural beings—divine or otherwise.) In his view, the pattern of pain and pleasure that we in fact observe isn't what we would naturally expect if pain existed (say) to serve the purpose of punishing sinners, or of building moral character. Rather, it is systematically connected with reproductive success, which is what we would expect on the supposition that naturalism and evolutionary theory are both true. Thus, on his view, the fact that pain and pleasure are systematically connected with reproductive success, together with the truth of evolutionary theory, provides evidence in support of naturalism.

The fourth reading in this section, an excerpt from Grace M. Jantzen's *Becoming Divine*, issues an important feminist challenge to the traditional framing of the problem of evil. As we have seen, the problem of evil is standardly presented as an objection against *belief* in a particular *kind of deity*—the traditionally male-gendered "omni-everything" God of Western monotheism. Within the traditional framing, discussions of the problem of evil typically leave unquestioned the "valorization" of power and knowledge in the traditional conception of God; alternative ways of envisioning the divine are commonly ignored; and questions about where evil comes from and what can be done with it are, as a rule, left off the table. But, Jantzen argues, there is no methodological reason why matters ought to be so. There is no reason why the *intellectual* challenge posed to religious belief by the existence of evil ought to take center stage in philosophical discussions about God, religion, and evil rather than some of these other issues. Thus, she advocates for a reframing of the problem from what she takes to be a distinctively feminist perspective. On her view, the problem of evil viewed from a feminist perspective will be concerned not so much with the question of how a perfect deity can permit evil as with questions like "How are the resources of religion … used by those who inflict evil on others?" and "How are those resources used by those who resist?" Above all, she says, treating the problem from a feminist perspective would ask, "What does the face of the Other require of me, and how can I best respond for love of the world?" (The phrase "the face of the Other" is an allusion to the work of French philosopher Emmanuel Levinas [1906–1995], who uses that term in reference not to the outward appearance—the literal *face*—of another person but rather to the person as she is in her inmost,indefinable self. Levinas is particularly concerned with the ethical demands made upon us by the so-called face of the Other.[*])

In this section's final reading, we turn to the problem of divine hiddenness as formulated by J. L. Schellenberg. Schellenberg's *Divine Hiddenness and Human Reason* (1993) has largely set the agenda for discussions of the hiddenness of God over the past two decades. In the present article he offers a simplified account of his reasons for thinking that divine hiddenness justifies disbelief in God. As we saw in the general introduction to Part III, the problem in short is that one would expect an all powerful, all knowing, perfectly loving God to ensure that divine hiddenness does not occur—that evidence sufficient for belief in God is always widely available. And yet divine hiddenness does occur. Thus, Schellenberg concludes, we are justified in believing that God does not exist.

---

[*]For discussion, see R. Burggraeve, "Violence and the Vulnerable Face of the Other: The Vision of Emmanuel Levinas on Moral Evil and Our Responsibility," *Journal of Social Research* 30 (1999): 29–45.

5

Evil and Omnipotence

J. L. MACKIE

John L. Mackie (1917–1981) was born in Australia and taught at Oxford University until his death. He made important contributions to the fields of metaphysics, epistemology, ethics, and philosophy of religion. Among his works are The Cement of the Universe *(1974),* Ethics: Inventing Right and Wrong *(1977), and* The Miracle of Theism *(1982). In this essay, Mackie argues that the argument from evil demonstrates the incoherence of theism. If there is a God who is all-powerful and completely good, he will be able and willing to eliminate all evil in the world. But there is evil, so no God exists.*

The traditional arguments for the existence of God have been fairly thoroughly criticised by philosophers. But the theologian can, if he wishes, accept this criticism. He can admit that no rational proof of God's existence is possible. And he can still retain all that is essential to his position, by holding that God's existence is known in some other, non-rational way. I think, however, that a more telling criticism can be made by way of the traditional problem of evil. Here it can be shown, not that religious beliefs lack rational support, but that they are positively irrational, that the several parts of the essential theological doctrine are inconsistent with one another, so that the theologian can maintain his position as a whole only by a much more extreme rejection of reason than in the former case. He must now be prepared to believe, not merely what cannot be proved, but what can be *disproved* from other beliefs that he also holds.

The problem of evil, in the sense in which I shall be using the phrase, is a problem only for someone who believes that there is a God who is both omnipotent and wholly good. And it is a logical problem, the problem of clarifying and reconciling a number of beliefs: it is not a scientific problem that might be solved by further observations, or a practical problem that might be solved by a decision or an action. These points are obvious; I mention them only because they are sometimes ignored by theologians, who sometimes parry a statement of the problem with such remarks as "Well, can you solve the problem yourself?" or "This is a mystery which may be revealed to us later" or "Evil is something to be faced and overcome, not to be merely discussed."

In its simplest form the problem is this: God is omnipotent; God is wholly good; and yet evil exists. There seems to be some contradiction between these three propositions, so that if any two of them were true the third would be false. But at the same time all three are essential parts of most theological positions: the theologian, it seems, at once *must* adhere and *cannot consistently* adhere to all three. (The problem does not arise only for theists, but I shall discuss it in the form in which it presents itself for ordinary theism.)

However, the contradiction does not arise immediately; to show it we need some additional

From *Mind*, 64 (1955): 200–212. Reprinted by permission of Oxford University Press.

premises, or perhaps some quasi-logical rules connecting the terms "good, evil," and "omnipotent." These additional principles are that good is opposed to evil, in such a way that a good thing always eliminates evil as far as it can, and that there are no limits to what an omnipotent thing can do. From these it follows that a good omnipotent thing eliminates evil completely, and then the propositions that a good omnipotent thing exists, and that evil exists, are incompatible.

A. ADEQUATE SOLUTIONS

Now once the problem is fully stated it is clear that it can be solved, in the sense that the problem will not arise if one gives up at least one of the propositions that constitute it. If you are prepared to say that God is not wholly good, or not quite omnipotent, or that evil does not exist, or that good is not opposed to the kind of evil that exists, or that there are limits to what an omnipotent thing can do, then the problem of evil will not arise for you.

There are, then, quite a number of adequate solutions of the problem of evil, and some of these have been adopted, or almost adopted, by various thinkers. For example, a few have been prepared to deny God's omnipotence, and rather more have been prepared to keep the term "omnipotence" but severely to restrict its meaning, recording quite a number of things that an omnipotent being cannot do. Some have said that evil is an illusion, perhaps because they held that the whole world of temporal, changing things is an illusion, and that what we call evil belongs only to this world, or perhaps because they held that although temporal things are much as we see them, those that we call evil are not really evil. Some have said that what we call evil is merely the privation of good, that evil in a positive sense, evil that would really be opposed to good, does not exist. Many have agreed with Pope that disorder is harmony not understood, and that partial evil is universal good. Whether any of these views is true is, of course, another question. But each of them gives an adequate solution of the problem of evil in the sense that if you accept it this problem does not arise for you, though you may, of course, have *other* problems to face.

But often enough these adequate solutions are only *almost* adopted. The thinkers who restrict God's power, but keep the term "omnipotence," may reasonably be suspected of thinking, in other contexts, that his power is really unlimited. Those who say that evil is an illusion may also be thinking, inconsistently, that this illusion is itself an evil. Those who say that "evil" is merely privation of good may also be thinking, inconsistently, that privation of good is an evil. (The fallacy here is akin to some forms of the "naturalistic fallacy" in ethics, where some think, for example, that "good" is just what contributes to evolutionary progress, and that evolutionary progress is itself good.) If Pope meant what he said in the first line of his couplet, that "disorder" is only harmony not understood, the "partial evil" of the second line must, for consistency, mean "that which, taken in isolation, falsely appears to be evil," but it would more naturally mean "that which, in isolation, really is evil." The second line, in fact, hesitates between two views, that "partial evil" isn't really evil, since only the universal quality is real, and that "partial evil" is really an evil, but only a little one.

In addition, therefore, to adequate solutions, we must recognise unsatisfactorily inconsistent solutions, in which there is only a half-hearted or temporary rejection of one of the propositions which together constitute the problem. In these, one of the constituent propositions is explicitly rejected, but it is covertly re-asserted or assumed elsewhere in the system.

B. FALLACIOUS SOLUTIONS

Besides these half-hearted solutions, which explicitly reject but implicitly assert one of the constituent propositions, there are definitely fallacious solutions which explicitly maintain all the constituent propositions, but implicitly reject at least one of them in the course of the argument that explains away the problem of evil.

There are, in fact, many so-called solutions which purport to remove the contradiction without abandoning any of its constituent propositions. These must be fallacious as we can see from the very statement of the problem, but it is not so easy to see in each case precisely where the fallacy lies. I suggest that in all cases the fallacy has the general form suggested above: in order to solve the problem one (or perhaps more) of its constituent propositions is given up, but in such a way that it appears to have been retained, and can therefore be asserted without qualification in other contexts. Sometimes there is a further complication: the supposed solution moves to and fro between, say, two of the constituent propositions, at one point asserting the first of these but covertly abandoning the second, at another point asserting the second but covertly abandoning the first. These fallacious solutions often turn upon some equivocation with the words "good" and "evil," or upon some vagueness about the way in which good and evil are opposed to one another, or about how much is meant by "omnipotence." I propose to examine some of these so-called solutions, and to exhibit their fallacies in detail. Incidentally, I shall also be considering whether an adequate solution could be reached by a minor modification of one or more of the constituent propositions, which would, however, still satisfy all the essential requirements of ordinary theism.

(1) "Good cannot exist without evil" or "Evil is necessary as a counterpart to good."

It is sometimes suggested that evil is necessary as a counterpart to good, that if there were no evil there could be no good either, and that this solves the problem of evil. It is true that it points to an answer to the question "Why should there be evil?" But it does so only by qualifying some of the propositions that constitute the problem.

First, it sets a limit to what God can do, saying that God *cannot* create good without simultaneously creating evil, and this means either that God is not omnipotent or that there are *some* limits to what an omnipotent thing can do. It may be replied that these limits are always presupposed, that omnipotence has never meant the power to do what is

logically impossible, and on the present view the existence of good without evil would be a logical impossibility. This interpretation of omnipotence may, indeed, be accepted as a modification of our original account which does not reject anything that is essential to theism, and I shall in general assume it in the subsequent discussion. It is, perhaps, the most common theistic view, but I think that some theists at least have maintained that God can do what is logically impossible. Many theists, at any rate, have held that logic itself is created or laid down by God, that logic is the way in which God arbitrarily chooses to think. (This is, of course, parallel to the ethical view that morally right actions are those which God arbitrarily chooses to command, and the two views encounter similar difficulties.) And this account of logic is clearly inconsistent with the view that God is bound by logical necessities—unless it is possible for an omnipotent being to bind himself, an issue which we shall consider later, when we come to the Paradox of Omnipotence. This solution of the problem of evil cannot, therefore, be consistently adopted along with the view that logic is itself created by God.

But, secondly, this solution denies that evil is opposed to good in our original sense. If good and evil are counterparts, a good thing will not "eliminate evil as far as it can." Indeed, this view suggests that good and evil are not strictly qualities of things at all. Perhaps the suggestion is that good and evil are related in much the same way as great and small. Certainly, when the term "great" is used relatively as a condensation of "greater than so-and-so," and "small" is used correspondingly, greatness and smallness are counterparts and cannot exist without each other. But in this sense greatness is not a quality, not an intrinsic feature of anything; and it would be absurd to think of a movement in favour of greatness and against smallness in this sense. Such a movement would be self-defeating, since relative greatness can be promoted only by a simultaneous promotion of relative smallness. I feel sure that no theists would be content to regard God's goodness as analogous to this—as if what he supports were not the *good* but the *better*, and if he had the paradoxical aim that all things should be better than other things.

This point is obscured by the fact that "great" and "small" seem to have an absolute as well as a relative sense. I cannot discuss here whether there is absolute magnitude or not, but if there is, there could be an absolute sense for "great," it could mean of at least a certain size, and it would make sense to speak of all things getting bigger, of a universe that was expanding all over, and therefore it would make sense to speak of promoting greatness. But in *this* sense great and small are not logically necessary counterparts: either quality could exist without the other. There would be no logical impossibility in everything's being small or in everything's being great.

Neither in the absolute nor in the relative sense, then, of "great" and "small" do these terms provide an analogy of the sort that would be needed to support this solution of the problem of evil. In neither case are greatness and smallness *both* necessary counterparts *and* mutually opposed forces or possible objects for support and attack.

It may be replied that good and evil are necessary counterparts in the same way as any quality and its logical opposite: redness can occur, it is suggested, only if non-redness also occurs. But unless evil is merely the privation of good, they are not logical opposites, and some further argument would be needed to show that they are counterparts in the same way as genuine logical opposites. Let us assume that this could be given. There is still doubt of the correctness of the metaphysical principle that a quality must have a real opposite: I suggest that it is not really impossible that everything should be, say, red, that the truth is merely that if everything were red we should not notice redness, and so we should have no word "red"; we observe and give names to qualities only if they have real opposites. If so, the principle that a term must have an opposite would belong only to our language or to our thought, and would not be an ontological principle, and correspondingly, the rule that good cannot exist without evil would not state a logical necessity of a sort that God would just have to put up with. God might have made everything good, though *we* should not have noticed it if he had.

But, finally, even if we concede that this is an ontological principle, it will provide a solution for the problem of evil only if one is prepared to say, "Evil exists, but only just enough evil to serve as the counterpart of good." I doubt whether any theist will accept this. After all, the ontological requirement that non-redness should occur would be satisfied even if all the universe, except for a minute speck, were red, and, if there were a corresponding requirement for evil as a counterpart to good, a minute dose of evil would presumably do. But theists are not usually willing to say, in all contexts, that all the evil that occurs is a minute and necessary dose.

(2) "Evil is necessary as a means to good."

It is sometimes suggested that evil is necessary for good not as a counterpart but as a means. In its simple form this has little plausibility as a solution of the problem of evil, since it obviously implies a severe restriction of God's power. It would be a *causal* law that you cannot have a certain end without a certain means, so that if God has to introduce evil as a means to good, he must be subject to at least some causal laws. This certainly conflicts with what a theist normally means by omnipotence. This view of God as limited by causal laws also conflicts with the view that causal laws are themselves made by God, which is more widely held than the corresponding view about the laws of logic. This conflict would, indeed, be resolved if it were possible for an omnipotent being to bind himself, and this possibility has still to be considered. Unless a favourable answer can be given to this question, the suggestion that evil is necessary as a means to good solves the problem of evil only by denying one of its constituent propositions, either that God is omnipotent or that "omnipotent" means what it says.

(3) "The universe is better with some evil in it than it could be if there were no evil."

Much more important is a solution which at first seems to be a mere variant of the previous one, that evil may contribute to the goodness of a whole in which it is found, so that the universe as a whole is better as it is, with some evil in it, than it would be if there were no evil. This solution may be developed in either of two ways. It may be supported by an aesthetic analogy, by the fact that contrasts heighten beauty, that in a musical work, for example, there may occur discords which somehow add to the beauty of the work as a whole. Alternatively, it may be worked out in connection with the notion of progress, that the best possible organization of the universe will not be static, but progressive, that the gradual overcoming of evil by good is really a finer thing than would be the eternal unchallenged supremacy of good.

In either case, this solution usually starts from the assumption that the evil whose existence gives rise to the problem of evil is primarily what is called physical evil, that is to say, pain. In Hume's rather half-hearted presentation of the problem of evil, the evils that he stresses are pain and disease, and those who reply to him argue that the existence of pain and disease makes possible the existence of sympathy, benevolence, heroism, and the gradually successful struggle of doctors and reformers to overcome these evils. In fact, theists often seize the opportunity to accuse those who stress the problem of evil of taking a low, materialistic view of good and evil, equating these with pleasure and pain, and of ignoring the more spiritual goods which can arise in the struggle against evils.

But let us see exactly what is being done here. Let us call pain and misery "first order evil" or "evil (1)." What contrasts with this, namely, pleasure and happiness, will be called "first order good" or "good (1)." Distinct from this is "second order good" or "good (2)" which somehow emerges in a complex situation in which evil (1) is a necessary component—logically not merely causally, necessary. (Exactly *how* it emerges does not matter: in the crudest version of this solution good (2) is simply the heightening of happiness by the contrast with misery, in other versions it includes sympathy with suffering, heroism in facing danger, and the gradual decrease of first order evil and increase of first order good.) It is also being assumed that second order good is more important than first order good or evil, in particular that it more than outweighs the first order evil it involves.

Now this is a particularly subtle attempt to solve the problem of evil. It defends God's

goodness and omnipotence on the ground that (on a sufficiently long view) this is the best of all logically possible worlds, because it includes the important second order goods, and yet it admits that real evils, namely first order evils, exist. But does it still hold that good and evil are opposed? Not, clearly, in the sense that we set out originally: good does not tend to eliminate evil in general. Instead, we have a modified, a more complex pattern. First order good (*e.g.* happiness) *contrasts with* first order evil (*e.g.* misery): these two are opposed in a fairly mechanical way; some second order goods (*e.g.* benevolence) try to maximize first order good and minimize first order evil; but God's goodness is not this, it is rather the will to maximize *second* order good. We might, therefore, call God's goodness an example of a third order goodness, or good (3). While this account is different from our original one, it might well be held to be an improvement on it, to give a more accurate description of the way in which good is opposed to evil, and to be consistent with the essential theist position.

There might, however, be several objections to this solution.

First, some might argue that such qualities as benevolence—and *a fortiori* the third order goodness which promotes benevolence—have a merely derivative value, that they are not higher sorts of good, but merely means to good (1), that is, to happiness, so that it would be absurd for God to keep misery in existence in order to make possible the virtues of benevolence, heroism, etc. The theist who adopts the present solution must, of course, deny this, but he can do so with some plausibility, so I should not press this objection.

Secondly, it follows from this solution that God is not in our sense benevolent or sympathetic: he is not concerned to minimize evil (1), but only to promote good (2); and this might be a disturbing conclusion for some theists.

But, thirdly, the fatal objection is this. Our analysis shows clearly the possibility of the existence of a *second* order evil, an evil (2) contrasting with good (2) as evil (1) contrasts with good (1). This would include malevolence, cruelty, callousness, cowardice, and states in which good

(1) is decreasing and evil (1) increasing. And just as good (2) is held to be the important kind of good, the kind that God is concerned to promote, so evil (2) will, by analogy, be the important kind of evil, the kind which God, if he were wholly good and omnipotent, would eliminate. And yet evil (2) plainly exists, and indeed most theists (in other contexts) stress its existence more than that of evil (1). We should, therefore, state the problem of evil in terms of second order evil, and against this form of the problem the present solution is useless.

An attempt might be made to use this solution again, at a higher level, to explain the occurrence of evil (2); indeed the next main solution that we shall examine does just this, with the help of some new notions. Without any fresh notions, such a solution would have little plausibility: for example, we could hardly say that the really important good was a good (3), such as the increase of benevolence in proportion to cruelty, which logically required for its occurrence the occurrence of some second order evil. But even if evil (2) could be explained in this way, it is fairly clear that there would be third order evils contrasting with this third order good: and we should be well on the way to an infinite regress, where the solution of a problem of evil, stated in terms of evil (n), indicated the existence of an evil ($n + 1$), and a further problem to be solved.

(4) "Evil is due to human free will."

Perhaps the most important proposed solution of the problem of evil is that evil is not to be ascribed to God at all, but to the independent actions of human beings, supposed to have been endowed by God with freedom of the will. This solution may be combined with the preceding one: first order evil (e.g. pain) may be justified as a logically necessary component in second order good (e.g. sympathy) while second order evil (e.g. cruelty) is not justified, but is so ascribed to human beings that God cannot be held responsible for it. This combination evades my third criticism of the preceding solution.

The free will solution also involves the preceding solution at a higher level. To explain why a wholly good God gave men free will although it would lead to some important evils, it must be argued that it is better on the whole that men should act freely, and sometimes err, than that they should be innocent automata, acting rightly in a wholly determined way. Freedom that is to say, is now treated as a third order good, and as being more valuable than second order goods (such as sympathy and heroism) would be if they were deterministically produced, and it is being assumed that second order evils, such as cruelty, are logically necessary accompaniments of freedom, just as pain is a logically necessary precondition of sympathy.

I think that this solution is unsatisfactory primarily because of the incoherence of the notion of freedom of the will: but I cannot discuss this topic adequately here, although some of my criticisms will touch upon it.

First I should query the assumption that second order evils are logically necessary accompaniments of freedom. I should ask this: if God has made men such that in their free choices they sometimes prefer what is good and sometimes what is evil, why could he not have made men such that they always freely choose the good? If there is no logical impossibility in a man's freely choosing the good on one, or on several, occasions, there cannot be a logical impossibility in his freely choosing the good on every occasion. God was not, then, faced with a choice between making innocent automata and making beings who, in acting freely, would sometimes go wrong: there was open to him the obviously better possibility of making beings who would act freely but always go right. Clearly, his failure to avail himself of this possibility is inconsistent with his being both omnipotent and wholly good.

If it is replied that this objection is absurd, that the making of some wrong choices is logically necessary for freedom, it would seem that "freedom" must here mean complete randomness or indeterminacy, including randomness with regard to the alternatives good and evil, in other words that men's choices and consequent actions can be "free" only if they are not determined by their characters. Only on this assumption can God escape the responsibility for men's actions; for if he made them as they are, but did not determine their wrong choices, this can only be because the wrong choices are not determined by men as they are. But then if freedom is randomness, how can it be a characteristic of *will*? And, still more, how can it be the most important good? What value or merit would there be in free choices if these were random actions which were not determined by the nature of the agent?

I conclude that to make this solution plausible two different senses of "freedom" must be confused, one sense which will justify the view that freedom is a third order good, more valuable than other goods would be without it, and another sense, sheer randomness, to prevent us from ascribing to God a decision to make men such that they sometimes go wrong when he might have made them such that they would always freely go right.

This criticism is sufficient to dispose of this solution. But besides this there is a fundamental difficulty in the notion of an omnipotent God creating men with free will, for if men's wills are really free this must mean that even God cannot control them, that is, that God is no longer omnipotent. It may be objected that God's gift of freedom to men does not mean that he *cannot* control their wills, but that he always *refrains* from controlling their wills. But why, we may ask, should God refrain from controlling evil wills? Why should he not leave men free to will rightly, but intervene when he sees them beginning to will wrongly? If God could do this, but does not, and if he is wholly good, the only explanation could be that even a wrong free act of will is not really evil, that its freedom is a value which outweighs its wrongness, so that there would be a loss of value if God took away the wrongness and the freedom together. But this is utterly opposed to what theists say about sin in other contexts. The present solution of the problem of evil, then, can be maintained only in the form that God has made men so free that he *cannot* control their wills.

This leads us to what I call the Paradox of Omnipotence: can an omnipotent being make things which he cannot subsequently control? Or, what is practically equivalent to this, can an omnipotent being make rules which then bind himself? (These are practically equivalent because any such rules could be regarded as setting certain things beyond his control, and *vice versa*.) The second of these formulations is relevant to the suggestions that we have already met, that an omnipotent God creates the rules of logic or causal laws, and is then bound by them.

It is clear that this is a paradox: the questions cannot be answered satisfactorily either in the affirmative or in the negative. If we answer "Yes," it follows that if God actually makes things which he cannot control, or makes rules which bind himself, he is not omnipotent once he has made them: there are then things which he cannot do. But if we answer "No," we are immediately asserting that there are things which he cannot do, that is to say that he is already not omnipotent.

It cannot be replied that the question which sets this paradox is not a proper question. It would make perfectly good sense to say that a human mechanic has made a machine which he cannot control: if there is any difficulty about the question it lies in the notion of omnipotence itself.

This, incidentally, shows that although we have approached this paradox from the free will theory, it is equally a problem for a theological determinist. No one thinks that machines have free will, yet they may well be beyond the control of their makers. The determinist might reply that anyone who makes anything determines its ways of acting, and so determines its subsequent behaviour: even the human mechanic does this by his *choice* of materials and structure for his machine, though he does not know all about either of these: the mechanic thus determines, though he may not foresee, his machine's actions. And since God is omniscient, and since his creation of things is total, he both determines and foresees the ways in which his creatures will act. We may grant this, but it is beside the point. The question is not whether God *originally* determined the future actions of his creatures, but whether he can *subsequently* control their actions, or whether he was able in his original creation to put things beyond his subsequent control. Even on determinist principles the answers "Yes" and "No" are equally irreconcilable with God's omnipotence.

Before suggesting a solution of this paradox, I would point out that there is a parallel Paradox of Sovereignty. Can a legal sovereign make a law restricting its own future legislative power? For example, could the British parliament make a law forbidding any future parliament to socialise banking, and also forbidding the future repeal of this law itself? Or could the British parliament, which was legally sovereign in Australia in, say, 1899, pass a valid law, or series of laws, which made it no longer sovereign in 1933? Again, neither the affirmative nor the negative answer is really satisfactory. If we were to answer "Yes," we should be admitting the validity of a law which, if it were actually made, would mean that parliament was no longer sovereign. If we were to answer "No," we should be admitting that there is a law, not logically absurd, which parliament cannot validly make, that is, that parliament is not now a legal sovereign. This paradox can be solved in the following way. We should distinguish between first order laws, that is laws governing the actions of individuals and bodies other than the legislature, and second order laws, that is laws about laws, laws governing the actions of the legislature itself. Correspondingly, we should distinguish two orders of sovereignty, first order sovereignty (sovereignty (1)) which is unlimited authority to make first order laws, and second order sovereignty (sovereignty (2)) which is unlimited authority to make second order laws. If we say that parliament is sovereign we might mean that any parliament at any time has sovereignty (1), or we might mean that parliament has both sovereignty (1) and sovereignty (2) at present, but we cannot without contradiction mean both that the present parliament has sovereignty (2) and that every parliament at every time has sovereignty (1), for if the present parliament has sovereignty (2) it may use it to take away the sovereignty (1) of later parliaments. What the paradox shows is that we cannot ascribe to any continuing institution legal sovereignty in an inclusive sense.

The analogy between omnipotence and sovereignty shows that the paradox of omnipotence can be solved in a similar way. We must distinguish between first order omnipotence (omnipotence (1)), that is unlimited power to act, and second order omnipotence (omnipotence (2)), that is unlimited power to determine what powers to act things shall have. Then we could consistently say that God all the time has omnipotence (1), but if so no beings at any time have powers to act independently of God. Or we could say that God at one time had omnipotence (2), and used it to assign independent powers to act to certain things, so that God thereafter did not have omnipotence (1). But what the paradox shows is that we cannot consistently ascribe to any continuing being omnipotence in an inclusive sense.

An alternative solution of this paradox would be simply to deny that God is a continuing being, that any times can be assigned to his actions at all. But on this assumption (which also has difficulties of its own) no meaning can be given to the assertion that God made men with wills so free that he could not control them. The paradox of omnipotence can be avoided by putting God outside time, but the free will solution of the problem of evil cannot be saved in this way, and equally it remains impossible to hold that an omnipotent God *binds himself* by causal or logical laws.

CONCLUSION

Of the proposed solutions of the problem of evil which we have examined, none has stood up to criticism. There may be other solutions which require examination, but this study strongly suggests that there is no valid solution of the problem which does not modify at least one of the constituent propositions in a way which would seriously affect the essential core of the theistic position.

Quite apart from the problem of evil, the paradox of omnipotence has shown that God's omnipotence must in any case be restricted in one way or another, that unqualified omnipotence cannot be ascribed to any being that continues through time. And if God and his actions are not in time, can omnipotence, or power of any sort, be meaningfully ascribed to him?

6

The Inductive Argument from Evil against the Existence of God

WILLIAM ROWE

William Rowe (1931–) is emeritus professor of philosophy at Purdue University and the author of numerous books and articles in the philosophy of religion. In the present selection, Rowe argues that an inductive or probabilistic version of the argument from evil justifies atheism. He concedes that deductive arguments against the existence of God on the basis of evil, such as J. L. Mackie uses (Reading 5), do not succeed. Nevertheless, he says it is reasonable to believe that there is no God. In the last part of his essay, Rowe defines his position as "friendly atheism" because he admits that a theist may be justified in rejecting the probabilistic argument from evil.

This paper is concerned with three interrelated questions. The first is: Is there an argument for atheism based on the existence of evil that may rationally justify someone in being an atheist? To this first question I give an affirmative answer and try to support that answer by setting forth a strong argument for atheism based on the existence of evil.[1] The second question is: How can the theist best defend his position against the argument for atheism based on the existence of evil? In response to this question I try to describe what may be an adequate rational defense for theism against any argument for atheism based on the existence of evil. The final question is: What position should the informed atheist take concerning the rationality of theistic belief? Three different answers an atheist may give to this question serve to distinguish three varieties of atheism: unfriendly atheism, indifferent atheism, and friendly atheism. In the final part of the paper I discuss and defend the position of friendly atheism.

Before we consider the argument from evil, we need to distinguish a narrow and a broad sense of the terms "theist," "atheist," and "agnostic." By a "theist" in the narrow sense I mean someone who believes in the existence of an omnipotent, omniscient, eternal, supremely good being who created the world. By a "theist" in the broad sense I mean someone who believes in the existence of some sort of divine being or divine reality. To be a theist in the narrow sense is also to be a theist in the broad sense, but one may be a theist in the broad sense— as was Paul Tillich—without believing that there is a supremely good, omnipotent, omniscient, eternal being who created the world. Similar distinctions must be made between a narrow and a broad sense of the terms "atheist" and "agnostic." To be an atheist in the broad sense is to deny the existence of any sort of divine being or divine reality. Tillich was not an atheist in the broad sense. But he was an atheist in the narrow sense, for he denied that there exists a divine being that is all-knowing,

Reprinted from "The Problem of Evil and Some Varieties of Atheism," *American Philosophical Quarterly* 16 (1979) by permission. Footnotes edited.

all-powerful and perfectly good. In this paper I will be using the terms "theism," "theist," "atheism," "atheist," "agnosticism," and "agnostic" in the narrow sense, not in the broad sense.

I

In developing the argument for atheism based on the existence of evil, it will be useful to focus on some particular evil that our world contains in considerable abundance. Intense human and animal suffering, for example, occurs daily and in great plenitude in our world. Such intense suffering is a clear case of evil. Of course, if the intense suffering leads to some greater good, a good we could not have obtained without undergoing the suffering in question, we might conclude that the suffering is justified, but it remains an evil nevertheless. For we must not confuse the intense suffering in and of itself with the good things to which it sometimes leads or of which it may be a necessary part. Intense human or animal suffering is in itself bad, an evil, even though it may sometimes be justified by virtue of being a part of, or leading to, some good which is unobtainable without it. What is evil in itself may sometimes be good as a means because it leads to something that is good in itself. In such a case, while remaining an evil in itself, the intense human or animal suffering is, nevertheless, an evil which someone might be morally justified in permitting.

Taking human and animal suffering as a clear instance of evil which occurs with great frequency in our world, the argument for atheism based on evil can be stated as follows:

1. There exist instances of intense suffering which an omnipotent, omniscient being could have prevented without thereby losing some greater good or permitting some evil equally bad or worse.[2]

2. An omniscient, wholly good being would prevent the occurrence of any intense suffering it could, unless it could not do so without thereby losing some greater good or permitting some evil equally bad or worse.

3. There does not exist an omnipotent, omniscient, wholly good being.

What are we to say about this argument for atheism, an argument based on the profusion of one sort of evil in our world? The argument is valid; therefore, if we have rotational grounds for accepting its premises, to that extent we have rational grounds for accepting atheism. Do we, however, have rational grounds for accepting the premises of this argument?

Let's begin with the second premise. Let s_1 be an instance of intense human or animal suffering which an omniscient, wholly good being could prevent. We will also suppose that things are such that s_1 will occur unless prevented by the omniscient, wholly good (OG) being. We might be interested in determining what would be a sufficient condition of OG failing to prevent s_1. But, for our purpose here, we need only try to state a necessary condition for OG failing to prevent s_1. That condition, so it seems to me, is this:

Either

(i)   there is some greater good, G, such that G is obtainable by OG only if OG permits s_1,

or

(ii) there is some greater good, G, such that G is obtainable by OG only if OG permits either s_1 or some evil equally bad or worse,

or

(iii) s_1 is such that it is preventable by OG only if OG permits some evil equally bad or worse.

It is important to recognize that (iii) is not included in (i). For losing a good greater than s_1 is not the same as permitting an evil greater than s_1. And this because the *absence* of a good state of affairs need not itself be an evil state of affairs. It is also important to recognize that s_1 might be such that it is preventable by OG *without* losing G (so condition (i) is not satisfied) but also such that if OG did prevent it, G would be lost unless OG permitted some evil equal to or worse than s_1. If this were so, it does not seem correct to require that OG prevent s_1.

Thus, condition (ii) takes into account an important possibility not encompassed in condition (i).

Is it true that if an omniscient, wholly good being permits the occurrence of some intense suffering it could have prevented, then either (i) or (ii) or (iii) obtains? It seems to me that it is true. But if it is true then so is premise (2) of the argument for atheism. For that premise merely states in more compact form what we have suggested must be true if an omniscient, wholly good being fails to prevent some intense suffering it could prevent. Premise (2) says that an omniscient, wholly good being would prevent the occurrence of any intense suffering it could, unless it could not do so without thereby losing some greater good or permitting some evil equally bad or worse. This premise (or something not too distant from it) is, I think, held in common by many atheists and nontheists. Of course, there may be disagreement about whether something is good, and whether, if it is good, one would be morally justified in permitting some intense suffering to occur in order to obtain it. Someone might hold, for example, that no good is great enough to justify permitting an innocent child to suffer terribly. Again, someone might hold that the mere fact that a given good outweighs some suffering and would be lost if the suffering were prevented, is not a morally sufficient reason for permitting the suffering. But to hold either of these views is not to deny (2). For (2) claims only that *if* an omniscient, wholly good being permits intense suffering *then* either there is some greater good that would have been lost, or some equally bad or worse evil that would have occurred, had the intense suffering been prevented. (2) does not purport to describe what might be a *sufficient* condition for an omniscient, wholly good being to permit intense suffering, only what is a *necessary* condition. So stated, (2) seems to express a belief that accords with our basic moral principles, principles shared by both theists and nontheists. If we are to fault the argument for atheism, therefore, it seems we must find some fault with its first premise.

Suppose in some distant forest lightning strikes a dead tree, resulting in a forest fire. In the fire a fawn is trapped, horribly burned, and lies in terrible agony for several days before death relieves its suffering. So far as we can see, the fawn's intense suffering is pointless. For there does not appear to be any greater good such that the prevention of the fawn's suffering would require either the loss of that good or the occurrence of an evil equally bad or worse. Nor does there seem to be any equally bad or worse evil so connected to the fawn's suffering that it would have had to occur had the fawn's suffering been prevented. Could an omnipotent, omniscient being have prevented the fawn's apparently pointless suffering? The answer is obvious, as even the theist will insist. An omnipotent, omniscient being could have easily prevented the fawn from being horribly burned, or, given the burning, could have spared the fawn the intense suffering by quickly ending its life, rather than allowing the fawn to lie in terrible agony for several days. Since the fawn's intense suffering was preventable and, so far as we can see, pointless, doesn't it appear that premise (1) of the argument is true, that there do exist instances of intense suffering which an omnipotent, omniscient being could have prevented without thereby losing some greater good or permitting some evil equally bad or worse?

It must be acknowledged that the case of the fawn's apparently pointless suffering does not prove that (1) is true. For even though we cannot see how the fawn's suffering is required to obtain some greater good (or to prevent some equally bad or worse evil), it hardly follows that it is not so required. After all, we are often surprised by how things we thought to be unconnected turn out to be intimately connected. Perhaps, for all we know, there is some familiar good outweighing the fawn's suffering to which that suffering is connected in a way we do not see. Furthermore, there may well be unfamiliar goods, goods we haven't dreamed of, to which the fawn's suffering is inextricably connected. Indeed, it would seem to require something like omniscience on our part before we could lay claim to *knowing* that there is no greater good connected to the fawn's suffering in such a manner than an omnipotent, omniscient being could not have achieved that good without permitting that suffering or some evil equally bad or worse. So the case of the fawn's suffering surely does not enable us to *establish* the truth of (1).

The truth is that we are not in a position to prove that (1) is true. We cannot know with certainty that instances of suffering of the sort described in (1) do occur in our world. But it is one thing to *know* or *prove* that (1) is true and quite another thing to have *rational grounds* for believing (1) to be true. We are often in the position where in the light of our experience and knowledge it is rational to believe that a certain statement is true, even though we are not in a position to prove or to know with certainty that the statement is true. In the light of our past experience and knowledge it is, for example, very reasonable to believe that neither Goldwater nor McGovern will ever be elected President, but we are scarcely in the position of knowing with certainty that neither will ever be elected President. So, too, with (1), although we cannot know with certainty that it is true, it perhaps can be rationally supported, shown to be a rational belief.

Consider again the case of the fawn's suffering. Is it reasonable to believe that there is some greater good so intimately connected to that suffering that even an omnipotent, omniscient being could not have obtained that good without permitting that suffering or some evil at least as bad? It certainly does not appear reasonable to believe this. Nor does it seem reasonable to believe that there is some evil at least as bad as the fawn's suffering such that an omnipotent being simply could not have prevented it without permitting the fawn's suffering. But even if it should somehow be reasonable to believe either of these things of the fawn's suffering, we must then ask whether it is reasonable to believe either of these things of *all* the instances of seemingly pointless human and animal suffering that occur daily in our world. And surely the answer to this more general question must be no. It seems quite unlikely that all the instances of intense suffering occurring daily in our world are intimately related to the occurrence of greater goods or the prevention of evils at least as bad; and even more unlikely, should they somehow all be so related, that an omnipotent, omniscient being could not have achieved at least some of those goods (or prevented some of those evils) without permitting the instances of intense suffering that are supposedly related to them. In the

light of our experience and knowledge of the variety and scale of human and animal suffering in our world, the idea that none of this suffering could have been prevented by an omnipotent being without thereby losing a greater good or permitting an evil at least as bad seems an extraordinary absurd idea, quite beyond our belief. It seems then that although we cannot prove that (1) is true, it is, nevertheless, altogether *reasonable* to believe that (1) is true, that (1) is a *rational* belief.

Returning now to our argument for atheism, we've seen that the second premise expresses a basic belief common to many theists and nontheists. We've also seen that our experience and knowledge of the variety and profusion of suffering in our world provides *rational support* for the first premise. Seeing that the conclusion, "There does not exist an omnipotent, omniscient, wholly good being" follows from these two premises, it does seem that we have *rational support* for atheism, that it is reasonable for us to believe that the theistic God does not exist.

II

Can theism be rationally defended against the argument for atheism we have just examined? If it can, how might the theist best respond to that argument? Since the argument from (1) and (2) to (3) is valid, and since the theist, no less than the nontheist, is more than likely committed to (2), it's clear that the theist can reject this atheistic argument only by rejecting its first premise, the premise that states that there are instances of intense suffering which an omnipotent, omniscient being could have prevented without thereby losing some greater good or permitting some evil equally bad or worse. How, then, can the theist best respond to this premise and the considerations advanced in its support?

There are basically three responses a theist can make. First, he might argue not that (1) is false or probably false, but only that the reasoning given in support of it is in some way *defective*. He may do this either by arguing that the reasons given in support of (1) are *in themselves* insufficient to justify accepting (1), or by arguing that there are other things we know which, when taken in conjunction with these reasons, do not justify us in accepting (1). I suppose some theists would be content with this rather modest response to the basic argument for atheism. But given the validity of the basic argument and the theist's likely acceptance of (2), he is thereby committed to the view that (1) is false, not just that we have no good reasons for accepting (1) as true. The second two responses are aimed at showing that it is reasonable to believe that (1) is false. Since the theist is committed to this view, I shall focus the discussion on these two attempts, attempts which we can distinguish as "the direct attack" and "the indirect attack."

By a direct attack, I mean an attempt to reject (1) by pointing out goods, for example, to which suffering may well be connected, goods which an omnipotent, omniscient being could not achieve without permitting suffering. It is doubtful, however, that the direct attack can succeed. The theist may point out that some suffering leads to moral and spiritual development impossible without suffering. But it's reasonably clear that suffering often occurs in a degree far beyond what is required for character development. The theist may say that some suffering results from free choices of human beings and might be preventable only by preventing some measure of human freedom. But, again, it's clear that much intense suffering occurs not as a result of human free choices. The general difficulty with this direct attack on premise (1) is twofold. First, it cannot succeed; for the theist does not know what greater goods might be served, or evils prevented, by each instance of intense human or animal suffering. Second, the theist's own religious tradition usually maintains that in this life it is not given to us to know God's purpose in allowing particular instances of suffering. Hence, the direct attack against premise (1) cannot succeed and violates basic beliefs associated with theism.

The best procedure for the theist to follow in rejecting premise (1) is the indirect procedure. This procedure I shall call "the G. E. Moore shift," so-called in honor of the twentieth century philosopher G. E. Moore, who used it to great effect in dealing with the arguments of the skeptics.

Skeptical philosophers such as David Hume have advanced ingenious arguments to prove that no one can know of the existence of any material object. The premises of their arguments employ plausible principles, principles which many philosophers have tried to reject directly, but only with questionable success. Moore's procedure was altogether different. Instead of arguing directly against the premises of the skeptic's arguments, he simply noted that the premises implied, for example, that he (Moore) did not know of the existence of a pencil. Moore then proceeded indirectly against the skeptic's premises by arguing:

> I do know that this pencil exists.
>
> If the skeptic's principles are correct I cannot know of the existence of this pencil.
>
> ∴ The skeptic's principles (at least one) must be incorrect.

Moore then noted that his argument is just as valid as the skeptic's, that both of their arguments contain the premise "If the skeptic's principles are correct Moore cannot know of the existence of this pencil," and concluded that the only way to choose between the two arguments (Moore's and the skeptic's) is by deciding which of the first premises it is more rational to believe—Moore's premise "I do know that this pencil exists" or the skeptic's premise asserting that his skeptical principles are correct. Moore concluded that his own first premise was the more rational of the two.

Before we see how the theist may apply the G. E. Moore shift to the basic argument of atheism, we should note the general strategy of the shift. We're given an argument: p, q, therefore, r. Instead of arguing directly against p, another argument is constructed not-r, q, therefore, not-p—which begins with the denial of the conclusion of the first argument, keeps its second premise, and ends with the denial of the first premise as its conclusion. Compare, for example, these two:

I.	p	II.	not-r
	q		q
	r		not-p

It is a truth of logic that if I is valid II must be valid as well. Since the arguments are the same so far as the second premise is concerned, any choice between them must concern their respective first premises. To argue against the first premise (*p*) by constructing the counter argument II is to employ the G. E. Moore shift.

Applying the G. E. Moore shift against the first premise of the basic argument for atheism, the theist can argue as follows:

not-3. There exists an omnipotent, omniscient, wholly good being.

2. An omniscient, wholly good being would prevent the occurrence of any intense suffering it could, unless it could not do so without thereby losing some greater good or permitting some evil equally bad or worse.

therefore,

not-1. It is not the case that there exist instances of intense suffering which an omnipotent, omniscient being could have prevented without thereby losing some greater good or permitting some evil equally bad or worse.

We now have two arguments: the basic argument for atheism from (1) and (2) to (3), and the theist's best response, the argument from (not-3) and (2) to (not-1). What the theist then says about (1) is that he has rational grounds for believing in the existence of the theistic God (not-3), accepts (2) as true, and sees that (not-1) follows from (not-3) and (2). He concludes, therefore, that he has rational grounds for rejecting (1). Having rational grounds for rejecting (1), the theist concludes that the basic argument for atheism is mistaken.

III

We've had a look at a forceful argument for atheism and what seems to be the theist's best response to that argument. If one is persuaded by the argument for atheism, as I find myself to be, how might one best view the position of the theist? Of course, he will view the theist as having a false belief, just as the theist will view the atheist as having a false belief. But what position should the atheist take concerning the *rationality* of the theist's belief? There are three major positions an atheist might take, positions which we may think of as some varieties of atheism. First, the atheist may believe that no one is rationally justified in believing that the theistic God exists. Let us call this position "unfriendly atheism." Second, the atheist may hold no belief concerning whether any theist is or isn't rationally justified in believing that the theistic God exists. Let us call this view "indifferent atheism." Finally, the atheist may believe that some theists are rationally justified in believing that the theistic God exists. This view we shall call "friendly atheism." In this final part of the paper I propose to discuss and defend the position of friendly atheism.

If no one can be rationally justified in believing a false proposition then friendly atheism is a paradoxical, if not incoherent position. But surely the truth of a belief is not a necessary condition of someone's being rationally justified in having that belief. So in holding that someone is rationally justified in believing that the theistic God exists, the friendly atheist is not committed to thinking that the theist has a true belief. What he is committed to is that the theist has rational grounds for his belief, a belief the atheist rejects and is convinced he is rationally justified in rejecting. But is this possible? Can someone, like our friendly atheist, hold a belief, be convinced that he is rationally justified in holding that belief, and yet believe that someone else is equally justified in believing the opposite? Surely this is possible. Suppose your friends see you off on a flight to Hawaii. Hours after take-off they learn that your plane has gone down at sea. After a twenty-four hour search, no survivors have been found. Under these circumstances they are rationally justified in believing that you have perished. But it is hardly rational for you to believe this, as you bob up and down in your life vest, wondering why the search planes have failed to spot you. Indeed, to amuse yourself while awaiting your fate, you might very well reflect on the fact that your friends are rationally justified in believing that you are now dead, a proposition you disbelieve and are rationally justified in disbelieving. So, too, perhaps an atheist may be rationally justified in his atheistic belief and yet hold that some theists are rationally justified in believing just the opposite of what he believes.

What sort of grounds might a theist have for believing that God exists? Well, he might endeavor to justify his belief by appealing to one or more of the traditional arguments: Ontological, Cosmological, Teleological, Moral, etc. Second, he might appeal to certain aspects of religious experience, perhaps even his own religious experience. Third, he might try to justify theism as a plausible theory in terms of which we can account for a variety of phenomena. Although an atheist must hold that the theistic God does not exist, can he not also believe, and be justified in so believing, that some of these "justifications of theism" do actually rationally justify some theists in their belief that there exists a supremely good, omnipotent, omniscient being? It seems to me that he can.

If we think of the long history of theistic belief and the special situations in which people are sometimes placed, it is perhaps as absurd to think that no one was ever rationally justified in believing that the theistic God exists as it is to think that no one was ever justified in believing that human beings would never walk on the moon. But in suggesting that friendly atheism is preferable to unfriendly atheism, I don't mean to rest the case on what some human beings might reasonably have believed in the eleventh or thirteenth century. The more interesting question is whether some people in modern society, people who are aware of the usual grounds for belief and disbelief and are acquainted to some degree with modern science, are yet rationally justified in accepting theism. Friendly

atheism is a significant position only if it answers this question in the affirmative.

It is not difficult for an atheist to be friendly when he has reason to believe that the theist could not reasonably be expected to be acquainted with the grounds for disbelief that he (the atheist) possesses. For then the atheist may take the view that some theists are rationally justified in holding to theism, but would not be so were they to be acquainted with the grounds for disbelief—those grounds being sufficient to tip the scale in favor of atheism when balanced against the reasons the theist has in support of his belief.

Friendly atheism becomes paradoxical, however, when the atheist contemplates believing that the theist has all the grounds for atheism that he, the atheist, has, and yet is rationally justified in maintaining his theistic belief. But even so excessively friendly a view as this perhaps can be held by the atheist if he also has some reason to think that the grounds for theism are not as telling as the theist is justified in taking them to be.

In this paper I've presented what I take to be a strong argument for atheism, pointed out what I think is the theist's best response to that argument, distinguished three positions an atheist might take concerning the rationality of theistic belief, and made some remarks in defense of the position called "friendly atheism." I'm aware that the central points of the paper are not likely to be warmly received by many philosophers. Philosophers who are atheists tend to be tough minded—holding that there are no good reasons for supposing that theism is true. And theists tend either to reject the view that the existence of evil provides rational grounds for atheism or to hold that religious belief has nothing to do with reason and evidence at all. But such is the way of philosophy.

NOTES

1. Some philosophers have contended that the existence of evil is *logically inconsistent* with the existence of the theistic God. No one, I think, has succeeded in establishing such an extravagant claim.

Indeed, granted incompatibilism, there is a fairly compelling argument for the view that the existence of evil is logically consistent with the existence of the theistic God. (For a lucid statement of this argument see Alvin Plantinga, *God, Freedom, and Evil* (New York, 1974), 29–59.) There remains, however, what we may call the *evidential* form—as opposed to the *logical* form—of the problem of evil; the view that the variety and profusion of evil in our world, although perhaps not logically inconsistent with the existence of the theistic God, provides, nevertheless, *rational support* for atheism. In this paper I shall be concerned solely with the evidential form of the problem, the form of the problem which, I think, presents a rather severe difficulty for theism. William L. Rowe, "The Problem of Evil and Some Varieties of Atheism," first published in *American Philosophical Quarterly*, 16 (1979), pp. 335–41. Used with permission.

2. If there is some good, *G*, greater than any evil, (1) will be false for the trivial reason that no matter what evil, *E*, we pick the conjunctive good state of affairs consisting of *G* and *E* will outweigh *E* and be such that an omnipotent being could not obtain it without permitting *E*. (See Alvin Plantinga, *God and Other Minds* [Ithaca, 1967], 167.) To avoid this objection we may insert "unreplaceable" into our premises (1) and (2) between "some" and "greater." If *E* isn't required for *G*, and *G* is better than *G* plus *E*, then the good conjunctive state of affairs composed of *G* and *E* would be replaceable by the greater good of *G* alone. For the sake of simplicity, however, I will ignore this complication both in the formulation and discussion of premises (1) and (2).

7

Evolution and the Problem of Evil

PAUL DRAPER

Paul Draper (1957–) is professor of philosophy at Purdue University and the author of several important essays in the philosophy of religion. In the present article, Draper notes that traditionally the problem of evil has been, with few exceptions, the only atheological argument against the existence of God. He argues that the naturalistic account of evolution can provide a cogent alternative to theism and that by combining that with the problem of evil, one can begin to build a cumulative case against theism.

I. INTRODUCTION

Naturalism and theism are powerful and popular worldviews. They suggest very different conceptions of the nature of human beings, our relationship to the world, and our future. Though I hope that theism is true, I believe that it faces a number of evidential problems, problems that prevent my

hope from becoming belief. In this paper I will examine two of those problems: evolution and evil. I will use certain known facts about the origin of complex life and the pattern of pain and pleasure in the world to construct a powerful *prima facie* case against theism.

By "theism" I mean the hypothesis[1] that God is the creator of the physical universe. I take the

This article appeared in print for the first time in the third edition of *Philosophy of Religion: An Anthology*, edited by Louis Pojman.
Copyright © Paul Draper 1997.

word "God" to be a title that, by definition, can be borne only by a perfect supernatural person. To claim that God is a "person" is to claim that God performs actions and has beliefs and purposes. "Supernatural" persons are not natural—they are neither a part nor a product of the physical universe—and yet they can affect natural objects. A "perfect" person is, among other things, perfect in power (omnipotent), perfect in knowledge (omniscient), and perfect in moral goodness (morally perfect). While some have dismissed this conception of God as religiously insignificant, I am convinced that, for millions of Jews, Christians, and Muslims, factual belief in a perfect supernatural person is essential for making sense of their forms of worship. By "naturalism" I mean the hypothesis that the physical universe is a "closed system" in the sense that nothing that is neither a part nor a product of it can affect it. So naturalism entails the nonexistence of all supernatural beings, including the theistic God.

Arguments against theism can be divided into two main types. *Logical* arguments attempt to show that theism is either self-contradictory or logically inconsistent with some known fact. *Evidential* arguments attempt to show that certain known facts that are (at least so far as we can tell) consistent with theism nevertheless provide evidence against it.[2] The arguments in this paper will be evidential. I will show that certain known facts support the hypothesis of naturalism over the hypothesis of theism because we have considerably more reason to expect them to obtain on the assumption that naturalism is true than on the assumption that theism is true. This is a threat to theism because naturalism and theism are alternative hypotheses—they cannot both be true. Thus, if (after considering all of the evidence) naturalism turns out to be more probable than theism, then theism is probably false.

II. EVOLUTION

Ever since the publication of Darwin's *On the Origin of Species*, countless theologians, philosophers, and scientists have pointed out that evolution could be the means by which God has chosen to create

human beings and the rest of the living world. This is thought to show that, while the truth of evolution does refute the biblical story of creation as told in the book of Genesis, it in no way threatens the more general belief that the universe was created by God. In other words, it provides no reason to doubt theism. The plausibility of this argument is reflected by the fact that many scientists are both evolutionists and theists. Commenting on this fact, Stephen Jay Gould says:

> Unless at least half my colleagues are dunces, there can be—on the most raw and direct empirical grounds—no conflict between science and religion. I know hundreds of scientists who share a conviction about the fact of evolution, and teach it in the same way. Among these people I note an entire spectrum of religious attitudes—from devout daily prayer and worship to resolute atheism. Either there's no correlation between religious belief and confidence in evolution—or else half these people are fools.[3]

What Gould neglects to mention is that many well-educated people, including many of Gould's colleagues on the irreligious end of the spectrum, reject theism precisely because they believe in evolution. For example, William B. Provine, a leading historian of science, maintains that those who retain their religious beliefs while accepting evolution "have to check [their] brains at the church-house door."[4]

So who is correct? Is it compatibilists like Gould and the liberal preacher Henry Ward Beecher, who claimed in 1885 that evolution "will change theology, but only to bring out the simple temple of God in clearer and more beautiful lines and proportions"[5]? Or is it incompatibilists like Provine and the fundamentalist preacher William Jennings Bryan, who once defined "theistic evolution" as "an anesthetic which deadens the patient's pain while atheism removes his religion"[6]? My own position, as my introductory remarks suggest, lies somewhere between the view that theistic evolution is a happy marriage and the view that it must end in divorce. I agree with the compatibilists that theism and evolution are logically consistent. What I disagree with is the compatibilist's inference from no inconsistency to no conflict. For while consistency implies that the truth of evolution does not disprove theism—that there is no good *logical* argument from evolution against theism just as there is no good logical argument from evil against theism—it does not imply that the truth of evolution is no evidence at all against theism. My position is that evolution is evidence favoring naturalism over theism. There is, in other words, a good *evidential* argument from evolution against theism.

By "evolution," I mean the conjunction of two theses. The first, which I will call "the genealogical thesis," asserts that evolution did in fact occur—complex life did evolve from relatively simple life. Specifically, it is the view that all multicellular organisms and all (relatively) complex unicellular organisms on earth (both present and past) are the (more or less) gradually modified descendents of a small number of relatively simple unicellular organisms. The second thesis, which I will call "the genetic thesis," addresses the issue of how evolution occurred. It states that all evolutionary change in populations of complex organisms either is or is the result of trans-generational genetic change (or, to be more precise, trans-generational change in nucleic acids). It is important to distinguish this claim about the mechanisms by which evolution takes place from the much more specific claim that natural selection operating on random genetic mutation is the principal mechanism driving evolutionary change (or the principal mechanism driving the evolutionary change that results in increased complexity). Let's call this more specific claim "Darwinism" and its conjunction with evolution "Darwinian evolution."

Many evolutionary arguments against theism appeal to Darwinian evolution rather than just to evolution. I believe that such arguments overestimate the strength of the evidence for Darwinism. Darwinism may be highly probable on the assumption that naturalism is true. But it is far less probable on the assumption that theism is true, because on theism it is a real possibility that God has guided evolution by directly causing various genetic changes

to occur. Thus, any argument against theism that is based on the truth of Darwinism is at best question-begging. This is why my argument appeals only to evolution rather than to Darwinian evolution. It is my belief (which I won't defend here) that the evidence for evolution, unlike the evidence for Darwinian evolution, is overwhelming—so overwhelming that evolution can legitimately be taken as fact rather than mere theory for the purpose of arguing against theism.

The specific claim I wish to defend is the following:

> Antecedently, evolution is much more probable on the assumption that naturalism is true than on the assumption that theism is true.

By "antecedently" I mean "independent of the observations and testimony that together constitute the primary evidence upon which what we know about evolution, as well as the connection between pain and pleasure and reproductive success, is based." Thus, I intend to abstract from our information about selective breeding and other changes within populations of animals, as well as what we know about the geographical distribution of living things, homologies, the fossil record, genetic and biochemical evidence, imperfect adaptations, and vestigial organs. The additional abstraction concerning pain and pleasure is necessary because eventually I will combine my argument concerning evolution with an argument concerning the systematic connection between pain and pleasure and reproductive success. The claim will be made that evolution and this connection are, taken together, antecedently much more likely on naturalism than on theism. One last point. No other abstraction from what we know is intended. For example, I do not intend to abstract from our knowledge that complex life of various forms exists nor from our knowledge that this life has not always existed. It is an interesting and difficult question whether these facts are evidence favoring theism over naturalism, but that issue is beyond the scope of this paper.

Let "T," "N," and "E" stand for theism, naturalism and evolution, let "Pr(p)" stand for the antecedent probability of p being true, and let "$Pr(p/q)$" stand for the antecedent probability of p being true on the assumption that q is true. Finally, let "$>!$" stand for "is much greater than." The claim I wish to defend can now be restated as follows:

$$Pr(E/N) >! Pr(E/T)$$

My strategy for proving this claim requires one more symbol and one more definition. Let "S" stand for special creationism, by which I mean the statement that some relatively complex living things did not descend from relatively simple single-celled organisms but rather were independently created by a supernatural person. (The use of the word "independently" here signifies not just that the creation in question violates genealogical continuity, but also that it involves the direct intervention of the deity in the natural order.) Since evolution entails that special creationism is false, some basic theorems of the probability calculus give us:

$$Pr(E/N) >! Pr(E/T) \text{ if and only if } Pr(\sim S/N) \times Pr(E/\sim S\&N) >! Pr(\sim S/T) \times Pr(E/\sim S\&T)^7$$

My strategy for establishing that $Pr(E/N) >! Pr(E/T)$ will be to show both that $Pr(\sim S/N) >! Pr(\sim S/T)$ and that $Pr(E/\sim S\&N) >! Pr(E/\sim S\&T)$. In other words, I will show both that special creationism is antecedently much more likely to be false on naturalism than on theism and that, even on the assumption that special creationism is false, evolution is still antecedently at least as likely to be true on naturalism as it is on theism.

Since naturalism entails that no supernatural beings exist, it entails that special creationism is false. Thus, the falsity of special creationism is antecedently certain on naturalism: $Pr(\sim S/N) = 1$. But on theism special creationism might, for all we know antecedently, be true: $Pr(\sim S/T) < 1$. Thus, the falsity of special creationism is antecedently more probable on naturalism than on theism, which implies that the falsity of special creationism is some evidence favoring naturalism over theism— it raises the ratio of the probability of naturalism to the probability of theism. But how strong is this evidence? Is the falsity of special creationism *much* more probable on naturalism than on theism? I will

show that $\sim S$ is at least twice as probable antecedently on naturalism as it is on theism, which implies that it at least doubles the ratio of the probability of naturalism to the probability of theism.[8] Since $Pr(\sim S/N) = 1$, my task is to show that $Pr(\sim S/T) \leq 1/2$, which is to say that $Pr(S/T) \geq 1/2$—that, independent of the evidence for evolution, special creationism is at least as likely as not on the assumption that theism is true. To defend this claim, I will first evaluate some antecedent reasons for believing that God, assuming he exists, did not create any complex living things independently. Then I will show that we have a very strong antecedent reason for believing that God, assuming he exists, did specially create.

At first glance, it seems that the evidence for evolution is the only strong reason theists have for believing that God is not a special creator (which is to say that we don't have any strong *antecedent* reasons for believing this). After all, for all we know antecedently, God might have chosen to create in a variety of different ways. For example, while he might have created life in a way consistent with genealogical continuity, he might also have created each species independently. Or he might have created certain basic types independently, allowing for evolutionary change, including change resulting in new species, within these types. Or he might have independently created only a few species or even only a single species, humans perhaps. Antecedently—that is, independent of the evidence for evolution—it appears we have no reason at all to think that an omnipotent, omniscient, and morally perfect creator would prefer evolution or any other "naturalistic" approach to one of these forms of special creation.

Some theists, however, are quite confident on purely *a priori* grounds that God is not a special creator. According to Diogenes Allen and Howard J. Van Till, for example, special creationism was implausible even before the evidence for evolution was discovered, because it is an implication of God's "rationality" or his status as creator rather than as "member of the universe" that God "creates a universe with members that are coherently connected."[9] This coherence precludes God's intervening in the natural order and hence precludes any sort of special creation, including the creation of those first simple life forms from which all subsequent life has evolved. Thus, according to these theists, the only sort of explanations of natural phenomena that theistic scientists should look for are ones that are consistent with naturalism. In short, these theists are committed methodological naturalists.

I don't find these arguments at all convincing. What possible justification could be given for thinking that if God were the immediate cause of a natural event that would reduce God's status from creator to "member of the universe"? Also, what does God's rationality have to do with this? Perhaps the idea is that, just as a perfectly rational car manufacturer would produce a car that never needed its gas tank filled or its air filter replaced, a perfectly rational creator would make a universe that ran on its own. But such a car would be preferable because filling up with gas or replacing parts has a cost in terms of time, energy, and so on. An omnipotent and omniscient creator wouldn't have such worries. In general, what counts as a rational or perfect or defective universe depends on the creator's goals. What goal or plan of God would be better served by a universe in which God never intervenes? Of course, human freedom may place limitations on the amount and type of God's interventions. But it doesn't rule out special creation. For all we know, God may have some goal that is furthered by the laws of nature we have, but those laws are such that they will not by themselves produce the sort of complex life God wants. If this were the case, then God would independently create that life. Surely such intervention in the course of nature would not conflict with God's status as creator or with his rationality. Nor would it imply that the universe is in some way defective or inferior to universes in which God never intervenes.

Another theist who holds that we have antecedent reasons for believing that God would not perform any special creative acts is the philosopher Ernan McMullin. In response to Alvin Plantinga's defense of special creationism, McMullin says that "from the theological and philosophical standpoints, such intervention is, if anything, antecedently *improbable*."[10] McMullin claims that "the eloquent texts of *Genesis, Job, Isaiah,* and *Psalms*" support his position, because "The Creator whose powers are gradually revealed in these texts is omnipotent and all-wise, far beyond the reach of human reckoning. His Providence extends to all His creatures; they are all part of His single plan, only a fragment of which we know, and that darkly."[11] But how this is supposed to support his position is never explained. It seems to do the opposite, since any claim to know that God would never intervene in the natural order will be difficult to justify if we are as much in the dark about God's plans as these texts suggest.[12]

Incidentally, I find it interesting that, when confronted with arguments against theism based on the idea that it is antecedently unlikely that God would permit heinous evil, theistic philosophers are quick to suggest that, since God is omniscient, humans are not in a position to make such a judgment. Yet, if we are to believe Allen and Van Till (McMullin has his doubts), then humans are in a position to judge that it is antecedently unlikely that God would create any life forms independently! Personally, I find the claim that the torturing of innocent children is antecedently improbable on theism vastly more plausible than the claim that special creationism is antecedently improbable on theism.

The problem with the theistic objections to special creationism considered so far is that they all involve *a priori* theological or philosophical speculation, the direction of which is influenced far too much by the conclusion desired.[13] Indeed, these attempts to make special creation seem incompatible with theism are no more objective and no more plausible than William B. Provine's attempt to make evolution seem incompatible with theism. While Allen, Van Till, and McMullin claim that God would never intervene in nature to create life, Provine claims that the idea of a God who "works through the laws of nature" is "worthless" and "equivalent to atheism."[14] How convenient!

A more serious attempt to show that special creationism is antecedently unlikely on theism is a posteriori in nature. We know by past experience that God, if he exists, has at least latent deistic tendencies. Teleology was, after all, eliminated from the physical sciences well before Darwin wrote *On the Origin of Species*. And even independent of the evidence for evolution there is considerable evidence that various biological processes work quite well without divine intervention. In general, even independent of the evidence on which evolution is based, the history of science is a history of success for naturalistic explanations and failure for supernaturalistic ones. Thus, we have a good antecedent *a posteriori* reason to believe that, assuming theism is true, God does not intervene in nature.

I believe that the past success of naturalistic science does provide some reason for theists to believe that God is not a special creator. But it is easy to overestimate the strength of this reason, especially for intellectual theists who must admit to living in a "post-mythological" era or else risk being held personally responsible for the plight of Galileo. But putting scientific propaganda aside, it is important to remember how little we actually know about the causal history of the universe! Were it not for the evidence for evolution, our sample of successful naturalistic explanations seems to me to be much too small to justify great confidence in the claim that, *assuming God exists*, God is not a special creator. Of course, it is worth mentioning that, if I am underestimating how successful the search for naturalistic explanations has been, then theists hardly escape unscathed. For if the search for such explanations has been so successful that any supernaturalistic explanation of a natural phenomenon is implausible even on the assumption that theism is true, then that would be powerful evidence against theism. For such extraordinary success would be antecedently much more likely on naturalism—which entails that all supernaturalistic explanations are false—than it would on theism.

More to the point, however, I believe theists have a very strong antecedent reason for believing that God did create at least some complex life independently. For the division between conscious and nonconscious life is enormously significant if theism is true. Theism implies an extreme metaphysical dualism—a mind existed prior to the physical world and was responsible for its existence. Thus, on the assumption that theism is true, it is antecedently likely that minds are fundamentally nonphysical entities and hence that conscious life is fundamentally different from nonconscious life. But this in turn makes it likely that conscious living things are not just the genetically modified descendents of nonconscious living things—that conscious life was created independently. And since special creationism is defined as the position that at least some complex life was created independently, it follows that, on the assumption that theism is true, it is antecedently likely that special creationism is true.

The dualism inherent in theism may explain why so many theists were drawn to the idea of special creationism before (and in many cases even after) the evidence for evolution was discovered. For this dualism supports a dualistic view of human nature—a view that must have made the idea that we are the effect of altering the nucleic acids of single-celled organisms seem ludicrous. Offspring don't have to be identical to their parents, but surely genetic change can't result in fundamental metaphysical lines being crossed! Thus, even if we know by past experience that God, assuming he exists, generally doesn't intervene in nature, the sort of metaphysics presupposed by theism makes it antecedently likely that God did intervene in the physical world in order to create a mental world within it. So it's hardly surprising that, before Darwin, many theists were special creationists. They had a good reason and we have a good *antecedent* reason to believe that God, assuming he or she exists, performed at least one special creative act. Thus, $\Pr(S/T) \geq 1/2$. And this implies that the falsity of special creationism is at least twice as probable antecedently on naturalism as it is on theism: $\Pr(\sim S/N) \geq 2 \times \Pr(\sim S/T)$.

Recall that, in order to show that $\Pr(E/N) >!$ $\Pr(E/T)$, it is sufficient to show first that $\Pr(\sim S/N)$ $>!$ $\Pr(\sim S/T)$ and second that $\Pr(E/\sim S\&N) \geq$ $\Pr(E/\sim S\&T)$. I have completed the first of these two tasks. Turning to the second, we are now assuming that special creationism is false and asking how likely evolution is on naturalism and on theism. Of course, naturalism entails that special creationism is false, so the denial of special creationism conjoined with naturalism (~S&N) just is naturalism (N). I will call the denial of special creationism conjoined with theism (~S&T) "regular theism." So my task is to show that evolution is antecedently at least as probable on naturalism as it is on regular theism.

It is important to recognize that the probabilities in question are to be assessed relative to the background knowledge that various complex life forms do exist. Thus, the issue is not whether complex life together with the evolutionary mechanisms that produce it are more surprising on theism or on naturalism. (Again, whether or not there is a good anthropic design argument supporting theism is beyond the scope of this paper.) Given that complex life exists, what makes evolution so likely on naturalism is the lack of plausible naturalistic alternatives to evolution. On naturalism, it is antecedently much more likely that all complex organisms descended from a small number of relatively simple organisms than that complex life descended from a large number of relatively simple single-celled organisms all of which arose independently from nonliving matter or that complex life arose directly from nonliving matter. Furthermore, given the genealogical thesis, it is antecedently likely on naturalism that all evolutionary change in complex life is or results from one basic sort of change like genetic change. On regular theism, alternatives to evolution are somewhat more likely, simply because there is less reason to assume that the complex must arise from the simple. When one starts with omnipotence and omniscience, so much is possible!

Even if the regular theist grants that these considerations favor naturalism, she might counter that it has never been proven that naturalistic evolution is biologically possible. Perhaps evolution could not have produced complex life without supernatural assistance. For example, it might be argued that, without some intelligent being guiding genetic change, such magnificent ordered systems as the human eye would never have evolved. The stronger the evidence for this, the lower the antecedent probability of evolution on naturalism. I do not believe, however, that the evidence for this is very strong. Admittedly, no one can describe in detail exactly how the eye or any other complex organic system could have come about without supernatural assistance. And it's hard to see how anyone could prove that evolution could produce complex life in a naturalistic universe. But neither has anyone provided good reason for thinking that it couldn't either. (Some special creationists have tried, but their arguments are very weak.[15]) This is not to say that there are no real difficulties for naturalistic evolution. (For example, it's notoriously difficult to explain how sexual reproduction evolved.) It's just to say that no one has given a good reason to believe that naturalistic solutions to these problems will not be found. Indeed, the fact that plausible solutions have been found to some of these problems (e.g., the problem of altruistic behavior) gives the naturalist reason for optimism. So any advantage that the problems faced by naturalistic evolution give to regular theism is more than offset by the considerations favoring naturalism mentioned above. All things considered, then, the modest conclusion that evolution is at least as probable antecedently on naturalism as it is on regular theism is justified. Therefore, since the falsity of special creationism is antecedently much more probable on naturalism than on theism, it follows for the reasons explained earlier that evolution is antecedently much more probable on naturalism than on theism.

III. PAIN AND PLEASURE

It is true by definition that a morally perfect God would permit an instance of pain only if he or she had a morally sufficient reason to do so. (By "pain" I mean any suffering, physical or mental.) Thus, the "logical" problem of pain is the problem of whether or not God's being both omnipotent and omniscient is logically compatible with God's having a morally sufficient reason to permit all of the suffering in the world. No one has been able to demonstrate an incompatibility because not even an omnipotent being can do the logically impossible and it might, for all we know or can prove, be logically impossible to bring about certain important goods without at least risking the existence of the suffering we find in our world. So demonstrative logical arguments from pain have been unsuccessful. And nondemonstrative or probabilistic logical arguments from pain have been challenged on the grounds that they involve questionable inductive generalizations, questionable inferences from there being no *known* morally sufficient reasons for an omnipotent and omniscient being to permit certain instances of suffering to their probably being no such morally sufficient reasons. But these discussions of the logical problem of pain leave unsettled the issue of whether or not the suffering in our world is evidence against theism or evidence favoring naturalism over theism. In other words, the failure of logical arguments from evil, including probabilistic ones, does not preclude a successful evidential argument from evil.

I do not, however, wish to consider suffering in isolation. Instead, I will address the issue of whether the pattern of both pain and pleasure in the world is evidence favoring naturalism over theism. The more common strategy of focusing only on evil, indeed only on a few particularly heinous evils, has its advantages. I choose not to pursue this strategy because the theist might counter such an argument by pointing out a few particularly glorious goods and plausibly claiming that they are equally strong evidence favoring theism over naturalism. So my argument will be based on both pain and pleasure. There may, of course, be other intrinsic evils and intrinsic goods besides pain and pleasure, but the issue of whether or not there are, and whether or not, if there are, their existence is evidence against theism, will not be addressed in this paper.

There are many facts about pain and pleasure that might provide the resources for an evidential argument against theism. Because I wish to explore how our knowledge of evolution affects the problem of evil, I will focus on the fact that much of the pain and pleasure we find in the world is systematically connected (in a variety of often complex ways) to reproductive success. For example, it is no accident that we find a warm fire on a cold night pleasurable and lying naked in a snowbank painful. Maintaining a constant body temperature increases our chances of (temporary) survival and thereby increases our chances of reproducing. Of course, the connections are not all this obvious or this direct. For example, children enjoy playing, which promotes the development of various physical, social, and intellectual skills, which in turn increases children's chances of surviving and reproducing. Even less obviously and less directly, adults find play pleasurable (though typically not as much as children do), which may or may not promote reproductive success, but which results from our capacity to enjoy play as children, which, as we have seen, does promote reproductive success. I could give countless other examples, but the connection between pain and pleasure and reproductive success and the systematic nature of that connection is so striking that additional examples aren't really needed. Instead, I will now turn to the task of showing that, antecedently, this connection is much more probable on evolutionary naturalism than it is on evolutionary theism. I will offer a two-part argument for this position, and then reply to two objections.

The first part of my argument appeals to natural selection. I suggested earlier that Darwinism is much more likely to be true if evolutionary naturalism is true than if evolutionary theism is true. Allow me to explain why. Darwinism is likely on evolutionary naturalism both because it explains the increase in the complexity of life over time better than other naturalistic mechanisms and, most importantly for our purposes, it solves an explanatory problem for naturalism: the problem of explaining teleological or "means–end" order in organic systems. Since evolutionary theism can explain teleological order in terms of God's conscious purposes, it wouldn't be at all surprising on theism if the principal mechanisms driving evolution themselves displayed teleological order—if, for example, organisms had built-in mechanisms that would produce precisely those genetic changes needed to solve a problem arising because of some environmental change. (Such mechanisms would have made William Paley a happy evolutionist!) On naturalism, natural selection is just the sort of process one would expect to drive evolution: a simple "blind" process that can explain the extremely complex teleological order in the living world without itself displaying such order. Notice also that, contrary to popular belief, natural selection does not generally promote the good of individual animals. Variations that result in reproductive success will be favored, regardless of the other consequences—good or bad—of the variation. For example, if walking upright gave our distant ancestors a reproductive advantage (e.g., by allowing them to carry tools while they walked), then this trait was selected despite the foot, back, heart, and numerous other ailments that resulted from it. Further, natural selection requires competition for scarce resources and thus entails that many living things will not flourish. So the claim that natural selection is the principal mechanism driving evolutionary change is much more probable on evolutionary naturalism than on evolutionary theism.

Of course, if natural selection is the principal mechanism driving evolution, then it is likely on evolutionary naturalism that it played a significant role in the evolution of pain and pleasure and so it is likely on evolutionary naturalism that pain and pleasure will, like anything produced by natural selection, be systematically connected to reproductive success. Thus, the fact that natural selection is antecedently much more likely to have governed the evolution of pain and pleasure if evolutionary naturalism is true than if evolutionary theism is true supports my position that the systematic connection between reproductive success and the pain and pleasure we find in the world is antecedently much more likely on evolutionary naturalism than on evolutionary theism.

This position is further supported by our antecedent knowledge that many other parts of organic systems are systematically connected to reproductive success. This gives us much more reason to believe that pain and pleasure will also be so connected if we assume that evolutionary naturalism is true than if we assume that evolutionary theism is true. To see why, consider the inductive inference from a sample consisting of other physical and mental parts of organic systems that are systematically connected

to reproductive success to the conclusion that pain and pleasure are also systematically connected to reproductive success. Although a good number of parts of organic systems lack such a connection, this inference is potentially quite strong given the suitability of pain and pleasure for promoting reproductive success. But the assumption that evolutionary theism is true undermines this inference, while the assumption that evolutionary naturalism is true does not. To see why, notice that this inference is an inductive inference from a sample to another member of a population, and the strength of any such inference depends on how much reason one has to believe that this other member is relevantly different from the members of the sample. Now pain and pleasure are strikingly different from other parts of organic systems in one way: They have a specific sort of moral significance that other parts lack. (Other parts of organic systems may have moral significance, but not of the same sort.) But is this a relevant difference? We have much more reason to believe it is on the assumption that evolutionary theism is true than on the assumption that evolutionary naturalism is true. For the biological goal of reproductive success does not provide an omnipotent omniscient creator with a morally sufficient reason for permitting humans and animals to suffer in the ways they do or for limiting their pleasure to the sorts and amounts we find. Thus, on evolutionary theism, pain and pleasure would be systematically connected to the biological goal of reproductive success only if this goal and some unknown justifying moral goal happened to coincide in such a way that each could be simultaneously satisfied. Such a coincidence is (to say the least) antecedently far from certain. So on the assumption that evolutionary theism is true, the inference to the conclusion that pain and pleasure are systematically connected to reproductive success from the premise that other parts of organic systems are so connected is very weak. This inference is much stronger on the assumption that evolutionary naturalism is true because evolutionary naturalism entails nothing that would undermine the inference—on evolutionary naturalism the moral significance of pain and pleasure provides no antecedent reason at all to doubt that they will resemble other parts of organic systems by being systematically connected to reproductive success. Therefore, our antecedent knowledge that pain and pleasure have a certain sort of moral significance adds further support to my position that the systematic connection between pain and pleasure and reproductive success is antecedently much more probable on evolutionary naturalism than on evolutionary theism.

One might object that my argument ignores the many instances of pain and pleasure that are, so far as we can tell, disconnected from the biological goal of reproductive success. For example, some aesthetic pleasures seem to have at most a very remote connection to reproductive success. But neither the existence of such pain and pleasure, nor the fact that, in general, such pain and pleasure is more common in animals that are psychologically complex, is at all surprising on evolutionary naturalism. For the greater the complexity of a system, the more likely that some of its characteristics will be epiphenomenal. Also, much biologically gratuitous pain and pleasure is pathological—it results from the failure of an organic system to function properly. And the existence of this sort of pain and pleasure is also unsurprising on evolutionary naturalism. So on evolutionary naturalism, what we know about biologically gratuitous pain and pleasure is not surprising, while on evolutionary theism, the excess pleasure is perhaps to be expected, but this advantage is offset by the limited amount of such pleasure, by the existence of biologically gratuitous pain, and by the fact that a significant amount of biologically gratuitous pleasure and pain is pathological.

One might also object that theodicies undermine my argument; for theodicies make certain facts about pain antecedently more likely than they would otherwise be. The problem with existing theodicies, however, is that they explain certain facts at the price of making others even more mysterious. That is, they make certain facts more likely only by making others less likely. For example, if one of God's reasons for permitting pain is to punish sinners, then why do the innocent suffer as much as the guilty? Or, if we assume that God

wants to use pain to build moral character, then pain (and pleasure) that is demoralizing becomes even more surprising. If, instead of focusing on a few isolated cases, one looks at the overall pattern of pain and pleasure in the world, one cannot help but be struck by its apparent moral randomness. Pain and pleasure do not systematically promote justice or moral virtue. Nor are moral agents treated all that differently from nonmoral agents. Nonhuman animals suffer in many of the ways humans suffer (the more similar the animal, the more similar the suffering), despite the fact that such suffering cannot play a moral role in their lives, since they are not moral agents.

All of these facts, which might be summed up by saying that pain and pleasure do not systematically promote any discernible moral ends, are exactly what one would expect on evolutionary naturalism. For on evolutionary naturalism, the causes of good and evil are morally indifferent. Thus, on the assumption that evolutionary naturalism is true, it would be surprising in the extreme if pain and pleasure appeared to be anything but morally random. But a discernible moral pattern would be less surprising on theism even if, given the cognitive distance between humans and an omniscient being, it should not be expected. Notice that I am not claiming that the apparent moral randomness of pain and pleasure is antecedently unlikely on evolutionary theism. I'm just claiming that it is antecedently less likely on evolutionary theism than on evolutionary naturalism. And it seems to me that this is obvious. But that means that this apparent randomness adds to the evidence favoring evolutionary naturalism over evolutionary theism. It may not add a lot, but it certainly offsets any advantage evolutionary theism has as a result of the moral roles that pain and pleasure admittedly do play in human lives.

IV. CONCLUSION

I have argued both that evolution is antecedently much more probable on naturalism than on theism and that the systematic connection between pain, as well as pleasure, and reproductive success is antecedently much more probable on evolutionary naturalism than on evolutionary theism. This entails that the conjunction of evolution and the statement that pain and pleasure are systematically connected to reproductive success is antecedently very much more probable on naturalism than on theism. And since neither the truth nor falsity of naturalism or theism is certain, it follows that this conjunction substantially raises the ratio of the probability of naturalism to the probability of theism. Of course, if naturalism were far less plausible than theism (or if it were compatible with theism), then this sort of evidence would be worthless. But naturalism is a very serious alternative to theism. Neither evolution nor anything about pain and pleasure is built into it in an *ad hoc* way. (It is not as if I were claiming, for example, that *evolution* is antecedently more probable on *evolutionary* naturalism than on theism.) Also, naturalism doesn't deny the existence of all nonnatural beings—it only denies the existence of supernatural beings. And surely this is no less plausible than asserting the existence of a very specific sort of supernatural being. So naturalism is at least as plausible as theism.

Therefore, it follows from my arguments concerning evil and evolution that, other evidence held equal, naturalism is very much more probable than theism. And since naturalism and theism are alternative hypotheses—they cannot both be true—this implies that, other evidence held equal, it is highly likely that theism is false. So the evidence discussed in this paper provides a powerful *prima facie* case against theism. To put it another way, if one looks only at the evidence discussed here—evolution, the ability of natural selection to explain complex biological order without purpose, the systematic connection between pain and pleasure and reproductive success, and the apparent moral randomness of pain and pleasure—then Hume's words ring true: "The whole presents nothing but the idea of a blind nature, impregnated by a great vivifying principle, and pouring forth from her lap, without discernment or parental care, her maimed and abortive children."[16,17]

APPENDIX

My argument in this paper is based on the following two theorems of the probability calculus:

$$A : \frac{\Pr(N/E\&P)}{\Pr(T/E\&P)} = \frac{\Pr(N)}{\Pr(T)} \times \frac{\Pr(E\&P/N)}{\Pr(E\&P/T)}$$

$$B : \frac{\Pr(E\&P/N)}{\Pr(E\&P/T)} = \frac{\Pr(E/N)}{\Pr(E/T)} \times \frac{\Pr(P/E\&N)}{\Pr(P/E\&T)}$$

In using these two equations, I assume that neither naturalism nor theism is certainly true or certainly false.

$\Pr(N/E\&P)$ is the antecedent probability of naturalism given the conjunction of evolution and the statement (P) that pain and pleasure are systematically connected to reproductive success. In other words, it is the probability of naturalism, all things considered. (I assume here that the "given E&P" puts back everything of significance that the "antecedent" takes out.) Similarly, $\Pr(T/E\&P)$ is the probability of theism, all things considered. So the left side of equation A is the ratio of the probability of naturalism to the probability of theism. If this ratio is greater than 1, then naturalism is more probable than theism and hence theism is probably false.

Now consider the right side of equation A. The main purpose of my paper was to evaluate the second ratio here: The ratio of the antecedent probability of evolution conjoined with P given naturalism to the antecedent probability of this conjunction given theism. This ratio was evaluated using equation B. The first of the two ratios on the right side of B is the ratio of the antecedent probability of evolution given naturalism to the antecedent probability of evolution given theism. And the second is the ratio of the antecedent probability of P given evolutionary naturalism to the antecedent probability of P given evolutionary theism. I argued that each of these two ratios is much greater than 1. From this it follows (using equation B) that the ratio of $\Pr(E\&P/N)$ to $\Pr(E\&P/T)$ is very much greater than 1.

Now look at the first ratio on the right side of equation A. $\Pr(N)$ is the antecedent probability of naturalism. In other words, it is the probability of naturalism independent of our knowledge of E&P. And

Pr(T) is the probability of theism independent of our knowledge of E&P. So the first ratio on the right side of equation A depends on the plausibility of naturalism and theism as well as on other evidence (propositional or nonpropositional) for and against naturalism and theism (e.g., the existence of life on earth, the success of science, religious experiences, immorality, etc.). I argued very briefly that considerations of plausibility do not give us any reason to believe that this ratio is less than one. But I did not, of course, evaluate all of the other relevant evidence for and against theism and naturalism. So I did not come to any conclusion about this first ratio. This is why my case against theism is a *prima facie* one. I am entitled to conclude only that, other evidence held equal, the ratio on the left side of equation A is very much greater than 1. And this implies that, other evidence held equal, it is highly probable that theism is false.

The following summarizes my argument:

(1) Evolution is antecedently much more probable on the assumption that naturalism is true than on the assumption that theism is true [i.e., Pr(E/N) >! Pr(E/T)].

(2) The statement that pain and pleasure are systematically connected to reproductive success is antecedently much more probable on the assumption that evolutionary naturalism is true than on the assumption that evolutionary theism is true [i.e., Pr(P/E&N) >! Pr(P/E&T)].

(3) Therefore, evolution conjoined with this statement about pain and pleasure is antecedently very much more probable on the assumption that naturalism is true than on the assumption that theism is true [i.e., Pr(E&P/N) >!! Pr(E&P/T)]. (From 1 and 2)

(4) Naturalism is at least as plausible as theism [i.e., other evidence held equal, Pr(N) ≥ Pr(T)].

(5) Therefore, other evidence held equal, naturalism is very much more probable than theism [i.e., other evidence held equal, Pr(N/ E&P) >!! Pr(T/E&P)]. (From 3 and 4)

(6) Naturalism entails that theism is false.

(7) Therefore, other evidence held equal, it is highly probable that theism is false [i.e., other evidence held equal, Pr(T/E&P) <!! 1/2]. (From 5 and 6)

NOTES

1. By "hypothesis" I mean a statement that is neither certainly true nor certainly false.

2. It is worth noting that, although "probabilistic" arguments from evil are usually classified as evidential, many such arguments are logical—they attempt to show that theism is probably inconsistent with some known fact about evil.

3. "Darwinism Defined: The Difference Between Fact and Theory," *Discover*, Jan. 1987, p. 70. Quoted in James Rachels, *Created from Animals: The Moral Implications of Darwinism* (Oxford University Press, 1990), p. 100.

4. Quoted in Phillip E. Johnson, *Darwin on Trial* (InterVarsity Press, 1993), p. 126.

5. "The Two Revelations," in Gail Kennedy, *Evolution and Religion* (D. C. Heath and Company, 1957), p. 20. Also quoted on p. xiv.

6. Quoted in Kennedy, p. xiv.

7. Proof: Since E entails S, E is logically equivalent to ∼S&E. Thus, since it is a theorem of the probability calculus that logically equivalent statements are equally probable, it follows that Pr(E/N) >! Pr(E/T) if and only if Pr(∼S&E/N) >! Pr(∼S&E/T). But it is also a theorem of the probability calculus that Pr(p&q/r) = Pr(p/r) × Pr(q/p&r). Therefore, Pr(E/N) >! Pr(E/T) if and only if Pr(∼S/N) × Pr(E/∼S&N) >! × Pr(E/∼S&T).

8. Of course, whether this strong evidence is also significant depends on what the ratio of the probability of naturalism to the probability of theism is prior to considering the fact that special creationism is false. If it is extremely high or low, then the falsity of special creationism will not be significant evidence favoring naturalism. If, on the other hand, the other evidence is nearly balanced and both hypotheses are plausible, then this evidence will be significant. For example, if theism

starts out twice as probable as naturalism, then the two hypotheses will end up being equally probable.

9. Diogenes Allen, *Christian Belief in a Postmodern World* (Westminster: John Knox Press, 1989), p. 59. Quoted with approval in Howard J. Van Till, "When Faith and Reason Cooperate," *Christian Scholar's Review* 21.1 (1991), p. 43.

10. "Plantinga's Defense of Special Creation," *Christian Scholar's Review* 21.1 (1991), p. 74. Plantinga refers to McMullin's position as "semideism." McMullin complains that this terminology is loaded, yet he describes his own position as believing in "the integrity of the natural order." It would seem then that Christians have a dilemma. No good Christian wants to be called a "deist," but no good Christian would want to deny that God's creation has "integrity"!

11. Ibid., p. 75.

12. For additional criticisms of the positions of Van Till and McMullin, see Alvin Plantinga, "Evolution, Neutrality, and Antecedent Probability: A Reply to Van Till and McMullin," *Christian Scholar's Review* 21.1 (1991), pp. 80–109.

13. Cf. Plantinga, p. 100.

14. Review of "Trial and Error: The American Controversy over Creation and Evolution," *Academe* 73.1 (1987), 50–52. Quoted in McMullin, p. 58.

15. For an excellent defense of evolution against special creationist objections, see Philip Kitcher, *Abusing Science: The Case Against Creationism* (Cambridge, Massachusetts: The MIT Press, 1982).

16. *Dialogues Concerning Natural Religion*, ed. Norman Kemp Smith (Macmillan Publishing Co., 1947), p. 211.

17. I am grateful to Kai Draper, Daniel Howard Snyder, James Keller, George Mavrodes, Wes Morriston, William L. Rowe, Michael Tooley, and Stephen J. Wykstra for helpful comments on earlier versions of this paper.

8

Whose Problem Is the "Problem of Evil"?

GRACE M. JANTZEN

Grace M. Jantzen (1948–2006) was professor of religion, culture, and gender at the University of Manchester and was a leading feminist philosopher and theologian. Her most influential work lies at the intersection of French continental philosophy, feminist theology, and philosophy of religion; she has also made important contributions to the study of Western medieval mysticism. She is the author of numerous articles and several important books, including Julian of Norwich: Mystic and Theologian *(Paulist Press, 1987) and* Becoming Divine: Toward a Feminist Philosophy of Religion *(Indiana University Press, 1999). In this excerpt from* Becoming Divine, *she provides a feminist critique of the traditional framing of the problem of evil, arguing that not only have important alternative conceptions of God been neglected on both sides of the discussion, but important philosophical questions about the relationships between God, religion, and evil have been too long ignored. Note that her essay makes use of three terms*

From *Becoming Divine: Towards a Feminist Philosophy of Religion* by Grace M. Jantzen. (Indiana University Press, 1999). © 1999 by Grace Jantzen. Used with permission of Indiana University Press, Manchester University Press, and the estate of Grace Jantzen.

that may be unfamiliar to readers: (1) Natals is a term she uses for methodological reasons in place of the term mortals. Whereas mortals are "beings who die," natals are "beings who are born." She makes this distinction because she thinks philosophy of religion tends to be overly concerned with death and the afterlife, rather than with birth and this present life. (2) The term onto-theology refers to a way of doing theology that treats God as a being posited to explain phenomena in the world (e.g., the appearance of design), and that also presupposes that human reason is a reliable tool for arriving at clear and accurate knowledge of God. (3) The term the face of the Other was explained earlier, in the introduction to the present section of this book.

The problem of evil is normally set out in traditional philosophy of religion as a conundrum for the orthodox believer who cannot avoid mutually incompatible beliefs: that God, being omnipotent and omniscient, could have created a world without evil if "he" chose (or could eradicate the evil in this world); that God, being wholly good, would choose to eradicate evil; and yet that evil exists (Peterson 1992: 3). This argument is then used by those who would discredit theism as a way of showing that such a God cannot exist (Mackie 1982). Those who wish to retain their belief in God, however, try to show how the apparently incompatible beliefs can be reconciled after all. One standard form of such a strategy is known as the "free-will defence," which aims to show that omnipotence requires only that God be able to do all logically possible things. However, it is not logically possible to create a world which is simultaneously free of evil and contains human beings with freedom of choice, and such freedom allegedly outweighs the evils of the world (Swinburne 1979: 200; Plantinga 1992). Another form is to argue that the world is a "veil of soul-making," in which evil and suffering are a necessary condition for moral progress, individual or collective (Hick 1968); or, less frequently in philosophical literature but still often found in popular writings, that what is apparently evil is not really so in the overall divine plan. The variations and combinations of these themes are then discussed with considerable vigour and ever-increasing intellectual sophistication, as also are the arguments against them (cf. Peterson 1992).

The discussion is clearly framed within the realist assumptions of onto-theology rather than from the perspective of a religious symbolic, let alone one which takes process, becoming divine, seriously. As has frequently been noted in the course of this

book, it is the God of the west that is once again central to the philosophical discussion of the problem of evil: the conundrum does not arise unless the attributes of omnipotence, omniscience, and goodness are explicitly accepted as those of the God of the western onto-theological tradition. I have already discussed in several different ways the valorization of power and control which this account of God assumes and perpetuates, whether or not one believes that such a God exists: those same valorizations repeat themselves here. Even the term "theodicy," which is usually given to attempted resolutions of the problem of evil, means "to justify God"—that is, to show how a morally good omni-everything deity can be justified in permitting evil. The assumption throughout is that this is the only God worth talking about. But as we have seen, if we were to proceed by criteria of trustworthiness, thinking in terms of justice in the face of the natals and acting for love of the world, then such onto-theological assumptions are heavily problematized.

To be more specific, the outrageously unjust contextual values of the masculinist symbolic implicit in discussions of the problem of evil quickly show themselves when we ask what sorts of evils are suffered, and by whom; who inflicts them, and who benefits. What sort of flourishing is possible for natals in relation to these evils? Thus for example in "veil of soul-making" or "free-will" theodicies, where evil and suffering are held to be permitted for the overall moral progress or flourishing of humanity, it is important to ask whose face is the face of the Other. Are those who suffer the same as those who make progress? If so, then obviously the suffering has not been so great as to kill them or to incapacitate them for positive moral choices: those who are dead or mad or utterly demoralized cannot make moral progress. Yet much suffering kills or maddens. It does not lead to flourishing, even of this rarefied moral/spiritual variety. Are the lives of those who suffer to such acute degrees expendable for "our" moral progress? This point has of course often been raised, classically by Dostoevsky in *The Brothers Karamazov*, where Ivan protests that all the moral progress of the world stinks of corruption if it is bought at the price of the suffering of even one innocent victim.

Nevertheless, there is in many discussions of the "problem of evil" an implicit assumption that "they" suffer—in earthquakes, famines, wars, extermination camps—and that "we" learn from this suffering: "we" who are paradigmatically white, wealthy, highly privileged, and often male philosophers of religion. The obscenity of the idea that horrendous suffering for "them" is morally justified if it brings about the moral progress of "mankind"—read "us"—is matched by the iniquitous effect of this sort of discussion of the "problem of evil" in the first place. By making it an intellectual problem to be solved, concentration on the adequacy or inadequacy of the preferred solution can take up all the time and energy that could otherwise be devoted to doing something about the suffering itself. It is a classic case of the effect of prioritizing the onto-theological above the ethical, against which Levinas pitted himself.

The values of the symbolic which form the way in which the problem of evil is presented and discussed in fact exact a high moral cost in several respects. In the first place, as Ken Surin has eloquently shown in his book *Theology and the Problem of Evil* (1986), the assumption that the central significance of the problem of evil is its bearing on the God of the west, and on whether or not such a God could be justified in permitting the evil and suffering of the world, all too easily falls from an attempt to justify God into an implicit justification of the evil itself. After all, if evil is necessary in order to produce a greater good, such as "our" moral progress, then the urgency to eradicate evil is considerably undermined. Why should "we" be overly concerned to eliminate the political causes of homelessness or of the deprivation of people in materially deprived countries, if these forms of suffering contribute to

"our" development of generosity and compassion (to say nothing of "our" affluence)? If there are good reasons why a good and omnipotent God should permit evil, then surely that evil is permissible, and it would be futile for "us" to struggle against it.

Moreover, the discussion of whether God could be justified in permitting evil is regularly focused in such a way as to divert attention away from the question of where the evil comes from: who is it that is causing suffering, and to whom? Which natals, whose faces, present themselves? In traditional philosophy of religion the distinction is regularly made, of course, between natural and moral evil. Moral evil is what humans inflict on one another; natural evil is that which brings about suffering without any human agency being involved: disease, earthquake, and natural disaster are frequently cited examples, though with human interference in the natural world from genetics to the ozone layer, the line between natural and moral evil is ever thinner. However, in either case the "problem of evil" focuses on God rather than on human agency: why does God permit natural evils? Why does God permit human beings to do evil? Again, whatever the answers to these questions, and whether those evaluating the answers think them adequate or not, the focus of attention is diverted within this presentation away from what human beings are doing or might be doing to inflict or prevent evil, away from the earth and into the transcendent realm. It is a study in necrophilia.

Of course, it would be possible to object that while it is important to work against evil in every way we can, this is not the same thing as asking the philosophical question, and although the former task is incomparably more urgent than the latter, this does not mean that the latter is not important at all. Both are significant: there is no need to choose between them. Yet I suggest that while there is some plausibility in this response, it also masks important issues. The plausibility arises from the fact that it is indeed important, perhaps especially so at a time when the religious right is steadily gaining ground, for those attracted to belief in an omni-everything God to confront the question of whether that belief is actually compatible with the suffering of this world, and to explore the values implicit in the symbolic of such an onto-theological system. However, such an exploration could occur most helpfully in conjunction with actual engagement with evil and its causes. The face of the Other presents itself daily as people sleep rough, battered women seek refuge, and thousands are displaced by war and maimed by landmines. If we dare to face the Other, the intellectual questions will come thick and fast in such contexts, and the plausibility of answers will immediately be tested. There is much less scope for disengaged intellectual gymnastics, and much less patience with answers trotted out by privileged academics. It is, in short, more trustworthy to the flourishing of natals. When academics discussing the problem of evil begin to encourage the participants in that discussion to be actively involved in the struggle with suffering rather than defending themselves by saying that these are two separate issues, then their claim that active engagement and philosophical reflection are both important and should not be set up as false alternatives will be much more deserving of respect. As things stand, however, even the insistence that these are false alternatives slips readily into embracing the intellectual questions at the expense of active engagement, and thereby aligns itself with an expression of death rather than promoting the love of the world.

Moreover, if the response is that the problem of evil, or the development of a theodicy, just is the central philosophical question, then it is necessary to ask (again!) *why* this is so. Why is it not at least as important to ask who is committing evil, and against whom? If the reply is that these are, of course, important issues, but they do not belong to the philosophy of religion, then we are back again to the question of how the boundaries of the discipline are drawn up, and by whom. I have indicated more than once in this book that a study of the strategies of power and gender in the disciplining of religion is long overdue; and I hope to turn to it in another book. Here I can only repeat what I have already urged, namely that since religions concern themselves in large part with human propensity to evil and to good, surely it should be central to the philosophy of religion to take seriously questions about perpetrators and victims, and especially the ways in which religion itself fosters or inhibits the infliction of evil and enables or impedes resistance to it. By any standards, western christendom, which has to a large extent been the religion of the dominant, has a great deal to answer for; and philosophers and theologians have been its intellectual servants. By refusing to engage with the question of the human distribution of evil and focusing instead on theodicy, it is possible to evade questions of domination and victimization while still appearing to "deal with" the problem of evil. It is parallel to the preoccupation noted in relation to the issues of morality and religion of being concerned only with one's own moral status rather than with its effects on others, keeping one's own hands clean though the rest of the world may go to hell; only here it is God's moral status that is being protected. What sort of symbolic of the divine does such a preoccupation bespeak?

From this perspective it is not surprising that the way the question is framed is not challenged by those on either side of the debate, and it is also apparent how a feminist critique can begin. Whether philosophers of religion believe that an adequate defence against the problem of evil can be developed or not, there is no large-scale demand among traditional philosophers of religion (exceptions like Ken Surin notwithstanding) that the whole issue be broadened to consider the human as well as the divine responsibility for suffering and how that responsibility is apportioned. What we find instead is a striking parallel to what we already noted in relation to the debates about the existence of God and about religion and morality: a collusion between those on both sides of the debate about how the question should be set out. As in the former cases there was substantial agreement about what sort of God was worth discussion, and any other concept of God was deemed unworthy of notice, so in this case there is agreement that debate centres on whether or not such a God could permit evil. Where the discussion of the problem of evil adds a further dimension is in the collusion of both sides to concentrate wholly on the issue of *divine* responsibility for evil and suffering and not investigate the human responsibility, and especially the unevenness of human responsibility between the powerful and the powerless. Nor is there willingness to consider the religious legitimation for that unevenness. Both sides proceed from a detached intellectual perspective, as privileged onlookers, rather than in solidarity with those in suffering. The technologies of dominance of largely privileged white male academics for the structuring of the philosophy of religion could hardly be clearer.

Process theologians with their emphasis on a God who suffers alongside the suffering of the world strike a somewhat different and welcome note here, since the obvious corollary of their position is the implication that solidarity with those who are suffering is of supreme importance. Yet in the works of such writers as Whitehead and Hartshorne, while there is obvious sensitivity and concern, there is little attention paid to actual suffering and how it comes about, who are the victims and who are the perpetrators. In this respect they are not different from other traditional philosophers of religion, in spite of the fact that they do tender a radically different concept of the divine, and thus are an exception to the general agreement that only the classical concept of God is worthy of discussion. Nevertheless, in their emphasis on divine becoming and their recognition that this divine becoming importantly includes involvement with the suffering of the world, there are implicit in their work aspects of a religious symbolic which can be appropriated for a feminist philosophy of religion.

From a feminist perspective, becoming divine is inseparable from solidarity with human suffering: a symbolic of the divine is a symbolic of outrage, imagination and desire, and compassionate action, not the detached and objective intellectual stance which traditional philosophers of religion assume and which they take also to be characteristic of God. A feminist approach to the "problem of evil" is first of all outrage and bewilderment at the suffering and evil itself: how *can* the world be like this? How *dare* some people make others suffer in the way that they do? What sort of divinity could we possibly be talking about if such suffering is allowed to continue? Now it is certainly true that some of the traditional discussion of the problem of evil does arise from the distress which philosophers of religion feel at the suffering and evil in the world. But whereas much of the traditional discussion of the problem seems to

transform that distress into intellectual hot air, a feminist strategy intent on becoming divine would be to use the power of that anger in the work of love (Harrison 1985: 3), transforming outrage into solidarity and compassionate action for love of the world, recognizing and accepting the solidarity and compassion of one another also in our own suffering. Such action for love of the world obviously includes theory, but theory where imaginative insight has an important place. Rather than the development of theory becoming a diversion from action, theory is a reflection upon action, an effort to enable the action to be intelligent and creative rather than simply reactive. Whereas standard treatments of the problem of evil in the philosophy of religion set out the intellectual problems and use examples of actual suffering to illustrate their case, a feminist approach would be to start from engagement with suffering at some concrete level and see what sorts of theory such engagement requires or would find helpful. The struggle against suffering and injustice and towards flourishing takes precedence, beyond comparison, to the resolution of intellectual problems; and although it is important that the struggle is an intelligent one, there is no excuse for theory ever becoming a distraction from the struggle for justice itself. This is another way of putting the point of the previous chapter: onto-theology must not take precedence over response to the face of the Other.

This means that a feminist philosophy of religion will concentrate on the very questions which tend to be silenced by traditional accounts of the "problem of evil" and skated over too quickly even by process philosophers. The issue is not so much "how can a good God permit evil?" as it is "how are the resources of religion, particularly christendom, used by those who inflict evil on others? How are they used by those who resist?" And above all, "what does the face of the Other require of me, and how can I best respond for love of the world?" Posing the questions in this way means paying attention to who actually are the perpetrators of suffering, considering both the individuals and the structures within which they are embedded. It means also considering both how traditional theistic doctrines of power, mastery, and hierarchical patterns of domination feed into the ideologies propping up the structures of domination and reinforce racism, sexism, poverty, and homophobia. The question of what religion has to do with evil and suffering is thus posed in much more concrete ways, with a refusal to distract attention from the specific acts of evil that some specific human beings inflict on other specific human beings to a generalized and supernaturalized account, as though "evil" were some abstract monolithic entity which "God" permits or not.

And if the objection returns that these are different questions from those which are normally asked in the philosophy of religion, in fact that this is not properly philosophy of religion at all, then the response is that indeed they are different questions, and about time too. It has been the burden of this book that part of what is wrong with traditional philosophy of religion is precisely that such questions are not normally asked, which is why the philosophy of religion as it stands requires radical critique. That a feminist philosophy of religion which seeks a new symbolic and social order requires an altered demarcation of the boundaries of the philosophy of religion is not an objection, it is part of the point. Philosophy of religion more intent on preserving the boundaries of the discipline than in engaging with issues of how particular religious beliefs perpetuate or alleviate suffering is in urgent need of exactly such radical revision, so that it can point the way, not towards a justification of the status quo, but towards becoming divine, towards the flourishing of natals.

REFERENCES

Mackie, J. L. 1982. *The Miracle of Theism: Arguments for and Against the Existence of God*. Oxford: Oxford University Press.

Peterson, Michael (ed.). 1992. *The Problem of Evil: Selected Readings*. Notre Dame, Ind.: University of Notre Dame Press.

Plantinga, Alvin. 1992. "Is Belief in God Properly Basic?" in R. Douglas Geivett and Brendan Sweetman (eds.), *Contemporary Perspectives in Religious Epistemology*. New York: Oxford University Press.

Surin, Kenneth. 1986. *Theology and the Problem of Evil*. Oxford: Blackwell.

Swinburne, Richard. 1979. *The Existence of God*. Oxford: Clarendon Press.

9

Divine Hiddenness Justifies Atheism

J. L. SCHELLENBERG

J. L. Schellenberg (1959–) is professor of philosophy at Mount Saint Vincent University in Canada. He has written numerous articles and books in the philosophy of religion, and is best known for his work on the hiddenness of God. In the present article, Schellenberg argues from the fact that divine hiddenness occurs to the conclusion that disbelief in God is justified.

Reprinted from *Contemporary Debates in Philosophy of Religion*, ed. Michael L. Peterson and Raymond VanArragon. © Blackwell, 2004. Reproduced with permission of Blackwell Publishing Ltd.

Arguments from divine hiddenness often go unnoticed in the consideration of arguments for and against the existence of God—where by "God" is meant the *traditional* God: a separate but infinite consciousness, a personal and perfect creator of the universe. Perhaps the most interesting variety of this oversight occurs when people find themselves unable to settle the question of God's existence and therefore inclined toward agnosticism without noticing that these facts are *themselves* relevant to their quest and may support atheism. Of course, we need to be careful here. If by "God is hidden" you mean "There is an actually existing God who hides from us," it will be short work proving that divine hiddenness provides no basis for atheism. For how could a premise asserting the *actual existence* of God lead to the conclusion that God *does not exist?* But perhaps the careful reader will be able to see that it is also possible to take the language of hiddenness less literally—as referring simply to the absence of convincing evidence for the existence of God, or, more specifically, to the absence of some kind of positive experiential result in the search for God. That is how it will be taken here. I begin with an argument from analogy focused on the latter, more specific form of hiddenness. The possibility of broadening and strengthening this argument through a closer look at the concept of divine love is then considered. The first argument will here be called "the Analogy Argument"; its sibling, naturally, is called "the Conceptual Argument."

1 THE ANALOGY ARGUMENT

Imagine yourself in the following situation. You're a child playing hide-and-seek with your mother in the woods at the back of your house. You've been crouching for some time now behind a large oak tree, quite a fine hiding place but not undiscoverable—certainly not for someone as clever as your mother. However, she does not appear. The sun is setting, and it will soon be bedtime, but still no mother. Not only isn't she finding you, but, more disconcerting, you can't *hear* her anywhere: she's not beating the nearby bushes, making those exaggerated

"looking for you" noises, and talking to you meanwhile as mothers playing this game usually do. Now imagine that you start *calling* for your mother. Coming out from behind the tree, you yell out her name, over and over again. "Mooooommmmm!" But no answer. You look everywhere: through the woods, in the house, down to the road. An hour passes, and you are growing hoarse from calling. Is she anywhere around? Would she fail to answer if she were around?

Now let's change the story a little. You're a child with amnesia—apparently because of a blow to the head (which of course you don't remember), your memory goes back only a few days—and you don't even know whether you *have* a mother. You see other children with their mothers and think it would sure be nice to have one. So you ask everyone you meet and look everywhere you can, but without forwarding your goal in the slightest. You take up the search anew each day, looking diligently, even though the strangers who took you in assure you that your mother must be dead. But to no avail. Is this what we should expect if you really have a mother and she is around, and aware of your search? When in the middle of the night you tentatively call out— "Mooooommmmm!"—would she not answer if she were really within earshot?

Let's change the story one more time. You're still a small child, and an amnesiac, but this time you're in the middle of a vast rain forest, dripping with dangers of various kinds. You've been stuck there for days, trying to figure out who you are and where you came from. You don't remember having a mother who accompanied you into this jungle, but in your moments of deepest pain and misery you call for her anyway: "MOOOOOMMMMM!" Over and over again. For days and days ... the last time when a jaguar comes at you out of nowhere ... but with no response. What should you think in this situation? In your dying moments, what should cross your mind? Would the thought that you have a mother who cares about you and hears your cry and *could* come to you but chooses *not* to even make it onto the list?

Now perhaps we could suppose, in each of these cases, that you *do* have a mother and that she *is* around, but that she simply *doesn't* care. We are inclined to think of mothers as almost by definition loving and caring, but just remember the mother of Hyde in *That 70s Show,* someone might say. Another possibility is that your mother has been prevented from doing what mothers tend naturally to do by factors external to her own desire and will: perhaps she fell into a deep well in the woods, or was kidnapped by that escaped convict who was spotted near town last week (from whose clutches you narrowly escaped, suffering only a memory-erasing blow to the head), or is fending off a crocodile even as you succumb to the jaguar. What we *can't* say is that a *loving* mother would in circumstances like these be hidden from her child *if she could help it.*

The first step in the Analogy Argument is the defense of this claim. As we might put it, our job is to find the proper filling for the blank at the end of the following sentence: "A loving mother would not be hidden from her child in circumstances like those mentioned if she could help it *because* —." What we need here are propositions specifying the properties of love *in virtue of which* the claim appearing in front of the "because" is true. These would, I suggest, include the following: (1) A loving mother would consider each of her child's serious requests important and seek to provide a quick response. (2) A loving mother would wish to spare her child needless trauma, or, more positively, would wish to foster her child's physical and emotional well-being. (3) A loving mother would seek to avoid encouraging in her child false or misleading thoughts about herself or about their relationship. (4) A loving mother would want personal interaction with her child whenever possible, for the joy it brings as well as for its own sake. (5) A loving mother would *miss* her child if separated from her. It is clear that each of these propositions is true. It is also clear that, *if* they are true, the claim we are defending is true—that no loving mother who could help it would be hidden from her child in circumstances like those mentioned. We may therefore conclude that the latter claim *is* true.

The next step in the Analogy Argument involves pointing out that there are, in the actual world, circumstances of *divine* hiddenness very

similar to the circumstances we have highlighted in respect of our fictional mother and child. The relevant circumstances in our stories are those in which the mother is sought by the child but not found. Well, just so, God is (and has often been) hidden from many human beings: sought but not found. Some persons start out assured of the power and presence of God in their lives, and then *lose* all this—in the typical case because of reasoning that engenders doubt about the reliability of the support they have for theistic belief. And though they grieve what they have lost and seek to regain it, looking for God in all the old familiar places as well as in new, unfamiliar locales, they fail to do so: God seems simply absent, and their belief is gone. The situation of such individuals is relevantly similar to that of the child in the first story. Other persons don't start out in what they consider to be a relationship with God but, nonetheless, are, in their wanderings and in their attempts to determine where they belong, open to finding and being found by a divine parent; some of them seek long and hard for God, wishing to be related in love to God. But though they seek, they do not find. Their situation is relevantly similar to that of the second child. And many seekers, because of the inhospitable place this world can sometimes be, are at one time or another in a lot of *trouble,* and so have not only the usual and obvious reasons to seek to be united (or reunited) with a divine parent: they are also in serious need of divine help, calling out to God in conditions of great suffering and pain. But a divine answer to their calls is not forthcoming. What we see here is clearly relevantly similar to the situation of the third child.

Additional stories can be imagined, with features equally troubling from the perspective of motherly care, corresponding to other aspects of the form of divine hiddenness we are considering. We might have our first child, after many calls for her mother, hearing sounds in the woods that she is sure mark her mother's presence, but which turn out to come from nothing more than leaves rolling in the wind. This is like the experience of those who think they have detected traces of God in some happening or argument, only to have the former's theological significance undermined by convincing reinterpretation or the latter proved unsound. Our second child might come to be adopted by the strangers who take her in, and brought up in a manner that leaves her predisposed to be suspicious instead of trusting, calculatingly self-centered instead of generous and giving; or perhaps she comes to have experiences which cause her to deny the importance of personal relationship with a parent in the development of a child. This can be compared to what happens in the life of a seeker who, because of the influence of those who *do* answer her calls, is led to develop a character contrary to that which the God of traditional theism is said to desire for us, or whose search leads to religious experiences all right, but *nontheistic* ones. Clearly, the analogies between our fictional situations of parental hiddenness and the actual facts of divine hiddenness are very close.

So what can be done with these analogies? Well, the next step in the argument involves showing that what we have said about a mother's love applies to God as well. This is fairly easily done. For God, on the traditional theistic view we are challenging, is not only loving and caring, but *unsurpassably* loving and caring. Indeed, it seems that each of our propositions (1) to (5) above must specify a property that applies as much to God as to the mother. If God gives birth to the human race and is related to its members in a manner that is unimaginably close, caring, and loving, then surely: (1′) God would consider each serious request submitted by God's human children important and seek to provide a quick response; (2′) God would wish to spare human beings needless trauma or, more positively, would wish to foster their physical and emotional well-being; (3′) God would seek not to encourage in human beings false or misleading thoughts about God or about the divine-human relationship; (4′) God would want personal interaction with human beings whenever possible, for the joy it brings as well as for its own sake; and (5′) God would *miss* such personal interaction if it were absent.

Now perhaps someone will say that God might be totally different from ourselves, and thus unlike a human mother. But there are certain conceptual constraints that need to be respected here. Of course we don't mean that God should be conceptualized as physical and as biologically female. But situations of human interaction and discussions of human interaction, including interaction between mothers and their children, do represent the primary contexts in which such concepts as those of "closeness," "care," and "love" are used and acquire their meanings. What, then, could justify the supposition that God's closeness, caring, and loving would not be like those of the ideal mother, displayed in a manner appropriate to the divine nature (e.g., through religious experience instead of physical touching)? The question is rhetorical. Clearly what we have said about the best mother's love must in this way apply to God as well.

An important conclusion may now be reached quite easily. Let *P* be the conjunction of the various loving properties picked out by the original five propositions about a mother's love and the five propositions referring to God. We saw earlier that, in virtue of *P*, a loving mother who could help it would never be hidden from her child in the fictional circumstances we described. We also saw that the analogies between the latter circumstances and those of divine hiddenness are very close. But then we may infer that, very probably, *a God who could help it would never be hidden in those circumstances:* the operation of *P* would prevent this in the case of God, just as it would in the case of our fictional mother.

Thus far the Analogy Argument proper. Certain plausible additional moves may be made to bring us from this conclusion to atheism. In the case of the mother, we saw that there might be external actors that prevent her from responding to her child despite the presence of *P*—that she might be hidden and *not* able to help it. But if omnipotence means anything, it means that God couldn't *ever* be prevented from responding to the cries of God's human children. The disanalogy we see here, far from weakening the argument that starts out from the analogy, permits us to *complete* it. For it means that we may justifiably remove the little qualifier "who could help it" from our earlier conclusion and say simply that *God would never be hidden in the circumstances in question.* In other words, the Analogy Argument in conjunction with what we know about divine resourcefulness gives us a powerful reason to say that, if God exists, this form of divine hiddenness does not occur. But it *does* occur. Therefore, we have a powerful reason to believe that God does *not* exist.

2 IS THE ANALOGY ARGUMENT A SUCCESS?

Before getting too excited—or upset—about this argument, the reader should consider whether it can be defeated by counter-argument. It will, I think, be hard to question the claims we have made about how a loving mother would behave in our fictional scenarios. Most objections will quite naturally focus instead on questioning the closeness of the analogies we have drawn *between* those scenarios and the facts of divine hiddenness.

This can be done in various ways. One might argue, for example, that persons who seek God are not very much like *children*—the vulnerability and immaturity we attach to the latter and need to be able to transfer to the former if the argument is to succeed are in fact not transferable in this way. But this objection appears to assume that all who seek God in the relevant way are adult humans, and this is not at all obvious: actual children may (and do) seek God too, without in every case finding their search rewarded with positive results. More important, because of the evil we face and the evident frailty of our natures, even human grown-ups are not appropriately construed, theologically speaking, as mature adults. Theology has traditionally pictured us this way (while also referring to us as "God's children"), but a close look at the world suggests that a better picture would portray us as young and unformed, still needing a home—in particular, still in need of parental support and encouragement in the development of a character and self-esteem that can withstand the pressures toward fragmentation and despair that life presents and make the achievement of our full potential possible.

It might also be claimed that God is not appropriately thought of as mother—that in our

application of human talk to the divine, non-motherly elements of human experience ought to predominate. Now it is clear that, traditionally, the notion of God as Father is much more common than that of God as Mother, but an appeal to "common practice" is always weak, especially when the practice in question has been (or can be) successfully challenged. Instead of getting into debates about feminism and patriarchy, though, let me simply point out that, whether presented under the label of "loving Father" or in some other way, such attributes as those of caring and closeness, compassion and empathy, are nonnegotiable in any theistic view that takes the moral perfection and worship-worthiness of God seriously. And these are the attributes at issue here. I have found it helpful to focus on the model of a mother because these attributes are still more closely linked in our experience and imagination with the notion of mother than with that of father. Indeed, the commonness in human experience of *distant* or *absent* fathers makes it possible for us to construe the connection between fatherhood and the attributes in question rather loosely. This fact, in conjunction with the tendency to think uncritically of God as Father, is, I think, a big part of the reason why so many are inclined to underestimate the force of arguments from divine hiddenness.

A third objection to our argument—a rather common sort—suggests that there is something presumptuous about *expecting* a response from God. God is not obligated to respond to our every whim; and if God responds, it will be in God's own way, not necessarily as we expect. Even if so-called seekers lack presumption, we ought still to consider that there may be some *other* human sin that prevents them from experiencing God. Perhaps God is hidden from us because of our *own* failings, instead of God's.

But the Analogy Argument, as you may have noticed, is not suggesting that God should satisfy our every *whim,* our every sudden, unreflective, unreasonable desire; only that God would respond to serious attempts to be united or reunited with God in a loving relationship. Observe how much more plausible the latter claim is than the former. The objection is here dealing with a caricature of our argument, not the real thing. As for presumption, the expectation of a seeker does not come in the form of a *demand*, but as anticipation or reasoned inference. Are we really to imagine seekers walking around demanding that God "show himself"? Some *philosophers* may do this, but these are usually individuals who have long since concluded that God does not exist and think the world is better off that way; it would be a mistake to confuse them with the earnest, hopeful seekers of our argument, or with those (perhaps the same individuals) who after careful reflection on all the available information conclude that it would be in the nature of God to be in some way revealed to anyone who calls upon God sincerely.

Turning now to the general reference to sin: this seems completely unsubstantiated—many who seek God seem in fact to be quite blameless in the relevant respects. It is important to notice here that beyond looking thoroughly and carefully for reason to believe in the existence of God and removing all observed impediments to success in the search, there is nothing the seeker *can do* to bring about belief. Belief as such is involuntary; it is something that happens to you when evidence adds up to a certain point, not something you can do directly (if you doubt this, just try to acquire right now, or to drop, as the case may be, the belief that God exists). Thus, if a search of the sort in question has been undertaken (as it often has), a nonbeliever cannot be "to blame" for not believing.

What about the possibility, also mentioned by the "sin" objection, that God *does* respond, and seekers simply miss the response, expecting something else—something other than what God has in mind? Well, what else might God have in mind? If the request is for the beginning or resumption of a loving relationship, and what is needed for this is, among other things, some measure of belief that there is someone there to relate *to,* what *could* count both as *loving* and as a *response* apart from some noticeable indication of God's presence? Certainly in the case of the unencumbered mother and her child, nothing apart from the mother actually coming to her child in a manner recognized by the child would qualify as a loving response. What

makes us think that something else would do in the case of God's immeasurably greater love? Perhaps it will be said that God, unlike the mother, is able to be present to us all the time without us noticing it and is, moreover, responsible for every single good thing we experience. This is indeed true, if God exists. But it still doesn't qualify as a *response* to the cry of those who seek God. And we need to recognize that the absence of love in one respect is not compensated for by *other* forms of love when what we're dealing with is not the love of a finite being but the perfect love of an unlimited God. Indeed, it's starting to look as though the relevant differences between God and ourselves make it *harder* to mount an "other response" objection, not easier.

But maybe we can press this notion of differences between ourselves and God a little further, in a different direction. Perhaps there is some *great good* for the seeker that depends on the continuation of her search, and thus prevents God from responding. Perhaps no loving human mother would ever have reason to consider continued separation from her child, in circumstances like those we have described, to be "for his own good," but God, the critic will say, is aware of so many more forms of goodness than we are, and has a design plan that spans incomprehensible distances in time and space. We are therefore not justified in concluding that God would do what the mother does, even if they share the loving properties we have discussed.

Now various possible goods we know of might be enumerated and discussed in response to this objection, but the objector would only reply by saying that the relevant goods may be *unknown* to us. Fortunately, there is a way around all this. First, let's notice that if the ultimate spiritual reality is a personal God, then all serious spiritual development must begin in personal relationship with God. And if God is infinitely deep and rich, then any such relationship must be multileveled and developmental—indeed, the development of it would surely be potentially unending. Third, such relationship with a perfect and infinitely rich personal reality would have to be the greatest good that any human being could experience, if God exists—certainly this is the claim of all theistic traditions. But then why this talk of some *other* good, for which God would *sacrifice* such relationship?

Perhaps it will be replied that God sacrifices only *some time* in the relationship, not the whole relationship, and that what is gained thereby may contribute to the *flourishing* of a *future* relationship with God. But it is hard to see how someone seeking God, desiring a loving personal relationship, could possibly be in a state such that experience of God or evidence of some other sort would inhibit or prevent the success of the relationship in the long term, as this point requires. Indeed, such individuals would seem to be in just the *right* position in this respect—a position emphasized as eminently desirable by theistic traditions. Certainly their state is no less appropriate to relationship with God than that of many who would be declared by those traditions to be enjoying it already.

Consider also, in this connection, the infinite *resourcefulness* of God. If God indeed possesses this attribute and is, moreover, unsurpassably deep and rich, then there must at any juncture be literally an *infinite number* of ways of developing in relationship with God, which omnipotence and omniscience could facilitate, despite obstacles to continuing relationship that might seem to present themselves. To say less than this, a theist must surely contradict what she believes about the greatness of God! Hence, even if we were *not* dealing with seekers, individuals optimally placed to benefit from God's presence, we would *still* lack reason to maintain the present objection.

One particular form that the exercise of God's resourcefulness might take may be highlighted here. Strange as it may seem, there is an important form of "hiddenness" that is quite compatible with—and indeed *requires*—a situation in which God is revealed to every seeker. To see this, suppose that God exists, and that our seeker finds reason to believe in God and responds by entering into a personal relationship with God ("conversing" with God in prayer, feeling God's presence, living her whole life in the context of divine-human communion). Suppose also that she subsequently lapses into some inappropriate state—say, arrogance or presumption. What can God do?

Well, there is still the possibility of a sort of divine withdrawal *within* the relationship. What I have in mind here is analogous to what has traditionally been called "the dark night of the soul"—a state in which there is evidence for God's existence on which the believer may rely, but in which God is not felt as directly present to her experience, and may indeed feel absent. While not removing the conditions of relationship, such a "withdrawal" would severely test the believer's faith, and, in particular, work against the sort of arrogance and presumption we have mentioned. Indeed, this form of hiddenness would seem capable of accomplishing much, perhaps all, of what theists sometimes say the *other* sort of hiddenness is designed to do! John Macquarrie, a Christian theologian, puts it nicely:

> As happens also in some of our deepest human relationships, the lover reveals himself enough to awaken the love of the beloved, yet veils himself enough to draw the beloved into an even deeper exploration of that love. In the love affair with God ... there is an alternation of consolation and desolation and it is in this way that the finite being is constantly drawn beyond self into the depths of the divine.[1]

If this sort of hiddenness can produce the goods in question and is compatible with God having been revealed to the seeker, what possible reason could we have for insisting that God would leave the seeker in *doubt and nonbelief* in order to further those goods?

A final objection, significantly different from the rest, should briefly be mentioned. This is the claim that there are *other* reasons *for* belief in God which counterbalance or outweigh the reason *against* such belief that our argument represents. Our Analogy Argument, it should be emphasized, is broadly inductive, claiming only that its conclusion is very probable (i.e., much more probable than not). So it is always at least conceivable that the probability we assess for our conclusion on the basis of analogy may need to be adjusted when arguments *supporting* God's existence are taken into account. Someone, for example, who was deeply convinced of the soundness of a simple *deductive* argument for

God's existence (an argument with premises *entailing* the claim that God exists) and had only our Analogy Argument to consider on the side of atheism might well justifiably conclude, on the strength of her apparent proof of God's existence, that despite the closeness and persuasive force of the analogies, there must be *something* wrong with our argument and that God certainly exists, even if she can not put her finger on what the mistake in our reasoning is.

For how many will this sort of move function as a successful defeater? It is hard to say: everything depends on how the independent evidence is assessed, and whether it is properly assessed. Even if we had the space for an exhaustive discussion of other evidence (and of course we do not), it would be possible for others to justifiably disagree with our assessment of it, given facts of personality, experience, time, intelligence, opportunity, and so on that nonculpably incline them in another direction. But some general points can be made, that are not without interest or effect. Most readers, it must be said, are likely to be *without* such proofs of God as were earlier mentioned—indeed, that such proofs are in short supply is one of the circumstances that helps to generate the problem of divine hiddenness in the first place! Certainly, anyone who finds that the other evidence for and against God's existence leaves her thinking that theism and atheism are about equally probable should find the balance tipping toward atheism when this *new* evidence is considered. And it is interesting to note that even those who came to this discussion convinced of the truth of theism may find their epistemic situation changing because of the apparent force of our argument. This is because its apparent force may *affect*—and *negatively* affect—the confidence with which other arguments or experiences are taken to support theism, especially in cases where this other evidence has not previously been carefully examined. We should therefore not suppose that just anyone who comes to these discussions justified in theistic belief will leave that way.

That concludes our discussion of objections to the Analogy Argument. Nothing we have seen takes away from its initial persuasiveness (even the last defeater we discussed must concede this much). Indeed, we have encountered points in this discussion that add to its force. Does the divine hiddenness referred to in its premises therefore justify atheism? Does it justify *you, the reader,* in believing atheism? Well, it seems plausible and would be accepted by most philosophers that the following proposition refers to conditions necessary and sufficient for justification of the relevant sort.

> An individual S is epistemically justified in believing that p in response to evidence e if and only if (i) S does to some degree believe that p on e, (ii) has considered all available epistemic reasons for not believing that p on e, (iii) finds none to be a good reason, and (iv) has fulfilled all relevant epistemic duties in the course of her investigation.

Thinking of yourself as S, of p as atheism, of e as the form of divine hiddenness we have discussed, of the defeaters we have considered (including the defeater relying on independent evidence) and any others known to you as the available reasons for *not* believing atheism because of divine hiddenness, and of the relevant epistemic duties as including such things as care, thoroughness, and openness to the truth, you may, by reference to this standard, work out for *yourself* whether our argument justifies you in believing that God does not exist.

3 THE CONCEPTUAL ARGUMENT

The Analogy Argument is not the only argument from divine hiddenness. Indeed, in my previous work on this topic it is only alluded to, and another form of argumentation is utilized instead.[2] I wanted to develop the Analogy Argument here, and had thought to leave the other aside. But after proceeding, I realized that in developing the former argument, a natural basis for an abbreviated but still forceful presentation of the latter would be laid. So let us briefly consider the additional moves which the latter argument requires.

The Conceptual Argument takes further a theme already touched upon: namely, the proper understanding of the concept of divine love. In examining this concept, developing our understanding of it as we must, by reference to what is best in human love, we are led to endorse claims from which it follows that, if God exists, evidence sufficient to form belief in God is available to everyone capable of a personal relationship with God and not inclined to resist such evidence. As can be seen, this argument not only focuses more closely on the concept of divine love (while drawing information from what we know of human love, including a mother's love) but embraces a wider range of nonbelievers in its premises. In this new argument, the notion of divine hiddenness is, as it were, *expanded* to include events (or the absence of certain events) in the lives of people who, without being closed toward the traditional God, are for one reason or another not aware of any need to seek God. If a label is desired, we may call all those belonging to this new and broader category of non-believers *nonresisters*. Nonresisters might include, in addition to seekers, individuals-in the West whose upbringing has been completely secular. They certainly include the vast number of persons in both past and present living in parts of the world where the very *idea* of such a God is distant from human thought and imagination.

Now why should we suppose that the absence of evidence sufficient to form belief in God in the lives of nonresisters presents a problem for theism? Well, because reflection on the concept of divine love shows that a perfectly loving God would necessarily seek personal relationship with *all* individuals belonging to this type, and because such seeking entails the provision of evidence sufficient for belief in the existence of God. (As can be seen, here the emphasis is not on human seekers but on *God* as seeker.)

In defense of the first of these claims, we may point out that the seeking of a personal relationship is an essential part of the best human love. The best human lover encourages her beloved to draw from relationship with herself what he may need to flourish, but also quite naturally aspires to a kind of closeness between herself and her beloved: she reaches out to the one she loves immediately and spontaneously, and not only because of some prior calculation of advantages or disadvantages for either party. Something similar must apply to God's love for us: clearly an explicit divine-human relationship

must do much to promote human flourishing, in which case God would seek it for that reason; and clearly God would also value personal relationship with human beings—creatures created in God's own image—for its own sake. No doubt God would not *force* such a loving relationship on anyone (the notion is logically contradictory and, in any case, contrary to love's respect for freedom), but surely a God who did not at least make such a relationship *available* to those who are *nonresisting* would not be perfectly loving.

This point sometimes has a hard time getting through. Due to a variety of social and religious factors, we seem to have got used to thinking of even God's love in a limited and limiting fashion, contrary to what all philosophical methods for working out an explication of the divine nature would indicate. But why suppose that if God exists there will be times when personal relationship with God will not be available to us? While a perfectly good and loving parent might occasionally stand to one side and let her child make the first move, and refuse to suffocate the child with her attentions, or even withdraw for a time to make a point, these are moments *within* the relationship, which *add* to its meaning. And while she might with deep sadness acknowledge that her child had completely cut himself off from the relationship, and not actively seek its resumption, it *would take* such resistance on the part of the child for the relationship to be put out of his immediate reach. What loving parent would ever willingly participate in bringing about such a state of affairs? And similar points apply to love as it occurs in the context of friendship and marriage relationships. So there seems no escaping this point: some form of personal relationship with God is always going to be available to nonresisters, if God is indeed loving.

A defense of our second claim—that for such relationship to be available, evidence sufficient for belief in God's existence would have to be similarly available—may now be added. The key point here is that it is logically impossible for you to hear God speaking to you or consciously to experience divine forgiveness and support or feel grateful to God or experience God's loving presence and respond thereto in love and obedience and worship or participate in any *other* element of a personal relationship with God while *not believing that there is a God*. Simply by looking at what it *means* to be in personal relationship with God, we can see that this is so. Since belief is involuntary, it follows that without evidence sufficient for belief in the existence of God, nonresisters are not in a position to relate personally to God. But where nonresisters are not in such a position, relationship with God has not been made available to them in the above sense. It follows that if relationship with God is to be made available to them, nonresisters must be provided with evidence sufficient for belief in God. This evidence, notice, would not need to be some thunderbolt from the sky or miracle or devastating theoretical proof. The quiet evidence of religious experience would do, and might also be most appropriate to the aims of any would-be divine relationship partner. But *some* such evidence must be available to nonresisters if they are to have the possibility of responding in love to God.

Taken in conjunction, the two points we have defended imply that if God exists, evidence sufficient for belief in God is *much more widely available than is in fact the case*. And from this it follows that God does *not* exist. Now this argument, like the other, has of course got to deal with objections. But as it turns out, the objections are pretty much the same ones, tailored to address the specifics of the new argument. And so are the replies. The reader is invited to go over the objections and replies again, this time with the Conceptual Argument in mind. She or he will see, I think, that the resources are there for a fully satisfying defense of the latter argument too. If so, we have not just the probable grounds of analogy but the more certain grounds of conceptual analysis for concluding that God does not exist.

4 CONSEQUENCES FOR THE PHILOSOPHY OF RELIGION

Suppose I am right and that the arguments we have discussed can be used to justify atheism. What should those who are convinced by them conclude with respect to God and religion? That neither matters, and that any reasonably intelligent inquirer will arrive at a place where concerns about such things no longer enter her head? That nature is all there is, and that we should limit our intellectual attention to the methods and results of the various sciences? Hardly. The perceptive reader will notice that our discussion has been restricted to the epistemic status of *traditional* theism. And anyone who thinks that traditional theism and naturalistic atheism are the only options worth exploring here has a woefully inadequate grasp of the range and diversity and complexity of religion. Indeed, there are intriguing religious possibilities that are only now beginning to receive the attention they deserve from Western philosophers. And as human beings continue to develop, intellectually and morally, as well as emotionally and socially, it may well be that new possibilities will come to light. The philosophy of religion is potentially far richer and far more wide-ranging in its explorations than it is at present. And so I conclude by suggesting that the hiddenness of the traditional God may ultimately only have the effect of allowing the *real* God—ultimate reality as it really is—to be more clearly revealed.

NOTES

1. John Macquarrie, *In Search of Deity* (London: SCM Press, 1984), p. 198.

2. See my *Divine Hiddenness and Human Reason* (Ithaca, NY: Cornell University Press, 1993). See also my "Response to Howard-Snyder" (and the paper to which it is a response), in *Canadian Journal of Philosophy,* 26/3 (1996), pp. 455–62, and my "What the Hiddenness of God Reveals: A Collaborative Discussion," in Daniel Howard-Snyder and Paul Moser (eds.), *Divine Hiddenness* (Cambridge: Cambridge University Press, 2001), pp. 33–61.

RESPONSES

Introduction

HAVING NOW CONSIDERED various different formulations of the problems of evil and divine hiddenness, we turn to responses.

In our first reading, Alvin Plantinga rebuts J. L. Mackie's defense of the "logical problem of evil." He argues that Mackie is wrong in thinking that the existence of evil is inconsistent with the existence of God, and he also argues that Mackie is wrong in thinking that every *possible* world is *creatable*. Unlike Leibniz, Plantinga is offering merely a defense rather than a theodicy. (See the General Introduction to this volume for the distinction between "defense" and "theodicy.") Central to Plantinga's defense are the following three ideas: (a) a perfectly good being might have morally sufficient reason to permit evil, (b) the value of free will might provide such a morally sufficient reason if it is impossible for God to guarantee that a world containing free creatures would be free from evil, and (c) for all we know, it *is* impossible for God to guarantee that a world containing free creatures would be free from evil. In defense of (c), Plantinga sets forth the hypothesis of *transworld depravity*. Roughly, to suffer from transworld depravity is to be such that, no matter what total creative act God had performed, if God had created you and left you free, you would freely have done something wrong. According to Plantinga, for all we know everyone in the actual world suffers from transworld depravity. If that's so, then no matter what creative act God had performed, if he had created just those creatures who in fact exist, the world would have contained moral evil. Thus, though there are *possible* worlds in which everyone who actually exists freely does what is right, those worlds are not *creatable*. They are not creatable because, in effect, free creatures *cooperate* with God in determining what sort of world will exist; and (given the hypothesis of transworld depravity) no matter what God had done, his creatures would not have cooperated in such a way as to keep the world free from evil.

Our second reading, John Hick's "Evil and Soul-Making," provides an example of a theodicy that is based on the free will defense. Hick distinguishes between two different types of theodicy. The Augustinian theodicy starts with the idea that God created humans without sin and set them in a sinless paradise and goes on to maintain that humanity fell into sin through the misuse of free will. So we are to blame, not God, for the existence of suffering in the world. God's grace will save some of us, but others will perish everlastingly. In this division, God's goodness is manifested, for his mercy redeems some and his justice is served on the rest. On the other hand, the Irenaean theodicy, stemming from Irenaeus (120–202 C.E.), views Adam not as a free agent rebelling against God, but as more akin to a very small child. The fall is humanity's first faulty step in the direction of freedom. God is still working with humanity in order to bring it from undeveloped life (*bios*) to a state of self-realization in divine love, spiritual life (*zoe*). This life is viewed as the "vale of soul-making." Spiritual development requires obstacles and the opportunity to fail as well as to succeed. Hick declares that those who are opposed to the challenge that our freedom grants us are looking for a hedonistic paradise in which every desire is gratified and we are treated by God as pet animals rather than autonomous agents. On the other hand, those who accept the challenge of freedom consider themselves to be coworkers with God in bringing forth the kingdom of God.

As should be clear by now, the typical strategy in both defense and theodicy is to look for *greater goods* that might somehow justify God in permitting the evils of this world. The next four readings in this section each in their own way offer correctives to this trend.

In the third selection, Daniel Howard-Snyder defends the skeptical theist strategy for responding to the problem of evil (although he vehemently rejects that label for the position). The skeptical theist, as we have seen in the General Introduction, maintains a kind of skepticism about human abilities to fathom the full range of possible goods and evils and relations among them. Because of this, she also maintains that there is no reason to think that we would be able to detect the goods that justify God in permitting the evils of this world even if there are such goods. Thus, the skeptical theist *as such* makes no effort to discover particular goods that might justify God in permitting various kinds of evil. However, opponents of the skeptical theist strategy commonly argue that the skeptical theist's views about the limits of human cognitive powers imply a much wider and unacceptable skepticism. If indeed the skeptical theist is right about how poorly we grasp the realm of value, then—so the objector argues—she has no good reason to accept many of the commonsense moral truths that we all wish to accept. The main goal of Howard-Snyder's paper is to provide a reply to this common and important objection.

In our fourth selection, Eleonore Stump notes that a great deal of human suffering comes from unfulfilled "desires of the heart"—desires that matter to us a great deal but whose satisfaction isn't strictly necessary for our flourishing as human beings. Traditional theodicies fail to accord sufficient value to this sort of suffering—as if it is rather easily outweighed, offset, or defeated by global goods (like the value of freedom) or by "replacement goods" (like a new family, to replace the old one that was lost in some catastrophe). To the extent that they do fail in this way, she argues, such theodicies are, at best, incomplete.

In a somewhat similar vein, Marilyn Adams argues that traditional responses to the problem of evil do not deal adequately with *horrendous evil*, where horrendous evil is (roughly) evil that we might intuitively regard as life-wrecking. The problem, she argues, is that, when it comes to accounting for horrendous evils, the standard responses to the problem of evil fail to accord these evils the weight they deserve, or they fail in other ways to respect our moral intuitions or our intuitions about value. She then goes on to sketch a way of responding to the problem of evil that does deal adequately with horrors. At the heart of her response is the idea that horrors in our lives are, or can be, defeated by a kind of intimacy and identification with God which is made possible by the incarnation.

In our sixth reading, Laura Waddell Ekstrom explores the idea that, far from constituting evidence *against* the existence of God (as the atheologians would have it), suffering may in fact be an avenue *to* knowledge of God. Finding affinities between her own (partial) theodicy and responses to the problem of evil offered by Eleonore Stump and Marilyn Adams, Ekstrom argues that some instances of suffering satisfy standard conceptions of religious experience (discussed more fully in Part IV of this volume) and serve as means of intimacy with God.

The final two readings in this section provide replies to the problem of divine hiddenness. In the seventh reading, Michael J. Murray offers a sustained critique of J. L. Schellenberg's argument for atheism from divine hiddenness. (The version of the argument that Murray engages is the one found in Schellenberg's *Divine Hiddenness and Human Reason* [1993].) Murray is particularly concerned to defend, against a critique offered by Schellenberg, the thesis that divine hiddenness is often a necessary condition for preserving free creatures' ability to fully undergo the process of soul making. What Murray offers, then, is what we might call a "greater human goods" response to the problem: divine hiddenness is justified because it is required for (or at least often importantly contributes to) some outweighing human good. By contrast, in our eighth selection Michael Rea argues that perhaps divine hiddenness is justified even independently of whatever goods it might bring to human beings.

10

The Free Will Defense

ALVIN PLANTINGA

Alvin Plantinga (1932–) was, until his retirement, professor of philosophy at the University of Notre Dame and is one of the most important figures in the fields of metaphysics, epistemology, and the philosophy of religion. His works include God and Other Minds *(1957),* The Nature of Necessity *(1974), and* God, Freedom, and Evil *(1974). In the present selection, Plantinga argues that Mackie and other atheologians (those who argue against the existence of God) are mistaken in thinking that the existence of evil is inconsistent with the existence of a perfectly good and powerful God.*

2. DOES THE THEIST CONTRADICT HIMSELF?

In a widely discussed piece entitled "Evil and Omnipotence" John Mackie makes this claim:

> I think, however, that a more telling criticism can be made by way of the traditional problem of evil. Here it can be shown, not

that religious beliefs lack rational support, but that they are positively irrational, that the several parts of the essential theological doctrine are *inconsistent* with one another....[1]

Is Mackie right? Does the theist contradict himself? But we must ask a prior question: just what is being claimed here? That theistic belief contains an inconsistency or contradiction, of course. But what, exactly, is an inconsistency or contradiction? There

From *God, Freedom, and Evil* by Alvin Plantinga (Harper & Row, 1974). Reprinted by permission of the author. Footnotes edited.

are several kinds. An *explicit* contradiction is a *proposition* of a certain sort—a conjunctive proposition, one conjunct of which is the denial or negation of the other conjunct. For example:

> Paul is a good tennis player, and it's false that Paul is a good tennis player.

(People seldom assert explicit contradictions.) Is Mackie charging the theist with accepting such a contradiction? Presumably not; what he says is

> In its simplest form the problem is this: God is omnipotent; God is wholly good; yet evil exists. There seems to be some contradiction between these three propositions, so that if any two of them were true the third would be false. But at the same time all three are essential parts of most theological positions; the theologian, it seems, at once *must* adhere and *cannot consistently* adhere to all three.

According to Mackie, then, the theist accepts a group or set of three propositions; this set is inconsistent. Its members, of course, are

(1) God is omnipotent

(2) God is wholly good

and

(3) Evil exists.

Call this set *A*; the claim is that *A* is an inconsistent set. But what is it for a *set* to be inconsistent or contradictory? Following our definition of an explicit contradiction, we might say that a set of propositions is explicitly contradictory if one of the members is the denial or negation of another member. But then, of course, it is evident that the set we are discussing is not explicitly contradictory; the denials of (1), (2), and (3), respectively, are

(1′) God is not omnipotent (or it's false that God is omnipotent)

(2′) God is not wholly good

and

(3′) There is no evil

none of which is in set *A*.

Of course many sets are pretty clearly contradictory, in an important way, but not explicitly contradictory. For example, set *B*:

(4) If all men are mortal, then Socrates is mortal

(5) All men are mortal

(6) Socrates is not mortal.

This set is not explicitly contradictory; yet surely *some* significant sense of that term applies to it. What is important here is that by using only the rules of ordinary logic—the laws of propositional logic and quantification theory found in any introductory text on the subject—we can deduce an explicit contradiction from the set. Or to put it differently, we can use the laws of logic to deduce a proposition from the set, which proposition, when added to the set, yields a new set that is explicitly contradictory. For by using the law *modus ponens* (if *p,* then *q*; *p*; therefore *q*) we can deduce

(7) Socrates is mortal

from (4) and (5). The result of adding (7) to *B* is the set {(4), (5), (6), (7)}. This set, of course, is explicitly contradictory in that (6) is the denial of (7). We might say that any set which shares this characteristic with set *B* is *formally* contradictory. So a formally contradictory set is one from whose members an explicit contradiction can be deduced by the laws of logic. Is Mackie claiming that set *A* is formally contradictory?

If he is, he's wrong. No laws of logic permit us to deduce the denial of one of the propositions in *A* from the other members. Set *A* isn't formally contradictory either.

But there is still another way in which a set of propositions can be contradictory or inconsistent. Consider set *C*, whose members are

(8) George is older than Paul

(9) Paul is older than Nick

and

(10) George is not older than Nick.

This set is neither explicitly nor formally contradictory; we can't, just by using the laws of logic, deduce the denial of any of these propositions from the others. And yet there is a good sense in which it is inconsistent or contradictory. For clearly it is *not possible* that its three members all be true. It is *necessarily true* that

(11) If George is older than Paul, and Paul is older than Nick, then George is older than Nick.

And if we add (11) to set *C*, we get a set that is formally contradictory; (8), (9), and (11) yield, by the laws of ordinary logic, the denial of (10).

I said that (11) is *necessarily true*; but what does *that* mean? Of course we might say that a proposition is necessarily true if it is impossible that it be false, or if its negation is not possibly true. This would be to explain necessity in terms of possibility. Chances are, however, that anyone who does not know what necessity is, will be equally at a loss about possibility; the explanation is not likely to be very successful. Perhaps all we can do by way of explanation is to give some examples and hope for the best. In the first place many propositions can be established by the laws of logic alone—for example,

(12) If all men are mortal and Socrates is a man, then Socrates is mortal.

Such propositions are truths of logic; and all of them are necessary in the sense of question. But truths of arithmetic and mathematics generally are also necessarily true. Still further, there is a host of propositions that are neither truths of logic nor truths of mathematics but are nonetheless necessarily true; (11) would be an example, as well as

(13) Nobody is taller than himself

(14) Red is a color

(15) No numbers are persons

(16) No prime number is a prime minister

and

(17) Bachelors are unmarried.

So here we have an important kind of necessity—let's call it "broadly logical necessity." Of course there is a correlative kind of *possibility*: a proposition *p* is possibly true (in the broadly logical sense) just in case its negation or denial is not necessarily true (in that same broadly logical sense). This sense of necessity and possibility must be distinguished from another that we may call *causal* or *natural* necessity and possibility. Consider

(18) Henry Kissinger has swum the Atlantic.

Although this proposition has an implausible ring, it is not necessarily false in the broadly logical sense (and its denial is not necessarily true in that sense). But there is a good sense in which it is impossible: it is *causally* or *naturally* impossible. Human beings, unlike dolphins, just don't have the physical equipment demanded for this feat. Unlike Superman, furthermore, the rest of us are incapable of leaping tall buildings at a single bound or (without auxiliary power of some kind) traveling faster than a speeding bullet. These things are *impossible* for us—but not *logically* impossible, even in the broad sense.

So there are several senses of necessity and possibility here. There are a number of propositions, furthermore, of which it's difficult to say whether they are or aren't possible in the broadly logical sense; some of these are subjects of philosophical controversy. Is it possible, for example, for a person never to be conscious during his entire existence? Is it possible for a (human) person to exist *disembodied*? If that's possible, is it possible that there be a person who *at no time at all* during his entire existence has a body? Is it possible to see without eyes? These are propositions about whose possibility in that broadly logical sense there is disagreement and dispute.

Now return to set *C*. . . . What is characteristic of it is the fact that the conjunction of its members—the proposition expressed by the result of putting "and's" between (8), (9), and (10)—is necessarily false. Or we might put it like this: what characterizes set *C* is the fact that we can get a formally contradictory set by adding a necessarily true proposition— namely (11). Suppose we say that a set is *implicitly contradictory* if it resembles *C* in this respect. That is, a set *S* of propositions is implicitly contradictory if there is a necessary proposition *p* such that the result of adding *p* to *S* is a formally contradictory set. Another way to put it: *S* is implicitly contradictory if there is some necessarily true proposition p such that by using just the laws of ordinary logic, we can deduce an explicit contradiction from p together with the members of S. And when Mackie says that set A is contradictory, we may properly take him, I think, as holding that it is implicitly contradictory in the explained sense. As he puts it:

> However, the contradiction does not arise immediately; to show it we need some additional premises, or perhaps some quasi-logical rules connecting the terms "good" and "evil" and "omnipotent." These additional principles are that good is opposed to evil, in such a way that a good thing always eliminates evil as far as it can, and that there are no limits to what an omnipotent thing can do. From these it follows that a good omnipotent thing eliminates evil completely, and then the propositions that a good omnipotent thing exists, and that evil exists, are incompatible.[2]

Here Mackie refers to "additional premises"; he also calls them "additional principles" and "quasi-logical rules"; he says we need them to show the contradiction. What he means, I think, is that to get a formally contradictory set we must add some more propositions to set A; and if we aim to show that set A is implicitly contradictory, these propositions must be necessary truths—"quasi-logical rules" as Mackie calls them. The two additional principles he suggests are

(19)   A good thing always eliminates evil as far as it can

and

(20)   There are no limits to what an omnipotent being can do.

And, of course, if Mackie means to show that set A is implicitly contradictory, then he must hold that (19) and (20) are not merely *true* but *necessarily true*.

But, are they? What about (20) first? What does it mean to say that a being is omnipotent? That he is *all-powerful*, or *almighty*, presumably. But

are there no limits at all to the power of such a being? Could he create square circles, for example, or married bachelors? Most theologians and theistic philosophers who hold that God is omnipotent, do not hold that He can create round squares or bring it about that He both exists and does not exist. These theologians and philosophers may hold that there are no *nonlogical* limits to what an omnipotent being can do, but they concede that not even an omnipotent being can bring about logically impossible states of affairs or cause necessarily false propositions to be true. Some theists, on the other hand—Martin Luther and Descartes, perhaps—have apparently thought that God's power is unlimited even by the laws of logic. For these theists the question whether set A is contradictory will not be of much interest. As theists they believe (1) and (2), and they also, presumably, believe (3). But they remain undisturbed by the claim that (1), (2), and (3) are jointly inconsistent—because, as they say, God can do what is logically impossible. Hence He can bring it about that the members of set A are all true, even if that set is contradictory (concentrating very intensely upon this suggestion is likely to make you dizzy). So the theist who thinks that the power of God isn't *limited at all*, not even by the laws of logic, will be unimpressed by Mackie's argument and won't find any difficulty in the contradiction set A is alleged to contain. This view is not very popular, however, and for good reason; it is quite incoherent. What the theist typically means when he says that God is omnipotent is not that there are *no* limits to God's power, but at most that there are no nonlogical limits to what He can do; and given this qualification, it is perhaps initially plausible to suppose that (20) is necessarily true.

But what about (19), the proposition that every good thing eliminates every evil state of affairs that it can eliminate? Is that necessarily true? Is it true at all? Suppose, first of all, that your friend Paul unwisely goes for a drive on a wintry day and runs out of gas on a deserted road. The temperature dips to $-10°$, and a miserably cold wind comes up. You are sitting comfortably at home (twenty-five miles from Paul) roasting chestnuts in a roaring blaze.

Your car is in the garage; in the trunk there is the full five-gallon can of gasoline you always keep for emergencies. Paul's discomfort and danger are certainly an evil, and one which you could eliminate. You don't do so. But presumably you don't thereby forfeit your claim to being a "good thing"—you simply didn't know of Paul's plight. And so (19) does not appear to be necessary. It says that every good thing has a certain property—the property of eliminating every evil that it can. And if the case I described is possible—a good person's failing through ignorance to eliminate a certain evil he can eliminate—then (19) is by no means necessarily true.

But perhaps Mackie could sensibly claim that if you *didn't know* about Paul's plight, then in fact you were not, at the time in question, able to eliminate the evil in question; and perhaps he'd be right. In any event he could revise (19) to take into account the kind of case I mentioned:

(19a) Every good thing always eliminates every evil that *it knows about* and can eliminate.

{(1), (2), (3), (20), (19a)}, you'll notice is not a formally contradictory set—to get a formal contradiction we must add a proposition specifying that God knows about every evil state of affairs. But most theists do believe that God is omniscient or all-knowing; so if this new set—the set that results when we add to set A the proposition that God is omniscient—is implicitly contradictory then Mackie should be satisfied and the theist confounded. (And, henceforth, set A will be the old set A together with the proposition that God is omniscient.)

But is (19a) necessary? Hardly. Suppose you know that Paul is marooned as in the previous example, and you also know another friend is similarly marooned fifty miles in the opposite direction. Suppose, furthermore, that while you can rescue one or the other, you simply can't rescue both. Then each of the two evils is such that it is within your power to eliminate it; and you know about them both. But you can't eliminate *both*; and you don't forfeit your claim to being a good person by eliminating only one—it wasn't within your power to do more. So the fact that you don't doesn't mean that you are not a good person. Therefore (19a) is false; it is not a necessary truth or even a truth that every good thing eliminates every evil it knows about and can eliminate.

We can see the same thing another way. You've been rock climbing. Still something of a novice, you've acquired a few cuts and bruises by inelegantly using your knees rather than your feet. One of these bruises is fairly painful. You mention it to a physician friend, who predicts the pain will leave of its own accord in a day or two. Meanwhile, he says, there's nothing he can do, short of amputating your leg above the knee, to remove the pain. Now the pain in your knee is an evil state of affairs. All else being equal, it would be better if you had no such pain. And it is within the power of your friend to eliminate this evil state of affairs. Does his failure to do so mean that he is not a good person? Of course not; for he could eliminate this evil state of affairs only by bringing about another, much worse evil. And so it is once again evident that (19a) is false. It is entirely possible that a good person fail to eliminate an evil state of affairs that he knows about and can eliminate. This would take place, if, as in the present example, he couldn't eliminate the evil without bringing about a *greater* evil.

A slightly different kind of case shows the same thing. A really impressive good state of affairs G will outweigh a trivial E—that is, the conjunctive state of affairs G and E is itself a good state of affairs. And surely a good person would not be obligated to eliminate a given evil if he could do so only by eliminating a good that outweighed it. Therefore (19a) is not necessarily true; it can't be used to show that set A is implicitly contradictory.

These difficulties might suggest another revision of (19); we might try

(19b) A good being eliminates every evil E that it knows about and that it can eliminate without either bringing about a greater evil or eliminating a good state of affairs that outweighs E.

Is this necessarily true? It takes care of the second of the two difficulties afflicting (19a) but leaves the first untouched. We can see this as follows. First, suppose we say that a being *properly eliminates* an evil state of affairs if it eliminates that evil without either eliminating an outweighing good or bringing about a greater evil. It is then obviously possible that a person find himself in a situation where he could properly eliminate an evil E and could also properly eliminate another evil E', but couldn't properly eliminate them *both*. You're rock climbing again, this time on the dreaded north face of the Grand Teton. You and your party come upon Curt and Bob, two mountaineers stranded 125 feet apart on the face. They untied to reach their cigarettes and then carelessly dropped the rope while lighting up. A violent, dangerous thunderstorm is approaching. You have time to rescue one of the stranded climbers and retreat before the storm hits; if you rescue both, however, you and your party and the two climbers will be caught on the face during the thunderstorm, which will very likely destroy your entire party. In this case you can eliminate one evil (Curt's being stranded on the face) without causing more evil or eliminating a greater good; and you are also able to properly eliminate the other evil (Bob's being thus stranded). But you can't properly eliminate them *both*. And so the fact that you don't rescue Curt, say, even though you could have, doesn't show that you aren't a good person. Here, then, each of the evils is such that you can properly eliminate it; but you can't properly eliminate them both, and hence can't be blamed for failing to eliminate one of them.

So neither (19a) nor (19b) is necessarily true. You may be tempted to reply that the sort of counterexamples offered—examples where someone is able to eliminate an evil A and also able to eliminate a different evil B, but unable to eliminate them both—are irrelevant to the case of a being who, like God, is both omnipotent and omniscient. That is, you may think that if an omnipotent and omniscient being is able to eliminate each of two evils, it follows that he can eliminate them *both*. Perhaps this is so; but it is not strictly to the point. The fact is the counterexamples show that (19a) and (19b) are not necessarily true and hence can't be used to show that set A is implicitly inconsistent.

What the reply does suggest is that perhaps the atheologian will have more success if he works the properties of omniscience and omnipotence into (19). Perhaps he could say something like

(19c) An omnipotent and omniscient good being eliminates every evil that it can properly eliminate.

And suppose, for purposes of argument, we concede the necessary truth of (19c). Will it serve Mackie's purposes? Not obviously. For we don't get a set that is formally contradictory by adding (20) and (19c) to set A. This set (call it A') contains the following six members:

(1)   God is omnipotent

(2)   God is wholly good

(2′)   God is omniscient

(3)   Evil exists

(19c) An omnipotent and omniscient good being eliminates every evil that it can properly eliminate

and

(20)   There are no nonlogical limits to what an omnipotent being can do.

Now if A' were formally contradictory, then from any five of its members we could deduce the denial of the sixth by the laws of ordinary logic. That is, any five would *formally entail* the denial of the sixth. So if A' were formally inconsistent, the denial of (3) would be formally entailed by the remaining five. That is, (1), (2), (2′), (19c), and (20) would formally entail

(3′)   There is no evil.

But they don't; what they formally entail is not that there is no evil *at all* but only that

(3″)   There is no evil that God can properly eliminate.

So (19c) doesn't really help either—not because it is not necessarily true but because its addition [with (20)] to set A does not yield a formally contradictory set.

Obviously, what the atheologian must add to get a formally contradictory set is

(21) If God is omniscient and omnipotent, then he can properly eliminate every evil state of affairs.

Suppose we agree that the set consisting in A plus (19c), (20), and (21) is formally contradictory. So if (19c), (20), and (21) are all necessarily true, then set A is implicitly contradictory. We've already conceded that (19c) and (20) are indeed necessary. So we must take a look at (21). Is this proposition necessarily true?

No. To see this let us ask the following question. Under what conditions would an omnipotent being be unable to eliminate a certain evil E without eliminating an outweighing good? Well, suppose that E is *included in* some good state of affairs that outweighs it. That is, suppose there is some good state of affairs G so related to E that it is impossible that G obtain or be actual and E fail to obtain. (Another way to put this: a state of affairs S includes S' if the conjunctive state of affairs S *but not S'* is impossible, or if it is necessary that S' obtains if S does.) Now suppose that some good state of affairs G includes an evil state of affairs E that it outweighs. Then not even an omnipotent being could eliminate E without eliminating G. But are there any cases where a good state of affairs includes, in this sense, an evil that it outweighs?[3] Indeed there are such states of affairs. To take an artificial example, let's suppose that E is Paul's suffering from a minor abrasion and G is your being deliriously happy. The conjunctive state of affairs, G *and* E—the state of affairs that obtains if and only if both G and E obtain—is then a good state of affairs: it is better, all else being equal, that you be intensely happy and Paul suffer a mildly annoying abrasion than that this state of affairs not obtain. So G *and* E is a good state of affairs. And clearly G *and* E includes E: obviously it is necessarily true that if you are deliriously happy and Paul is suffering from an abrasion, then Paul is suffering from an abrasion.

But perhaps you think this example trivial, tricky, slippery, and irrelevant. If so, take heart; other examples abound. Certain kinds of values, certain familiar kinds of good states of affairs, can't

exist apart from evil of some sort. For example, there are people who display a sort of creative moral heroism in the face of suffering and adversity—a heroism that inspires others and creates a good situation out of a bad one. In a situation like this the evil, of course, remains evil; but the total state of affairs—someone's bearing pain magnificently, for example—may be good. If it is, then the good present must outweigh the evil; otherwise the total situation would not be *good*. But, of course, it is not possible that such a good state of affairs obtain unless some evil also obtain. It is a necessary truth that if someone bears pain magnificently, then someone is in pain.

The conclusion to be drawn, therefore, is that (21) is not necessarily true. And our discussion thus far shows at the very least that it is no easy matter to find necessarily true propositions that yield a formally contradictory set when added to set A.[4] One wonders, therefore, why the many atheologians who confidently assert that this set is contradictory make no attempt whatever to *show* that it is. For the most part they are content just to *assert* that there is a contradiction here. Even Mackie, who sees that some "additional premises" or "quasi-logical rules" are needed, makes scarcely a beginning towards finding some additional premises that are necessarily true and that together with the members of set A formally entail an explicit contradiction.

3. CAN WE SHOW THAT THERE IS NO INCONSISTENCY HERE?

To summarize our conclusions so far: although many atheologians claim that the theist is involved in contradiction when he asserts the members of set A, this set, obviously, is neither *explicitly nor formally* contradictory; the claim, presumably, must be that it is *implicitly* contradictory. To make good this claim the atheologian must find some necessarily true proposition p (it could be a conjunction of several propositions) such that the addition of p to set A yields a set that is formally contradictory. No atheologian has produced even a plausible candidate for this role, and it certainly is not easy to see what such a proposition might be. Now we might think we should simply declare set *A* implicitly consistent on the principle that a proposition (or set) is to be presumed consistent or possible until proven otherwise. This course, however, leads to trouble. The same principle would impel us to declare the atheologian's claim—that set *A* is inconsistent—possible or consistent. But the claim that a given set of propositions is implicitly contradictory, is itself either necessarily true or necessarily false; so if such a claim is *possible*, it is not necessarily false and is, therefore, true (in fact, necessarily true). If we followed the suggested principle, therefore, we should be obliged to declare set *A* implicitly consistent (since it hasn't been shown to be otherwise), but we should have to say the same thing about the atheologian's claim, since we haven't shown *that* claim to be inconsistent or impossible. The atheologian's claim, furthermore, is necessarily true if it is possible. Accordingly, if we accept the above principle, we shall have to declare set *A* both implicitly consistent and implicitly inconsistent. So all we can say at this point is that set *A* has not been shown to be implicitly inconsistent.

Can we go any further? One way to go on would be to try to *show* that set *A* is implicitly consistent or possible in the broadly logical sense. But what is involved in showing such a thing? Although there are various ways to approach this matter, they all resemble one another in an important respect. They all amount to this: to show that a set *S* is consistent you think of a *possible state of affairs* (it needn't *actually obtain*) which is such that if it were actual, then all of the members of *S* would be true. This procedure is sometimes called *giving a model of S*. For example, you might construct an axiom set and then show that it is consistent by giving a model of it; this is how it was shown that the denial of Euclid's parallel postulate is formally consistent with the rest of his postulates.

There are various special cases of this procedure to fit special circumstances. Suppose, for example, you have a pair of propositions *p* and *q* and wish to show them consistent. And suppose we say that a proposition *p1* entails a proposition *p2* if

it is impossible that *p1* be true and *p2* false—if the conjunctive proposition *p1* and not *p2* is necessarily false. Then one way to show that *p* is consistent with *q* is to find some proposition *r* whose conjunction with *p* is both possible, in the broadly logical sense, and entails *q*. A rude and unlettered behaviorist, for example, might hold that thinking is really nothing but movements of the larynx; he might go on to hold that

P   Jones did not move his larynx after April 30 is inconsistent (in the broadly logical sense) with

Q   Jones did some thinking during May.

By way of rebuttal, we might point out that *P* appears to be consistent with

R   While convalescing from an April 30 laryngotomy, Jones whiled away the idle hours by writing (in May) a splendid paper on Kant's *Critique of Pure Reason*.

So the conjunction of *P* and *R* appears to be consistent; but obviously it also entails *Q* (you can't write even a passable paper on Kant's *Critique of Pure Reason* without doing some thinking); so *P* and *Q* are consistent.

We can see that this is a special case of the procedure I mentioned above as follows. This proposition *R* is consistent with *P*; so the proposition *P and R* is possible, describes a possible state of affairs. But *P and R* entails *Q*; hence if *P and R* were true, *Q* would also be true, and hence both *P* and *Q* would be true. So this is really a case of producing a possible state of affairs such that, if it were actual, all the members of the set in question (in this case the pair set of *P* and *Q*) would be true.

How does this apply to the case before us? As follows, let us conjoin propositions (1), (2), and (2') and henceforth call the result (1):

(1)   God is omniscient, omnipotent, and wholly good.

The problem, then, is to show that (1) and (3) (evil exists) are consistent. This could be done, as we've seen, by finding a proposition *r* that is consistent with (1) and such that (1) and (*r*) together entail (3). One proposition that might do the trick is

(22) God creates a world containing evil and has a good reason for doing so.

If (22) is consistent with (1), then it follows that (1) and (3) (and hence set *A*) are consistent. Accordingly, one thing some theists have tried is to show that (22) and (1) are consistent.

One can attempt this in at least two ways. On the one hand, we could try to apply the same method again. Conceive of a possible state of affairs such that, if it obtained, an omnipotent, omniscient, and wholly good God would have a good reason for permitting evil. On the other, someone might try to specify *what God's reason is* for permitting evil and try to show, if it is not obvious, that it is a good reason. St. Augustine, for example, one of the greatest and most influential philosopher-theologians of the Christian Church, writes as follows:

> ... some people see with perfect truth that a creature is better if, while possessing free will, it remains always fixed upon God and never sins; then, reflecting on men's sins, they are grieved, not because they continue to sin, but because they were created. They say: He should have made us such that we never willed to sin, but always to enjoy the unchangeable truth.
>
> They should not lament or be angry. God has not compelled men to sin just because He created them and gave them the power to choose between sinning and not sinning. There are angels who have never sinned and never will sin.
>
> Such is the generosity of God's goodness that He has not refrained from creating even that creature which He foreknew would not only sin, but remain in the will to sin. As a runaway horse is better than a stone which does not run away because it lacks self-movement and sense perception, so the creature is more excellent which sins by free will than that which does not sin only because it has no free will.[5]

In broadest terms Augustine claims that God could create a better, more perfect universe by permitting evil than He could by refusing to do so:

> Neither the sins nor the misery are necessary to the perfection of the universe, but souls as such are necessary, which have the power to sin if they so will, and become miserable if they sin. If misery persisted after their sins had been abolished, or if there were misery before there were sins, then it might be right to say that the order and government of the universe were at fault. Again, if there were sins but no consequent misery, that order is equally dishonored by lack of equity.[6]

Augustine tries to tell us *what God's reason is* for permitting evil. At bottom, he says, it's that God can create a more perfect universe by permitting evil. A really top-notch universe requires the existence of free, rational, and moral agents; and some of the free creatures He created went wrong. But the universe with the free creatures it contains and the evil they commit is better than it would have been had it contained neither the free creatures nor this evil. Such an attempt to specify God's reason for permitting evil is what I earlier called a *theodicy*; in the words of John Milton it is an attempt to "justify the ways of God to man," to show that God is just in permitting evil. Augustine's kind of theodicy might be called a Free Will Theodicy, since the idea of rational creatures with free will plays such a prominent role in it.

A theodicist, then, attempts to tell us why God permits evil. Quite distinct from a Free Will Theodicy is what I shall call a Free Will Defense. Here the aim is not to say what God's reason *is*, but at most what God's reason *might possibly be*. We could put the difference like this. The Free Will Theodicist and Free Will Defender are both trying to show that (1) is consistent with (22), and of course if so, then set *A* is consistent. The Free Will Theodicist tries to do this by finding some proposition *r* which in conjunction with (1) entails (22); he claims, furthermore, that this proposition is true, not just consistent with (1). He tries to tell us what God's reason for permitting evil *really is*. The Free Will Defender, on the other hand, though he also tries to find a proposition *r* that is consistent with (1) and in conjunction with it entails (22), does *not* claim to know or even believe that *r* is true. And here, of course, he is perfectly within his rights. His aim is to show that (1) is consistent with (22); all he need do then is find an *r* that is consistent with (1) and such that (1) and (*r*) entail (22); whether *r* is true is quite beside the point.

So there is a significant difference between a Free Will Theodicy and a Free Will Defense. The latter is sufficient (if successful) to show that set *A* is consistent; in a way a Free Will Theodicy goes beyond what is required. On the other hand, a theodicy would be much more satisfying, if possible to achieve. No doubt the theist would rather know what God's reason is for permitting evil than simply that it's possible that He has a good one. But in the present context (that of investigating the consistency of set *A*), the latter is all that's needed. Neither a defense or a theodicy, of course, gives any hint to what God's reason for some *specific* evil—the death or suffering of someone close to you, for example— might be. And there is still another function[7]—a sort of pastoral function—in the neighborhood that neither serves. Confronted with evil in his own life or suddenly coming to realize more clearly than before the *extent* and *magnitude* of evil, a believer in God may undergo a crisis of faith. He may be tempted to follow the advice of Job's "friends"; he may be tempted to "curse God and die." Neither a Free Will Defense nor a Free Will Theodicy is designed to be of much help or comfort to one suffering from such a storm in the soul (although in a specific case, of course, one or the other could prove useful). Neither is to be thought of first of all as a means of pastoral counseling. Probably neither will enable someone to find peace with himself and with God in the face of the evil the world contains. But then, of course, neither is intended for that purpose.

4. THE FREE WILL DEFENSE

In what follows I shall focus attention upon the Free Will Defense. I shall examine it more closely, state it more exactly, and consider objections to it;

and I shall argue that in the end it is successful. Earlier we saw that among good states of affairs there are some that not even God can bring about without bringing about evil: those goods, namely, that *entail* or *include* evil states of affairs. The Free Will Defense can be looked upon as an effort to show that there may be a very different kind of good that God can't bring about without permitting evil. These are good states of affairs that don't include evil; they do not entail the existence of any evil whatever; nonetheless God Himself can't bring them about without permitting evil.

So how does the Free Will Defense work? And what does the Free Will Defender mean when he says that people are or may be free? What is relevant to the Free Will Defense is the idea of *being free with respect to an action*. If a person is free with respect to a given action, then he is free to perform that action and free to refrain from performing it; no antecedent conditions and/or causal laws determine that he will perform the action, or that he won't. It is within his power, at the time in question, to take or perform the action and within his power to refrain from it. Freedom so conceived is not to be confused with unpredictability. You might be able to predict what you will do in a given situation even if you are free, in that situation, to do something else. If I know you well, I may be able to predict what action you will take in response to a certain set of conditions; it does not follow that you are not free with respect to that action. Secondly, I shall say that an action is *morally significant*, for a given person, if it would be wrong for him to perform the action but right to refrain or vice versa. Keeping a promise, for example, would ordinarily be morally significant for a person, as would refusing induction into the army. On the other hand, having Cheerios for breakfast (instead of Wheaties) would not normally be morally significant. Further, suppose we say that a person is *significantly free*, on a given occasion, if he is then free with respect to a morally significant action. And finally we must distinguish between *moral evil* and *natural evil*. The former is evil that results from free human activity; natural evil is any other kind of evil.[8]

Given these definitions and distinctions, we can make a preliminary statement of the Free Will Defense as follows. A world containing creatures who are significantly free (and freely perform more good than evil actions) is more valuable, all else being equal, than a world containing no free creatures at all. Now God can create free creatures, but He can't *cause* or *determine* them to do only what is right. For if He does so, then they aren't significantly free after all; they do not do what is right *freely*. To create creatures capable of *moral good*, therefore, He must create creatures capable of moral evil; and He can't give these creatures the freedom to perform evil and at the same time prevent them from doing so. As it turned out, sadly enough, some of the free creatures God created went wrong in the exercise of their freedom; this is the source of moral evil. The fact that free creatures sometimes go wrong, however, counts neither against God's omnipotence nor against His goodness; for He could have forestalled the occurrence of moral evil only by removing the possibility of moral good.

I said earlier that the Free Will Defender tries to find a proposition that is consistent with

(1)   God is omniscient, omnipotent, and wholly good

and together with (1) entails that there is evil. According to the Free Will Defense, we must find this proposition somewhere in the above story. The heart of the Free Will Defense is the claim that it is *possible* that God could not have created a universe containing moral good (or as much moral good as this world contains) without creating one that also contained moral evil. And if so, then it is possible that God has a good reason for creating a world containing evil.

Now this defense has met with several kinds of objections. For example, some philosophers say that *causal determinism* and *freedom*, contrary to what we might have thought, are not really incompatible.[9] But if so, then God could have created free creatures who were free, and free to do what is wrong, but nevertheless were causally determined to do only what is right. Thus He could have created creatures who were free to do what was wrong, while nevertheless preventing them from ever performing any wrong actions—simply by seeing to it that they were causally determined to do only what is right. Of course this contradicts the Free Will Defense, according to which there is inconsistency in supposing that God determines free creatures to do only what is right. But is it really possible that all of a person's actions are causally determined while some of them are free? How could that be so? According to one version of the doctrine in question, to say that George acts freely on a given occasion is to say only this: *if George had chosen to do otherwise, he would have done otherwise.* Now George's action *A* is causally determined if some event *E*—some event beyond his control—has already occurred, where the state of affairs consisting in *E*'s occurrence conjoined with George's *refraining* from performing *A*, is a causally impossible state of affairs. Then one can consistently hold both that all of a man's actions are causally determined and that some of them are free in the above sense. For suppose that all of a man's actions are causally determined and that he *couldn't*, on any occasion, have made any choice or performed any action different from the ones he did make and perform. It could still be true that if he *had* chosen to do otherwise, he would have done otherwise. Granted, he couldn't have chosen to do otherwise; but this is consistent with saying that *if* he had, things would have gone differently.

This objection to the Free Will Defense seems utterly implausible. One might as well claim that being in jail doesn't really limit one's freedom on the grounds that if one were *not* in jail, he'd be free to come and go as he pleased. So I shall say no more about this objection here.[10]

A second objection is more formidable. In essence it goes like this. Surely it is possible to do only what is right, even if one is free to do wrong. It is *possible*, in that broadly logical sense, that there would be a world containing free creatures who always do what is right. There is certainly no *contradiction* or *inconsistency* in this idea. But God is omnipotent; his power has no nonlogical limitations. So if it's possible that there be a world containing creatures who are free to do what is wrong but never in fact do so, then it follows that an omnipotent God could create such a world. If so, however, the Free Will Defense must be mistaken in its insistence upon the possibility that God is omnipotent but unable to create a world containing moral good without permitting moral evil. J. L. Mackie ... states this objection:

> If God has made men such that in their free choices they sometimes prefer what is good and sometimes what is evil, why could he not have made men such that they always freely choose the good? If there is no logical impossibility in a man's freely choosing the good on one, or on several occasions, there cannot be a logical impossibility in his freely choosing the good on every occasion. God was not, then, faced with a choice between making innocent automata and making beings who, in acting freely, would sometimes go wrong; there was open to him the obviously better possibility of making beings who would act freely but always go right. Clearly, his failure to avail himself of this possibility is inconsistent with his being both omnipotent and wholly good.[11]

Now what, exactly, is Mackie's point here? This. According to the Free Will Defense, it is possible both that God is omnipotent and that He was unable to create a world containing moral good without creating one containing moral evil. But, replies Mackie, this limitation on His power to create is inconsistent with God's omnipotence. For surely it's *possible* that there be a world containing perfectly virtuous persons—persons who are significantly free but always do what is right. Surely there are *possible worlds* that contain moral good but no moral evil. But God, if He is omnipotent, can create any possible world He chooses. So it is *not* possible, contrary to the Free Will Defense, both that God is omnipotent and that He could create a world containing moral good only by creating one containing moral evil. If He is omnipotent, the only limitations of His power are *logical* limitations;

in which case there are no possible worlds He could not have created.

This is a subtle and important point. According to the great German philosopher G. W. Leibniz, *this* world, the actual world, must be the best of all possible worlds. His reasoning goes as follows. Before God created anything at all, He was confronted with an enormous range of choices; He could create or bring into actuality any of the myriads of different possible worlds. Being perfectly good, He must have chosen to create the best world He could; being omnipotent, He was able to create any possible world He pleased. He must, therefore, have chosen the best of all possible worlds; and hence *this* world, the one He did create, must be the best possible. Now Mackie, of course, agrees with Leibniz that God, if omnipotent, could have created any world He pleased and would have created the best world he could. But while Leibniz draws the conclusion that this world, despite appearances, must be the best possible, Mackie concludes instead that there is no omnipotent, wholly good God. For, he says, it is obvious enough that this present world is not the best of all possible worlds.

The Free Will Defender disagrees with both Leibniz and Mackie. In the first place, he might say, what is the reason for supposing that there is such a thing as the best of all possible worlds? No matter how marvelous a world is—containing no matter how many persons enjoying unalloyed bliss—isn't it possible that there be an even better world containing even more persons enjoying even more unalloyed bliss? But what is really characteristic and central to the Free Will Defense is the claim that God, though omnipotent, could not have actualized just any possible world He pleased.

5. WAS IT WITHIN GOD'S POWER TO CREATE ANY POSSIBLE WORLD HE PLEASED?

This is indeed the crucial question for the Free Will Defense. If we wish to discuss it with insight and authority, we shall have to look into the idea of *possible worlds.* And a sensible first question is this: what sort of thing is a possible world? The basic idea is that a possible world is *a way things could have been*; it is a *state of affairs* of some kind. Earlier we spoke of states of affairs, in particular of good and evil states of affairs. Suppose we look at this idea in more detail. What sort of thing is a state of affairs? The following would be examples:

> Nixon's having won the 1972 election
>
> 7 + 5's being equal to 12
>
> All men's being mortal

and

> Gary, Indiana's, having a really nasty pollution problem.

These are *actual* states of affairs: states of affairs that do in fact obtain. And corresponding to each such actual state of affairs there is a true proposition—in the above cases, the corresponding propositions would be *Nixon won the 1972 presidential election, 7 + 5 is equal to 12, all men are mortal, and Gary, Indiana, has a really nasty pollution problem.* A proposition *p corresponds* to a state of affairs s_1, in this sense, if it is impossible that *p* be true and s_1 fail to obtain and impossible that s_1 obtain and *p* fail to be true.

But just as there are false propositions, so there are states of affairs that do *not* obtain or are *not* actual. *Kissinger's having swum the Atlantic* and *Hubert Horatio Humphrey's having run a mile in four minutes* would be examples. Some states of affairs that do not obtain are impossible: e.g., *Hubert's having drawn a square circle, 7 + 5's being equal to 75,* and *Agnew's having a brother who was an only child.* The propositions corresponding to these states of affairs, of course, are necessarily false. So there are states of affairs that *obtain* or are *actual* and also states of affairs that don't obtain. Among the latter some are *impossible* and others are possible. And a possible world is a possible state of affairs. Of course not every possible state of affairs is a possible world; *Hubert's having run a mile in four minutes* is a possible state of affairs but not a possible world. No doubt it is an *element* of many possible worlds, but it isn't itself inclusive enough to be one. To be a possible world, a state of affairs must be very large—so large as to be *complete* or *maximal.*

To get at this idea of completeness we need a couple of definitions. As we have already seen . . . a state of affairs *A includes* a state of affairs *B* if it is not possible that *A* obtain and *B* not obtain or if the conjunctive state of affairs *A but not B*—the state of affairs that obtains if and only if *A* obtains and *B* does not—is not possible. For example, *Jim Whittaker's being the first American to climb Mt. Everest* includes *Jim Whittaker's being an American.* It also includes *Mt. Everest's being climbed, something's being climbed, no American's having climbed Everest before Whittaker did,* and the like. *Inclusion* among states of affairs is like *entailment* among propositions; and where a state of affairs *A* includes a state of affairs *B,* the proposition corresponding to *A* entails the one corresponding to *B.* Accordingly, *Jim Whittaker is the first American to climb Everest* entails *Mt. Everest has been climbed, something has been climbed,* and *no American climbed Everest before Whittaker did.* Now suppose we say further that a state of affairs *A precludes* a state of affairs *B* if it is not possible that *both* obtain, or if the conjunctive state of affairs *A and B* is impossible. Thus *Whittaker's being the first American to climb Mt. Everest* precludes *Luther Jerstad's being the first American to climb Everest,* as well as Whittaker's never having climbed any mountains. If *A* precludes *B,* than *A's* corresponding proposition entails the denial of the one corresponding to *B.* Still further, let's say that the *complement* of a state of affairs is the state of affairs that obtains just in case *A* does not obtain. [Or we might say that the complement (call it $\bar{A}$) of *A* is the state of affairs corresponding to the *denial* or *negation* of the proposition corresponding to *A.*] Given these definitions, we can say what it is for a state of affairs to be *complete*: *A* is a complete state of affairs if and only if for every state of affairs *B,* either *A includes B* or *A precludes B.* (We could express the same thing by saying that if *A* is a complete state of affairs, then for every state of affairs *B,* either *A* includes *B* or *A* includes $\bar{B}$, the complement of *B.*) And now we are able to say what a possible world is: a possible world is any possible state of affairs that is complete. If *A* is a possible world, then it says something about everything; every state of affairs *S* is either included in or precluded by it.

Corresponding to each possible world W, furthermore, there is a set of propositions that I'll call the book on W. A proposition is in the book on W just in case the state of affairs to which it corresponds is included in W. Or we might express it like this. Suppose we say that a proposition P *is true in a world W* if and only if *P would have been true if W had been actual*—if and only if, that is, it is not possible that W be actual and P be false. Then the book on W is the set of propositions true in W. Like possible worlds, books are *complete*; if B is a book, then for any proposition P, either P or the denial of P will be a member of B. A book is a *maximal consistent set* of propositions; it is so large that the addition of another proposition to it always yields an explicitly inconsistent set.

Of course, for each possible world there is exactly one book corresponding to it (that is, for a given world W there is just one book B such that each member of B is true in M; and for each book there is just one world to which it corresponds). So every world has its book.

It should be obvious that exactly one possible world is actual. At *least* one must be, since the set of true propositions is a maximal consistent set and hence a book. But then it corresponds to a possible world, and the possible world corresponding to this set of propositions (since it's the set of *true* propositions) will be actual. On the other hand there is at *most* one actual world. For suppose there were two: W and W'. These worlds cannot include all the very same states of affairs; if they did, they would be the very same world. So there must be at least one state of affairs S such that W includes S and W' does not. But a possible world is maximal; W', therefore, includes the complement $\bar{S}$ of S. So if both W and W' were actual, as we have supposed, then both S and $\bar{S}$ would be actual—which is impossible. So there can't be more than one possible world that is actual.

Leibniz pointed out that a proposition p is necessary if it is true in every possible world. We may add that p is possible if it is true in one world and impossible if true in none. Furthermore, p *entails* q if there is no possible world in which p is true and q is false, and p *is consistent with* q if there is at least one world in which both p and q are true.

A further feature of possible worlds is that people (and other things) exist in them. Each of us exists in the actual world, obviously; but a person also exists in many worlds distinct from the actual world. It would be a mistake, of course, to think of all of these worlds as somehow "going on" at the same time, with the same person reduplicated through these worlds and actually existing in a lot of different ways. This is not what is meant by saying that the same person exists in different possible worlds. What is meant, instead, is this: a person Paul exists in each of those possible worlds W which is such that, if W *had been actual,* Paul would have existed—actually existed. Suppose Paul had been an inch taller than he is, or a better tennis player. Then the world that does in fact obtain would not have been actual; some other world— W', let's say— would have obtained instead. If W' had been actual, Paul would have existed; so Paul exists in W'. (Of course there are still other possible worlds in which Paul does not exist—worlds, for example, in which there are no people at all.) Accordingly, when we say that Paul exists in a world W, what we mean is that Paul *would have* existed had W been actual. Or we could put it like this: Paul exists in each world W that includes the state of affairs consisting in Paul's existence. We can put this still more simply by saying that Paul exists in those worlds whose books contain the proposition *Paul exists*.

But isn't there a problem here? *Many* people are named "Paul": Paul the apostle, Paul J. Zwier, John Paul Jones, and many other famous Pauls. So who goes with "Paul exists"? Which Paul? The answer has to do with the fact that books contain *propositions*—not sentences. They contain the sort of thing sentences are used to express and assert. And the same sentence—"Aristotle is wise," for example—can be used to express many different propositions. When Plato used it, he asserted a proposition predicating wisdom of his famous pupil; when Jackie Onassis uses it, she asserts a proposition predicating wisdom of her wealthy husband. These are distinct propositions (we might even think they differ in truth value); but they are expressed by the same sentence. Normally (but not always) we don't have much trouble determining which of the several propositions expressed by a given sentence is relevant in the context at hand. So in this case a given person, Paul, exists in a world *W* if and only if *W'* book contains the proposition that says that *he*—that particular person—exists. The fact that the sentence we use to express this proposition can also be used to express *other* propositions is not relevant.

After this excursion into the nature of books and worlds we can return to our question. Could God have created just any world He chose? Before addressing the question, however, we must note that God does not, strictly speaking, *create* any possible worlds or states of affairs at all. What He creates are the heavens and the earth and all that they contain. But He has not created states of affairs. There are, for example, the state of affairs consisting in God's existence and the state of affairs consisting in His nonexistence. That is, there is such a thing as the state of affairs consisting in the existence of God, and there is also such a thing as the state of affairs consisting in the nonexistence of God, just as there are the two propositions *God exists* and *God does not exist*. The theist believes that the first state of affairs is actual and the first proposition true; the atheist believes that the second state of affairs is actual and the second proposition true. But, of course, both propositions *exist*, even though just one is true. Similarly, there are two states of affairs here, just one of which is actual. So both states of affairs *exist*, but only one *obtains*. And God has not created either one of them since there never was a time at which either did not exist. Nor has he created the state of affairs consisting in the earth's existence; there was a time when *the earth* did not exist, but none when the state of affairs consisting in the earth's existence didn't exist. Indeed, God did not bring into existence any states of affairs at all. What He did was to perform actions of a certain sort—creating the heavens and the earth, for example—which resulted in the *actuality* of certain states of affairs. God *actualizes* states of affairs. He actualizes the possible world that does in fact obtain; He does not create it. And while He has created Socrates, He did not create the state of affairs consisting in Socrates' existence.[12]

Bearing this in mind, let's finally return to our question. Is the atheologian right in holding that if God is omnipotent, then he could have actualized or created any possible world He pleased? Not obviously. First, we must ask ourselves whether God is a *necessary* or a *contingent* being. A necessary being is one that exists in every possible world—one that would have existed no matter which possible world had been actual; a contingent being exists only in some possible worlds. Now if God is not a necessary being (and many, perhaps most, theists think that He is not), then clearly enough there will be many possible worlds He could not have actualized—all those, for example, in which He does not exist. Clearly, God could not have created a world in which He doesn't even exist.

So, if God is a contingent being then there are many possible worlds beyond His power to create. But this is really irrelevant to our present concerns. For perhaps the atheologian can maintain his case if he revises his claim to avoid this difficulty; perhaps he will say something like this: if God is omnipotent, then He could have actualized any of these possible worlds *in which He exists*. So if He exists and is omnipotent, He could have actualized (contrary to the Free Will Defense) any of those possible worlds in which He exists and in which there exist free creatures who do no wrong. He could have actualized worlds containing moral good but no moral evil. Is this correct?

Let's begin with a trivial example. You and Paul have just returned from an Australian hunting expedition: your quarry was the elusive double-waffled cassowary. Paul captured an aardvark, mistaking it for a cassowary. The creature's disarming ways have won it a place in Paul's heart; he is deeply attached to it. Upon your return to the States you offer Paul $500 for his aardvark, only to be rudely turned down. Later you ask yourself, "What would he have done if I'd offered him $700?" Now what is it, exactly, that you are asking? What you're really asking in a way is whether, under a *specific set of conditions*, Paul would have sold it. These conditions include your having offered him $700 rather than $500 for the aardvark, everything else being as much as possible like the conditions that did in fact obtain. Let S' be this set of conditions or state of affairs. S' includes the state of affairs consisting in your offering Paul $700 (instead of the $500 you did offer him); of course it does not include his *accepting* your offer, and it does not include his *rejecting* it; for the rest, the conditions it includes are just like the ones that did obtain in the actual world. So, for example, S' includes Paul's being free to accept the offer and free to refrain; and if in fact the going rate for an aardvark was $650, then S' includes the state of affairs consisting in the going rate's being $650. So we might put your question by asking which of the following conditionals is true:

(23)   If the state of affairs S' had obtained, Paul would have accepted the offer

(24)   If the state of affairs S' had obtained, Paul would not have accepted the offer.

It seems clear that at least one of these conditionals is true, but naturally they can't both be; so exactly one is.

Now since S' includes neither Paul's accepting the offer nor his rejecting it, the antecedent of (23) and (24) does not entail the consequent of either. That is,

(25) S' *obtains* does not entail either

(26)   Paul accepts the offer

or

(27)   Paul does not accept the offer.

So there are possible worlds in which both (25) and (26) are true, and other possible worlds in which both (25) and (27) are true.

We are now in a position to grasp an important fact. Either (23) or (24) is in fact true; and either way there are possible worlds God could not have actualized. Suppose, first of all, that (23) is true. Then it was beyond the power of God to create a world in which (1) Paul is free to sell his aardvark and free to refrain, and in which the other states of affairs included in S' obtain, and (2) Paul does not sell. That is, it was beyond His power to create a world in which (25) and (27) are both true.

There is at least one possible world like this, but God, despite His omnipotence, could not have brought about its actuality. For let W be such a world. To actualize W, God must bring it about that Paul is free with respect to this action, and that the other states of affairs included in S' obtain. But (23), as we are supposing, is true; so if God had actualized S' and left Paul *free* with respect to this action, he would have sold: in which case W would not have been actual. If, on the other hand, God had *brought it about* that Paul didn't sell or had *caused him to* refrain from selling, then Paul would not have been free with respect to this action; then S' would not have been actual (since S' includes Paul's being free with respect to it), and W would not have been actual since W includes S'.

Of course if it is (24) rather than (23) that is true, then another class of worlds was beyond God's power to actualize—those, namely, in which S' obtains and Paul *sells* his aardvark. These are the worlds in which both (25) and (26) are true. But either (23) or (24) is true. Therefore, there are possible worlds God could not have actualized. If we consider whether or not God could have created a world in which, let's say, both (25) and (26) are true, we see that the answer depends upon a peculiar kind of fact; it depends upon what Paul would have freely chosen to do in a certain situation. So there are any number of possible worlds such that it is partly up to Paul whether God can create them.[13]

That was a past tense example. Perhaps it would be useful to consider a future tense case, since this might seem to correspond more closely to God's situation in choosing a possible world to actualize. At some time t in the near future Maurice will be free with respect to some insignificant action—having freeze-dried oatmeal for breakfast, let's say. That is, at time t Maurice will be free to have oatmeal but also free to take something else—shredded wheat, perhaps. Next, suppose we consider S', a state of affairs that is included in the actual world and includes Maurice's being free with respect to taking oatmeal at time t. That is, S' includes Maurice's being free at time t to take oatmeal and free to reject it. S' does not include

Maurice's taking oatmeal, however; nor does it include his rejecting it. For the rest S' is as much as possible like the actual world. In particular there are many conditions that do in fact hold at time t and are *relevant* to his choice—such conditions, for example, as the fact that he hasn't had oatmeal lately, that his wife will be annoyed if he rejects it, and the like; and S' includes each of these conditions. Now God no doubt knows what Maurice will do at time t, if S obtains; He knows which action Maurice would freely perform if S were to be actual. That is, God knows that one of the following conditionals is true:

(28) If S' were to obtain, Maurice will freely take the oatmeal

or

(29) If S' were to obtain, Maurice will freely reject it.

We may not know which of these is true, and Maurice himself may not know; but presumably God does.

So either God knows that (28) is true, or else He knows that (29) is. Let's suppose it is (28). Then there is a possible world that God, though omnipotent, cannot create. For consider a possible world W' that shares S' with the actual world (which for ease of reference I'll name "Kronos") and in which Maurice does not take oatmeal. (We know there is such a world, since S' does not include Maurice's taking the oatmeal.) S' obtains in W' just as it does in Kronos. Indeed, everything in W' is just as it is in Kronos up to time t. But whereas in Kronos Maurice takes oatmeal at time t, in W' he does not. Now W' is a perfectly possible world; but it is not within God's power to create it or bring about its actuality. For to do so He must actualize S'. But (28) is in fact true. So if God actualizes S' (as He must to create W') and leaves Maurice free with respect to the action in question, then he will take the oatmeal; and then, of course, W' will not be actual. If, on the other hand, God causes Maurice to *refrain* from taking the oatmeal, then he is not free to take it. That means, once again, that W' is not actual; for in W' Maurice is

free to take the oatmeal (even if he doesn't do so). So if (28) is true, then this world W' is one that God can't actualize, it is not within His power to actualize it even though He is omnipotent and it is a possible world.

Of course, if it is (29) that is true, we get a similar result; then too there are possible worlds that God can't actualize. These would be worlds which share S' with Kronos and in which Maurice *does* take oatmeal. But either (28) or (29) is true; so either way there is a possible world that God can't create. If we consider a world in which S' obtains and in which Maurice freely chooses oatmeal at time t, we see that whether or not it is within God's power to actualize it depends upon what Maurice would do if he were free in a certain situation. Accordingly, there are any number of possible worlds such that it is partly up to Maurice whether or not God can actualize them. It is, of course, up to God whether or not to create Maurice and also up to God whether or not to make him free with respect to the action of taking oatmeal at time t. (God could, if He chose, cause him to succumb to the dreaded *equine obsession*, a condition shared by some people and most horses, whose victims find it *psychologically impossible* to refuse oats or oat products.) But if He creates Maurice and creates him free with respect to this action, then whether or not he actually performs the action is up to Maurice—not God.[14]

Now we can return to the Free Will Defense and the problem of evil. The Free Will Defender, you recall, insists on the possibility that it is not within God's power to create a world containing moral good without creating one containing moral evil. His atheological opponent—Mackie, for example—agrees with Leibniz in insisting that *if* (as the theist holds) God is omnipotent, then it *follows* that He could have created any possible world He pleased. We now see that this contention—call it "Leibniz' Lapse"—is a mistake. The atheologian is right in holding that there are many possible worlds containing moral good but no moral evil; his mistake lies in endorsing Leibniz' Lapse. So one of his premises—that God, if omnipotent, could have actualized just any world He pleased—is false.

6. COULD GOD HAVE CREATED A WORLD CONTAINING MORAL GOOD BUT NO MORAL EVIL?

Now suppose we recapitulate the logic of the situation. The Free Will Defender claims that the following is possible:

(30)   God is omnipotent, and it was not within His power to create a world containing moral good but no moral evil.

By way of retort the atheologian insists that there are possible worlds containing moral good but no moral evil. He adds that an omnipotent being could have actualized any possible world he chose. So if God is omnipotent, it follows that He could have actualized a world containing moral good but no moral evil, hence (30), contrary to the Free Will Defender's claim, is not possible. What we have seen so far is that his second premise—Leibniz' Lapse—is false.

Of course, this does not settle the issue in the Free Will Defender's favor. Leibniz' Lapse (appropriately enough for a lapse) is false; but this doesn't show that (30) is possible. To show this latter we must demonstrate the possibility that among the worlds God could not have actualized are all the worlds containing moral good but no moral evil. How can we approach this question?

Instead of choosing oatmeal for breakfast or selling an aardvark, suppose we think about a morally significant action such as taking a bribe. Curley Smith, the mayor of Boston, is opposed to the proposed freeway route; it would require destruction of the Old North Church along with some other antiquated and structurally unsound buildings. L. B. Smedes, the director of highways, asks him whether he'd drop his opposition for $1 million. "Of course," he replies. "Would you do it for $2?" asks Smedes. "What do you take me for?" comes the indignant reply. "That's already established," smirks Smedes; "all that remains is to nail down your price." Smedes then offers him a bribe of $35,000; unwilling to break with the fine old traditions of Bay State politics, Curley accepts.

Smedes then spends a sleepless night wondering whether he could have bought Curley for $20,000.

Now suppose we assume that Curley was free with respect to the action of taking the bribe—free to take it and free to refuse. And suppose, furthermore, that he would have taken it. That is, let us suppose that

(31)   If Smedes had offered Curley a bribe of $20,000, he would have accepted it.

If (31) is true, then there is a state of affairs S' that (1) includes Curley's being offered a bribe of $20,000; (2) does not include either his accepting the bribe or his rejecting it; and (3) is otherwise as much as possible like the actual world. Just to make sure S' includes every relevant circumstance, let us suppose that it is a *maximal world segment*. That is, add to S' any state of affairs compatible with but not included in it, and the result will be an entire possible world. We could think of it roughly like this: S' is included in at least one world W in which Curley takes the bribe and in at least one world W' in which he rejects it. If S' is a maximal world segment, then S' is what remains of W when *Curley's taking the bribe* is deleted; it is also what remains of W' when *Curley's rejecting the bribe* is deleted. More exactly, if S' is a maximal world segment, then every possible state of affairs that includes S', but isn't included by S', is a possible world. So if (31) is true, then there is a maximal world segment S' that (1) includes Curley's being offered a bribe of $20,000; (2) does not include either his accepting the bribe or his rejecting it; (3) is otherwise as much as possible like the actual world—in particular, it includes Curley's being free with respect to the bribe; and (4) is such that if it were actual then Curley would have taken the bribe. That is

(32)   if S' were actual, *Curley would have accepted the bribe* is true.

Now, of course, there is at least one possible world W' in which S' is actual and Curley does not take the bribe. But God could not have created W'; to do so, he would have been obliged to actualize S', leaving Curley free with respect to the action of taking the bribe. But under these conditions Curley, as (32) assures us, would have accepted the bribe, so that the world thus created would not have been S'.

Curley, as we see, is not above a bit of Watergating. But there may be worse to come. Of course, there are possible worlds in which he is significantly free (i.e., free with respect to a morally significant action) and never does what is wrong. But the sad truth about Curley may be this. Consider W', any of these worlds: in W' Curley is significantly free, so in W' there are some actions that are morally significant for him and with respect to which he is free. But at least one of these actions—call it A—has the following peculiar property. There is a maximal world segment S' that obtains in W' and is such that (1) S' includes Curley's being free *re* A but neither his performing A nor his refraining from A; (2) S' is otherwise as much as possible like W' and (3) if S' had been actual, Curley would have gone wrong with respect to A.[15] (Notice that this third condition holds in fact, in the actual world; it does not hold in that world W'.)

This means, of course, that God could not have actualized W'. For to do so He'd have been obliged to bring it about that S' is actual; but then Curley would go wrong with respect to A. Since in W' he always does what is right, the world thus actualized would not be W'. On the other hand, if God *causes* Curley to go right with respect to A or *brings it about* that he does so, then Curley isn't free with respect to A; and so once more it isn't W' that is actual. Accordingly God cannot create W'. But W' was just any of the worlds in which Curley is significantly free but always does only what is right. It therefore follows that it was not within God's power to create a world in which Curley produces moral good but no moral evil. Every world God can actualize is such that if Curley is significantly free in it, he takes at least one wrong action.

Obviously Curley is in serious trouble. I shall call the malady from which he suffers transworld depravity. (I leave as homework the problem of comparing transworld depravity with what Calvinists call "total depravity.") By way of explicit definition:

(33) A person P *suffers from transworld depravity* if and only if the following holds: for every world W such that P is significantly free in W and P does only what is right in W, there is

an action A and a maximal world segment S' such that

(1) S' includes A's being morally significant for P

(2) S' includes P's being free with respect to A

(3) S' is included in W and includes neither P's performing A nor P's refraining from performing A

and

(4)   If S' were actual, P would go wrong with respect to A.

(In thinking about this definition, remember that (4) is to be true in fact, in the actual world—not in that world W.)

What is important about the idea of transworld depravity is that if a person suffers from it, then it wasn't within God's power to actualize any world in which that person is significantly free but does no wrong—that is, a world in which he produces moral good but no moral evil.

We have been here considering a crucial contention of the Free Will Defender: the contention, namely, that

(30) God is omnipotent, and it was not within His power to create a world containing moral good but no moral evil.

How is transworld depravity relevant to this? As follows. Obviously it is possible that there be persons who suffer from transworld depravity. More generally, it is possible that *everybody* suffers from it. And if this possibility were actual, then God, though omnipotent, could not have created any of the possible worlds containing just the persons who do in fact exist, and containing moral good but no moral evil. For to do so He'd have to create persons who were significantly free (otherwise there would be no moral good) but suffered from transworld depravity. Such persons go wrong with respect to at least one action in any world God could have actualized and in which they are free with respect to morally significant actions; so the price for creating a world in which they produce moral good is creating one in which they also produce moral evil.

NOTES

1. John Mackie, "Evil and Omnipotence," in *The Philosophy of Religion*, ed. Basil Mitchell (London Oxford University Press:, 1971), p. 92. [See previous reading.]

2. Ibid., p. 93. [*Philosophy of Religion: Selected Readings, Second Edition*, p. 224.]

3. More simply, the question is really just whether any good state of affairs includes an evil; a little reflection reveals that no good state of affairs can include an evil that it does not outweigh.

4. In Plantinga, *God and Other Minds* (Ithaca, N.Y.: Cornell University Press, 1967), chap. 5, I explore further the project of finding such propositions.

5. *The Problem of Free Choice,* Vol. 22 of *Ancient Christian Writers* (Westminster, Md.: The Newman Press, 1955), bk. 2, pp. 14–15.

6. Ibid., bk. 3, p. 9.

7. I am indebted to Henry Schuurman (in conversation) for helpful discussion of the difference between this pastoral function and those served by a theodicy or a defense.

8. This distinction is not very precise (how, exactly, are we to construe "results from"?), but perhaps it will serve our present purposes.

9. See, for example, A. Flew, "Divine Omnipotence and Human Freedom," in *New Essays in Philosophical Theology*, eds. A. Flew and A. MacIntyre (London SCM:, 1955), pp. 150–53.

10. For further discussion of it see Plantinga, *God and Other Minds*, pp. 132–35.

11. Mackie, in *The Philosophy of Religion*, pp. 100–101.

12. Strict accuracy demands, therefore, that we speak of God as actualizing rather than creating possible worlds. I shall continue to use both locutions, thus sacrificing accuracy to familiarity. For more about possible worlds see my book *The Nature of Necessity* (Oxford The Clarendon Press:, 1974), chaps. 4–8.

13. For a fuller statement of this argument see Plantinga, *The Nature of Necessity*, chap. 9, secs. 4–6.

14. For a more complete and more exact statement of this argument see Plantinga, *The Nature of Necessity*, chap. 9, secs. 4–6.

15. A person goes wrong with respect to an action if he either wrongfully performs it or wrongfully fails to perform it.

11

Evil and Soul-Making

JOHN HICK

John Hick (1922 – 2012) was for many years professor of theology at the University of Birmingham in England and, until his retirement, was professor of philosophy at Claremont Graduate School. His book Evil and the God of Love *(1966), from which this selection is taken, is considered one of the*

Pp. 253–261 from *Evil and the God of Love*, revised edition, by John Hick. Copyright © 1966, 1977 by John Hick. Used with permission. Footnotes edited.

most thorough treatises on the problem of evil. "Evil and Soul-Making" is an example of a theodicy argument that is based on the free will defense. Theodicies can be of two differing types depending on how they justify the ways of God in the face of evil. The Augustinian position is that God created humans without sin and set them in a sinless, paradisical world. However, humanity fell into sin through the misuse of free will. God's grace will save some of us, but others will perish everlastingly. The second type of theodicy stems from the thinking of Irenaeus. The Irenaean tradition views Adam not as a free agent rebelling against God but as more akin to a small child. The fall is humanity's first faulty step in the direction of freedom. God is still working with humanity in order to bring it from undeveloped life (bios) to a state of self-realization in divine love, spiritual life (zoe). This life is viewed as the "vale of soul-making." Hick favors this version and develops it in this reading.

Fortunately there is another and better way. As well as the "majority report" of the Augustinian tradition, which has dominated Western Christendom, both Catholic and Protestant, since the time of Augustine himself, there is the "minority report" of the Irenaean tradition. This latter is both older and newer than the other, for it goes back to St. Irenaeus and others of the early Hellenistic Fathers of the Church in the two centuries prior to St. Augustine, and it has flourished again in more developed forms during the last hundred years.

Instead of regarding man as having been created by God in a finished state, as a finitely perfect being fulfilling the divine intention for our human level of existence, and then falling disastrously away from this, the minority report sees man as still in process of creation. Irenaeus himself expressed the point in terms of the (exegetically dubious) distinction between the "image" and the "likeness" of God referred to in Genesis i.26: "Then God said, Let us make man in our image, after our likeness." His view was that man as a personal and moral being already exists in the image, but has not yet been formed into the finite likeness of God. By this "likeness" Irenaeus means something more than personal existence as such; he means a certain valuable quality of personal life which reflects finitely the divine life. This represents the perfecting of man, the fulfillment of God's purpose for humanity, the "bringing of many sons to glory," the creating of "children of God" who are "fellow heirs with Christ" of his glory.

And so man, created as a personal being in the image of God, is only the raw material for a further and more difficult stage of God's creative work. This is the leading of men as relatively free and autonomous persons, through their own dealings with life in the world in which He has placed them, towards that quality of personal existence that is the finite likeness of God. The features of this likeness are revealed in the person of Christ, and the process of man's creation into it is the work of the Holy Spirit. In St. Paul's words, "And we all, with unveiled faces, beholding the glory of the Lord, are being changed into his likeness (εἰκών) from one degree of glory to another; for this comes from the Lord who is the Spirit";[1] or again, "For God knew his own before ever they were, and also ordained that they should be shaped to the likeness (εἰκών) of his Son."[2] In Johannine terms, the movement from the image to the likeness is a transition from one level of existence, that of animal life (*Bios*), to another and higher level, that of eternal life (*Zoe*), which includes but transcends the first. And the fall of man was seen by Irenaeus as a failure within the second phase of this creative process, a failure that has multiplied the perils and complicated the route of the journey in which God is seeking to lead mankind.

In the light of modern anthropological knowledge some form of two-stage conception of the creation of man has become an almost unavoidable Christian tenet. At the very least we must acknowledge as two distinguishable stages the fashioning of *homo sapiens* as a product of the long evolutionary process, and his sudden or gradual spiritualization as a child of God. But we may well extend the first stage to include the development of man as a rational and responsible person capable of personal relationship with the personal Infinite who has created him. This first stage of the creative process was, to our anthropomorphic imaginations, easy for divine omnipotence. By an exercise of creative power God caused the physical universe to exist, and in the course of countless ages to bring forth within it organic life, and finally to produce out of organic life personal life; and when man had thus emerged out of the evolution of the forms of organic life, a creature had been made who has the possibility of existing in conscious fellowship with God. But the second stage of the creative process is of a different kind altogether. It cannot be performed by omnipotent power as such. For personal life is essentially free and self-directing. It cannot be perfected by divine fiat, but only through the uncompelled responses and willing co-operation of human individuals in their actions and reactions in the world in which God has placed them. Men may eventually become the perfected persons whom the New Testament calls "children of God," but they cannot be created ready-made as this.

The value-judgment that is implicitly being invoked here is that one who has attained to goodness by meeting and eventually mastering temptations, and thus by rightly making responsible choices in concrete situations, is good in a richer and more valuable sense than would be one created *ab initio* in a state either of innocence or of virtue. In the former case, which is that of the actual moral achievements of mankind, the individual's goodness has within it the strength of temptation overcome, a stability based upon an accumulation of right choices, and a positive and responsible character that comes from the investment of costly personal effort. I suggest, then, that it is an ethically reasonable judgment, even though in the nature of the case not one that is capable of demonstrative proof, that human goodness slowly built up through personal histories of moral effort has a value in the eyes of the Creator which justifies even the long travail of the soul-making process.

The picture with which we are working is thus developmental and teleological. Man is in process of becoming the perfected being whom God is seeking to create. However, this is not taking place—it is important to add—by a natural and inevitable evolution, but through a hazardous adventure in individual freedom. Because this is a pilgrimage within the life of each individual, rather than a racial

evolution, the progressive fulfillment of God's purpose does not entail any corresponding progressive improvement in the moral state of the world. There is no doubt a development in man's ethical situation from generation to generation through the building of individual choices into public institutions, but this involves an accumulation of evil as well as of good. It is thus probable that human life was lived on much the same moral plane two thousand years ago or four thousand years ago as it is today. But nevertheless during this period uncounted millions of souls have been through the experience of earthly life, and God's purpose has gradually moved towards its fulfillment within each one of them, rather than within a human aggregate composed of different units in different generations.

If, then, God's aim in making the world is "the bringing of many sons to glory," that aim will naturally determine the kind of world that He has created. Antitheistic writers almost invariably assume a conception of the divine purpose which is contrary to the Christian conception. They assume that the purpose of a loving God must be to create a hedonistic paradise; and therefore to the extent that the world is other than this, it proves to them that God is either not loving enough or not powerful enough to create such a world. They think of God's relation to the earth on the model of a human being building a cage for a pet animal to dwell in. If he is humane he will naturally make his pet's quarters as pleasant and healthful as he can. Any respect in which the cage falls short of the veterinarian's ideal, and contains possibilities of accident or disease, is evidence of either limited benevolence or limited means, or both. Those who use the problem of evil as an argument against belief in God almost invariably think of the world in this kind of way. David Hume, for example, speaks of an architect who is trying to plan a house that is to be as comfortable and convenient as possible. If we find that "the windows, doors, fires, passages, stairs, and the whole economy of the building were the source of noise, confusion, fatigue, darkness, and the extremes of heat and cold" we should have no hesitation in blaming the architect. It would be in vain for him to prove that if this or that defect were corrected greater ills would result: "still you would assert in general, that, if the architect had had skill and good intentions, he might have formed such a plan of the whole, and might have adjusted the parts in such a manner, as would have remedied all or most of these inconveniences."[3]

But if we are right in supposing that God's purpose for man is to lead him from human *Bios*, or the biological life of man, to that quality of *Zoe*, or the personal life of eternal worth, which we see in Christ, then the question that we have to ask is not, Is this the kind of world that an all-powerful and infinitely loving being would create as an environment for his human pets? or, Is the architecture of the world the most pleasant and convenient possible? The question that we have to ask is rather, Is this the kind of world that God might make as an environment in which moral beings may be fashioned, through their own free insights and responses, into "children of God"?

Such critics as Hume are confusing what heaven ought to be, as an environment for perfected finite beings, with what this world ought to be, as an environment for beings who are in process of becoming perfected. For if our general conception of God's purpose is correct the world is not intended to be a paradise, but rather the scene of a history in which human personality may be formed towards the pattern of Christ. Men are not to be thought of on the analogy of animal pets, whose life is to be made as agreeable as possible, but rather on the analogy of human children, who are to grow to adulthood in an environment whose primary and overriding purpose is not immediate pleasure but the realizing of the most valuable potentialities of human personality.

Needless to say, this characterization of God as the heavenly Father is not a merely random illustration but an analogy that lies at the heart of the Christian faith. Jesus treated the likeness between the attitude of God to man, and the attitude of human parents at their best towards their children, as providing the most adequate way for us to think about God. And so it is altogether relevant to a Christian understanding of this world to ask, How does the best parental love express itself in its influence upon the environment in which children are to grow up? I think it is clear that a parent who loves his children,

and wants them to become the best human beings that they are capable of becoming, does not treat pleasure as the sole and supreme value. Certainly we seek pleasure for our children, and take great delight in obtaining it for them; but we do not desire for them unalloyed pleasure at the expense of their growth in such even greater values as moral integrity, unselfishness, compassion, courage, humour, reverence for the truth, and perhaps above all the capacity for love. We do not act on the premise that pleasure is the supreme end of life; and if the development of these other values sometimes clashes with the provision of pleasure, then we are willing to have our children miss a certain amount of this, rather than fail to come to possess and to be possessed by the finer and more precious qualities that are possible to the human personality. A child brought up on the principle that the only or the supreme value is pleasure would not be likely to become an ethically mature adult or an attractive or happy personality. And to most parents it seems more important to try to foster quality and strength of character in their children than to fill their lives at all times with the utmost possible degree of pleasure. If, then, there is any true analogy between God's purpose for his human creatures, and the purpose of loving and wise parents for their children, we have to recognize that the presence of pleasure and the absence of pain cannot be the supreme and overriding end for which the world exists. Rather, this world must be a place of soul-making. And its value is to be judged, not primarily by the quantity of pleasure and pain occurring in it at any particular moment, but by its fitness for its primary purpose, the purpose of soul-making.

In all this we have been speaking about the nature of the world considered simply as the God given environment of man's life. For it is mainly in this connection that the world has been regarded in Irenaean and in Protestant thought. But such a way of thinking involves a danger of anthropocentrism from which the Augustinian and Catholic tradition has generally been protected by its sense of the relative insignificance of man within the totality of the created universe. Man was dwarfed within the medieval worldview by the innumerable hosts of angels and archangels above him—unfallen rational natures which rejoice in the immediate presence of God, reflecting His glory in the untarnished mirror of their worship. However, this higher creation has in our modern world lost its hold upon the imagination. Its place has been taken, as the minimizer of men, by the immensities of outer space and by the material universe's unlimited complexity transcending our present knowledge. As the spiritual environment envisaged by Western man has shrunk, his physical horizons have correspondingly expanded. Where the human creature was formerly seen as an insignificant appendage to the angelic world, he is now seen as an equally insignificant organic excrescence, enjoying a fleeting moment of consciousness on the surface of one of the planets of a minor star. Thus the truth that was symbolized for former ages by the existence of the angelic hosts is today impressed upon us by the vastness of the physical universe, countering the egoism of our species by making us feel that this immense prodigality of existence can hardly all exist for the sake of man—though, on the other hand, the very realization that it is not all for the sake of man may itself be salutary and beneficial to man!

However, instead of opposing man and nature as rival objects of God's interest, we should perhaps rather stress man's solidarity as an embodied being with the whole natural order in which he is embedded. For man is organic to the world; all his acts and thoughts and imaginations are conditioned by space and time; and in abstraction from nature he would cease to be human. We may, then, say that the beauties and sublimities and powers, the microscopic intricacies and macroscopic vastnesses, the wonders and the terrors of the natural world and of the life that pulses through it, are willed and valued by their Maker in a creative act that embraces man together with nature. By means of matter and living flesh

God both builds a path and weaves a veil between Himself and the creature made in His image. Nature thus has permanent significance; for God has set man in a creaturely environment, and the final fulfilment of our nature in relation to God will accordingly take the form of an embodied life within "a new heaven and a new earth." And as in the present age man moves slowly towards that fulfillment through the pilgrimage of his earthly life, so also "the whole creation" is "groaning in travail," waiting for the time when it will be "set free from its bondage to decay."

And yet however fully we thus acknowledge the permanent significance and value of the natural order, we must still insist upon man's special character as a personal creature made in the image of God; and our theodicy must still centre upon the soul-making process that we believe to be taking place within human life.

This, then, is the starting-point from which we propose to try to relate the realities of sin and suffering to the perfect love of an omnipotent Creator. And as will become increasingly apparent, a theodicy that starts in this way must be eschatological in its ultimate bearings. That is to say, instead of looking to the past for its clue to the mystery of evil, it looks to the future, and indeed to that ultimate future to which only faith can look. Given the conception of a divine intention working in and through human time towards a fulfilment that lies in its completeness beyond human time, our theodicy must find the meaning of evil in the part that it is made to play in the eventual outworking of that purpose; and must find the justification of the whole process in the magnitude of the good to which it leads. The good that outshines all ill is not a paradise long since lost but a kingdom which is yet to come in its full glory and permanence.

NOTES

1. II Corinthians iii. 18.
2. Romans viii. 29. Other New Testament passages expressing a view of man as undergoing a process of spiritual growth within God's purpose are:

Ephesians ii. 21, iii. 16; Colossians ii. 19; I John iii. 2; II Corinthians iv. 16.

3. *Dialogues Concerning Natural Religion*, pt. xi. Kemp-Smith's ed. (Oxford: Clarendon Press, 1935), p. 251.

12

Epistemic Humility, Arguments from Evil, and Moral Skepticism

DANIEL HOWARD-SNYDER

Daniel Howard-Snyder (1959–) is professor of philosophy at Western Washington University and has written extensively in epistemology and the philosophy of religion. In this essay, he defends what is commonly (although, in his view, inappropriately) called the "skeptical theist" strategy for responding to the problem of evil. The skeptical theist maintains that we should be in doubt about whether the goods we know of constitute a representative sample of the goods there are. The skeptical theist offers this skeptical claim as a reason for doubting that we can infer that no good could possibly justify God in permitting some instance of evil from our inability to detect a good that might justify God in permitting that instance of evil. Howard-Snyder focuses in particular on replying to the objection that the skeptical theist's skepticism about our grasp of the realm of value leads to more widespread forms of moral skepticism.

Many arguments from evil at least tacitly rely on something like the following line of thought:

> *The Inference.* On sustained reflection, we don't see how any reason we know of would justify God in permitting all the evil in the world; therefore, there is no reason that would justify God.

The conclusion is frequently more nuanced: "it is very likely that there is no such reason" or "more likely than not" or "more likely than it otherwise would be." Some critics reject the premise: we do see how some reason would justify God. These are the theodicists. Others accept the premise but reject the conclusion: the evidence or non-evidential warrant for God's existence is much better than the evidence for no justifying reason. These are the natural theologians and Reformed epistemologists. Some critics, however, insist that *even if* the premise is true and *even if* there isn't better evidence

or non-evidential warrant for God's existence, we should not infer that there is no justifying reason. (Throughout the essay, keep the "even if"s in mind as definitive of agnosticism.) These are the agnostics about the Inference. In this essay I aim to assess an increasingly popular objection to agnosticism.

There are different versions of agnosticism about the Inference. The one I have in mind—henceforth *Agnosticism* with a capital *A*—affirms at least two theses:

> *Agnostic Thesis 1* (AT1). We should be in doubt about whether the Goods we know of constitute a representative sample of all the goods there are.
>
> *Agnostic Thesis 2* (AT2). We should be in doubt about whether each good we know of is such that the necessary conditions of its realization we know of are all there are.

Excerpted from "Epistemic Humility, Arguments from Evil, and Moral Skepticism", in Oxford Studies in *Philosophy of Religion*, vol. 2 (2009), edited by Jonathan Kvanvig. Used by permission of Oxford University Press.

(I will focus on AT1 although I will say a few words about AT2 shortly.) The Agnostic continues: since we should be in doubt about whether the goods we know of constitute a representative sample of all the goods there are, we should be in doubt about whether some good we don't know of figures in a reason that would justify God. But if we should be in doubt about that, then we should be in doubt about whether there is a reason that would justify God. And if we should be in doubt about that, we should not infer that there is no such reason, even if we don't see how any reason would justify God and even if there is no evidence and non-evidential warrant for God's existence.

The objection to Agnosticism that I aim to assess is the *Moral Skepticism Objection*, or the *Objection*, for short. There are different versions of the Objection. Here's a simple one. Let *Ashley's suffering* name the evil done to twelve-year-old Ashley Jones and what she suffered and lost in Stanwood, Washington, September 21, 1997, who while babysitting her neighbor's kids, was raped and bludgeoned to death by an escapee from a local juvenile detention center. Suppose we could have easily intervened to prevent Ashley's suffering without any cost to ourselves. In that case, it would be absurd to suppose that we should be in doubt about whether we should have intervened. *Obviously* we should have intervened. Agnosticism, however, implies otherwise. It tells us that since we should be in doubt about whether the goods we know of constitute a representative sample of all the goods there are, we should be in doubt about whether there is a reason that would justify God's nonintervention. But if that's right, then so is this: since we should be in doubt about whether the goods we know of constitute a representative sample of all the goods there are, we should also be in doubt about whether there is a reason that would justify *our* nonintervention, in which case we should be in doubt about whether *we* should have intervened. So Agnosticism implies that we should be in doubt about whether we should have intervened. But that's absurd. Obviously we should have. So Agnosticism is false.

It will prove useful to have before us the main thrust of this argument. I will call it the *simple version of the Objection*:

1. If Agnosticism is true, then we should be in doubt about whether we should have intervened to prevent Ashley's suffering.

2. We should not be in doubt about whether we should have intervened.

3. So, Agnosticism is false.

Here's the plan of the paper. In Section I, I clarify Agnosticism. In Sections II and III, I sketch a criticism of the simple version of the Objection. Absent qualification, it goes like this. Our assessment of the simple version of the Objection should reflect the epistemic implications of our moral theories or principles. There are two types of moral theory and principle: (i) those that posit right- and wrong-making features of an act that should leave us in doubt about its moral status and (ii) those that posit right- and wrong-making features of an act that should not leave us in doubt about its moral status. If we endorse an instance of the first type, then prior to our assessment of the simple version of the Objection we should already be in doubt about whether we should have intervened to prevent Ashley's suffering; in which case we should think that premise (2) is false. However, if we endorse an instance of the second type, then prior to our assessment of the simple version of the Objection we should deny that Agnosticism implies that we should be in doubt about whether we should have intervened; in which case we should think that premise (1) is false. Either way, the epistemic implications of our moral theories or principles imply that the simple version of the Objection is unsound. . . .

I . SOME PRELIMINARIES ABOUT AGNOSTICISM

Note, firstly, that Agnosticism is *not* a kind of theism. It is perfectly compatible with atheism. Thus, to call it "skeptical theism," as many people do, is to evince ineptitude at naming things.

Second, it is important to be clear about what the Agnostic means and does not mean when she says *we don't see* how any reason we know of would justify God in permitting all the evil in the world. She does not mean to comment on our visual capacities. Rather, she means that we don't understand or comprehend how any reason we know of would justify God. Furthermore, she does not mean that we don't see how any reason would justify God in permitting *any* of the evil in the world, nor does she mean that we don't see how any reason would *partially* justify God in permitting all of the evil in the world. She means that we don't see how any reason would *fully* justify God in permitting *all* of the evil in the world. Ashley's suffering is a case in point.

Sometimes the Agnostic will say "We don't see how any *good we know of* justifies God in permitting all the evil in the world." This is shorthand. What she means is, "We don't see how any *reason we know of that appeals to a good* justifies God in permitting all the evil in the world." I will frequently revert to the Agnostic's shorthand way of speaking. . . .

Fourth, it is important to be clear about what the Agnostic means and does not mean when she says that we should be in doubt about whether some good *we don't know of* would justify God in permitting all the evil in the world, including Ashley's suffering.

(a) I might know of something, in one sense, but not in another. I know of String Theory, in the sense that I know that it attempts to unite quantum mechanics and the theory of General Relativity, the most popular versions posit one-dimensional oscillating lines and eleven spatial dimensions, and so on. Anyone can know of String Theory in this sense by simply consulting an encyclopedia. But I don't know of String Theory in another sense, in the sense that would require me to have a substantive understanding of the mathematics of quantum mechanics, the theory of General Relativity, multi-dimensionality, and the like. Which sense does the Agnostic mean when she speaks of *goods we know of* and *goods we don't know of* (if there are any)? She means the second sense. When she speaks of goods we know of, she means goods we comprehend and understand in at least somewhat of a substantive way; and when she speaks of goods we don't know of, she means goods we don't comprehend or understand (if there are any), not even in a somewhat substantive way.

(b) When the Agnostic says that we should be *in doubt* about whether some good we don't know of would justify God in permitting all the evil in the world she does not mean that we should *doubt that* there is such a good. To be in doubt about something is not to doubt that it is so. To doubt that something is so is to be (at least) more inclined to think it is false rather than true; to be in doubt about something is to be of two minds about it, ambivalent, undecided. I am in doubt about whether there is sentient extra-terrestrial life, whether the United States will be a world power in a thousand years, and whether the number of Douglas firs in Lake Padden State Park is odd. But I am not in the least bit inclined to think these things are false. Rather, given what information I have at my disposal, I don't know what to think about them. According to the Agnostic, the same goes for the Inference. Given the information she has at her disposal, she is in doubt about whether there is a reason that would justify God even though she can't see how any reason she knows of would do the trick. She thinks she is in no position to make such a judgment. She is in the dark. She confesses ignorance on the matter.

(c) When the Agnostic says that we *should* be in doubt about whether some good we don't know of would justify God in permitting all the evil in the world she means either that we have a duty to be in doubt about it, that it is wrong not to be in doubt, that we're irresponsible if we are not in doubt, or, alternatively, she means that it is fitting for us to be in doubt about it, being in doubt is the appropriate state of mind. Speaking for myself, although I do not reject the first way, I tend to think in terms of the second way. I tend to think of the Agnostic as saying that it is proper for us to be in doubt about whether some good we don't know of would justify God, proper in the sense that being in doubt about the matter exhibits a humility that befits the range of our cognitive powers whereas not being in doubt exhibits excessive self-confidence. (Hence the first phrase in the title of this paper.) . . .

(d) When the Agnostic speaks of a *good*, she means to refer to an abstract state of affairs which, if it were to obtain, would be good. She does not mean to refer to a concrete object or event. Goods are abstracta not concreta. (Cp. Bergmann and Rea [2005: 242]) Thus, when she says that we should be in doubt about whether some unknown *good* would justify God, she means that we should be in doubt about whether some unknown *abstract state of affairs the obtaining of which would be good* would justify God.

(e) The Agnostic assumes that states of affairs are necessary beings. They exist at every possible world. So every good state of affairs exists. However, not every good state of affairs obtains. Some good states of affairs do not obtain. For example, if no one has ever been free with respect to being the sort of person that they are, then the state of affairs of our sometimes being free with respect to the sorts of persons we are *exists* but it does *not obtain*. . . .

Fifth, we need to understand what the Agnostic means and does not mean when she says we should be in doubt about whether the goods we know of constitute a *representative sample* of all the goods there are (which is AT1).

(a) In general, a sample can be representative of a population with respect to one feature but not another. For example, the employees at Microsoft are representative of the human population with respect to planet of origin but not annual income, place of residence, or nationality, among other things. When the Agnostic says we should be in doubt about whether the goods we know of constitute a representative sample of all the goods there are she means that we should be in doubt about whether the goods we know of are representative of all the goods there are with respect to *being apt for justifying God's permission of all the evil in the world*. In what follows, I will typically leave the qualification made in this paragraph tacit.

(b) In general, a sample, S, is representative of a population, P, with respect to feature F, if and only if the frequency of members in S that are F is almost the same as the frequency of members in P that are F. Thus, when the Agnostic says that we should be in doubt about whether the goods we know of constitute a representative sample of all the goods there are with respect to being apt for justifying God's permission of all the evil in the world she means that we should be in doubt about whether the frequency of members of the goods we know of that are apt for justifying God's permission of all the evil in the world is almost the same as the frequency of members of the total population of goods that are apt for justifying God's permission of all the evil in the world.

Sixth, what reason do we have to think that we should be in doubt about whether the goods we know of constitute a representative sample of all the goods there are? Excellent question! The first thing to note about it is that it presupposes that we *need* good evidence to be in doubt about the matter for it to be the case that we should be in doubt. That's arguably false, however. To be in doubt about something is the stance from which we need good evidence to move, to believing it or believing its denial. We don't need good evidence to be in doubt for it to be the case that we should be in doubt. So, absent good evidence to believe that the goods we know of are representative of all the goods there are (or its denial), we should be in doubt about the matter.

Even if we don't need good evidence to be in doubt about something for it to be the case that we should be in doubt about it, we might nevertheless have good evidence to be in doubt about it. In this connection, the Agnostic argues that evidence to think that the goods we know of are representative of the total population is bad evidence and that more general considerations in favor of the Inference fail. Moreover, she argues, several considerations properly induce doubt about whether there are God-justifying goods outside our ken. (See e.g. Wykstra [1984 and 1996], Alston [1991 and 1996], Howard-Snyder [1996a], Bergmann [2001].) Since my aim in this essay is to assess a specific objection to Agnosticism and not to assess the general case for it, I will say no more about the latter.

Except this: If the goods we know of constitute a random sample of the total population of goods, then our sample is generated by a process that gives every member of the total population of goods an equal chance of being selected into our sample. (. . . or else there is a subclass, C, of the total population of goods, P, such that C is not S and C is representative of P with respect to being apt for justifying God, from which S is generated by a process that gives every member of C an equal chance of being selected into S. See Hawthorne [2004: n. 15]. This way for a sample to be random need not concern us here.) But if our sample is generated by a process that gives every member of the total population of goods an equal chance of being selected into our sample *but we lack the concepts needed to comprehend or understand every member of the total population of goods*, then we might have selected from the total population of goods a member that we in fact lack the concepts to comprehend or understand, in which case our sample might have included a good we know of but lack the concepts to understand or comprehend. But that's impossible. It is impossible that we know of a good but lack the concepts to comprehend or understand it. (For, as I said earlier, in the present context a good that we know of is one that "we comprehend and understand in at least somewhat of a substantive way.") So if our sample is generated by a process that gives every member of the total population of goods an equal chance of being selected into our sample, then we possess the concepts needed to comprehend or understand *every* member of the total population of goods. Thus, if the goods we know of constitute a random sample of the total population of goods, then

(i) Each member of the total population of goods is such that we possess the concepts needed to comprehend or understand it. The Agnostic bids us to reflect on the fact that (i) is like some other

propositions in an epistemically relevant respect, for example

(ii) Each member of the total population of empirically adequate physical theories is such that we possess the concepts needed to comprehend or understand it,

and

(iii) Each member of the total population of ontologies of what we call "physical objects" is such that we have the concepts needed to comprehend or understand it.

We should be in doubt about (ii) and (iii) even if, unbeknownst to us, they are both true. It would be an extraordinary stroke of good epistemic luck if our evolutionary history to this point left us with every concept needed to comprehend and understand *every* physical theory and *every* ontology of physical objects. Similarly, says the Agnostic, and for the same reason, we should be in doubt about (i) even if, unbeknownst to us, it is true. Therefore, we have some good evidence to think that we should be in doubt about whether the goods we know of constitute a random sample of the total population of goods, and so we have some good evidence to think that we should be in doubt about whether the goods we know of constitute a representative sample of all the goods there are—which is exactly what AT1 says.

Finally, a word about AT2, the thesis that we should be in doubt about whether each good we know of is such that the necessary conditions of its realization we know of are all there are. As has been pointed out on occasion, we can *know of* a good without *seeing how* it would justify God in permitting horrific evil. This can happen in at least two ways. First, we might know of a good but fail to fully appreciate its goodness. Second, we might know of a good but fail to know of all the necessary conditions of its realization. (See Alston [1996: 315–6, 323–5], Howard-Snyder [1996a: 308 n. 13], and Bergmann [2001].) AT2 is about the second way.

What goods might be such that we know of them but fail to know of all the necessary conditions of their realization? Union with God is one candidate. It's hard to say whether or not created persons must be permitted to undergo horrific suffering in order to enter into the deepest union with God. To be sure, we have some idea of what it would require by way of understanding what union between human persons requires. But is our understanding of what union with God requires *complete*? Suppose we are in the following frame of mind: no aspect of God's nature that we know of is such that we think that by virtue of it, God cannot permit horrific suffering; moreover, for all we can tell, there are aspects of God's nature that we don't know of in virtue of which a created person can enter into the deepest union with God only if she is permitted to undergo horrific suffering. If we are in that frame of mind, then our understanding of what union with God required would be not only incomplete, it would be—much more importantly—incomplete in such a way that we should be in doubt about whether we know of all the necessary conditions of its realization. Are we in that frame of mind? I think I am. The Agnostic thinks you should be. If she's right, then we should be in doubt about whether union with God is such that the necessary conditions of its realization we know of are all there are. Thus, we should think AT2 is true.

So much for preliminaries. I now turn to my main task.

II. TAKING CONSEQUENCES VERY, *VERY* SERIOUSLY

Consider the following theory:

> *Objective Maximizing Act Consequentialism* (OMAC). An agent's act is permissible solely in virtue of the fact that its total consequences are no overall worse than those of any option open to him; otherwise, it is impermissible.

There are different concepts of consequence that might be plugged into OMAC and the resulting versions of OMAC will have different implications. Although I am not defending OMAC here, as will be apparent shortly I will assert that OMAC has certain epistemic implications. Whether I'm right or not will depend on what concept of consequence is deployed. So I have to say something about the matter.

Without trying to be precise, I have in mind a version of OMAC that most of my self-identifying maximizing consequentialist friends affirm. They say that what counts as a consequence of an act is *any* future event or fact causally downstream from the act. Some of them like a counterfactual condition on causation according to which A caused B only if B would not have occurred if A hadn't. In

that case, we can think of a chain of counterfactuals of the form *If A had not occurred then B would not have occurred* linking the act and the future event or fact. If you are happy with this concept of causal consequence, go with it. If not, go with whatever "link" you like *provided that* it has the implication that my maximizing friends want, namely, that what you do right now will have causal ramifications until the end of time and *all* of them are morally relevant. (Cp. Mason [2004: 317]: "consequentialism demands that we make decisions that have as their justification *the whole future*" [emphasis added]. Unless otherwise indicated explicitly or by context, in what follows all talk of consequences should be understood along these lines including talk of consequences in contexts other than OMAC.)

OMAC implies that the total consequences of intervening to prevent suffering and the total consequences of nonintervention make the difference as to whether we should intervene. If nonintervention in Ashley's case has overall better total consequences than intervention, then we should not intervene—even if the foreseeable consequences of intervention are vastly better than those of nonintervention. Now: since we are in no position to say what the unforeseeable consequences of intervention and nonintervention contain and the unforeseeable consequences swamp the foreseeable ones, we should be in doubt about whether the total consequences of intervention are overall worse than those of nonintervention. In that case, given OMAC, we should be in doubt about whether we should intervene to prevent Ashley's suffering. Thus, prior to assessing the simple version of the Objection, we should already be inclined to deny premise (2)—*if we endorse OMAC.*

In effect, I have just summarized the first step of the well-known Epistemic Objection to OMAC. Later steps connect that step with the denial of OMAC. I am not taking the later steps. I am only taking the first. Let me explain why I take the first step. What I have to say is not original.

The unforeseeable consequences of an act and its alternatives swamp the foreseeable consequences. Thus, what we can foresee is a minute fraction of the total consequences. Moreover, we are in the dark about what the unforeseeable consequences of an act and its alternatives contain. In an important article, James Lenman underscores how deeply darkness envelops us on this score by pointing out how much of our behavior has massive and inscrutable causal ramifications. (Lenman [2000]. I can't recommend this article strongly enough.) Killing and engendering, and refraining from killing and engendering, ramify in massive ways because they are directly identity-affecting actions. They directly "make a difference to the identities of future persons [that is, a difference to what people there will be] and these differences are apt to amplify exponentially down the generations." (Lenman [2000: 346].) Much of our other behavior is indirectly identity-affecting, as, for example, when a word harshly spoken, or eating raw garlic, or introducing your girlfriend to your best friend Ray makes a difference to who sleeps with whom tonight, or tomorrow morning, or next month. To illustrate the main point here, imagine Richard, a first-century bandit in southern Germany who, while raiding a small village, spares the life of a pregnant woman, Angie. (Lenman [2000: 344–6].) Angie, it turns out, is the great- great- ... (add 97 'great-'s) ... great-grandmother of Adolf Hitler. By permitting Angie to live, Richard played a role in the occurrence of the Holocaust. Moreover, anyone who refrained from killing any of the intermediate ancestors of Hitler before they engendered the relevant child, or assisted in introducing the parents of each generation, or refrained from introducing them to others, and so on, played a role as well. Which one of these people throughout the generations had an inkling that their behavior would contribute to such a horror?

Another source of massive causal ramification is causal systems that "are extremely sensitive to very small and localized variations or changes in their initial conditions." (Lenman [2000: 347].) Such sensitivity will underscore the skeptical implications of OMAC if such systems occur

> in even a small number of domains that have a significant influence on the human world. One such domain is perhaps the

> weather: differences in the weather make extremely widespread differences to the behavior of huge numbers of people. Such differences affect, for example, people's moods, the plans they make for any given day, and the way these plans evolve as the day goes on. For any significant difference in weather over a large populated area, some of these effects are certain to be identity-affecting. ([Lenman [2000: 348].)

Another such domain is financial markets:

> [T]hese are influenced by countless, often quite intrinsically insignificant, human actions, and probably—directly or indirectly—by a very high percentage of intrinsically more significant ones. And the effect of market movements on human life is again enormous and certainly often identity-affecting. (Lenman [2000: 348].)

As it was with Angie and Richard, so it is with Ashley and us. We are in the dark about the unforeseeable consequences of intervention and nonintervention; moreover, the foreseeable consequences are but a drop in the ocean of the total consequences, and all but that drop is inscrutable to us. So, *if we endorse OMAC*, then, when we turn to assess the simple version of the Objection, we should already be in doubt about whether we should prevent Ashley's suffering; that is, we should already be strongly inclined to deny premise (2).

OMAC posits right- and wrong-making features of an act which, given the limitations of our information and a sensible view about what is and is not of value, should leave us in doubt about its moral status. But perhaps appearances are deceiving. Perhaps there is a way friends of OMAC can avoid this skeptical implication. Let's look into the matter briefly.

A popular reply used to be that the consequences of our acts "approximate rapidly to zero like the furthermost ripples on a pond after a stone has been dropped in it." Or, ... "Consequences fizzle fast." (Smart and Williams [1973: 33]. See also Moore [1903: 153]). ... To be sure, there are some concepts of a consequence according to which this is true. But, as I intimated above, those concepts are none of my concern here. I am concerned with a version of OMAC according to which, as I said, "what you do right now will have causal ramifications until the end of time and *all* of them are morally relevant." We all know objective maximizing consequentialists who take this line. And my point is simply this: no one privy to the facts to which Lenman calls our attention can retain the view that consequences *in that sense* fizzle fast. (Cp. Lenman [2000: 350–1].)

An appeal to expected value might be a more promising strategy. Suppose act *A* is an alternative action open to me. There are many possible outcomes, *O1, O2, O3, . . ., On*, each of which might obtain, for all I can tell, if I were to perform *A*. Each outcome has a value, $V(Oi)$. Moreover, for each outcome, *Oi*, there is a conditional probability of its obtaining given that I perform *A*: $P(Oi/A)$. The expected value of *A* is the sum, for all of these outcomes, of all of the products determined by $V(Oi) \times P(Oi/A)$. Expected value can be put to use as follows. Although the foreseeable consequences of intervention and nonintervention in Ashley's case are a vanishingly small proportion of their total consequences, and although we are ignorant of their unforeseeable consequences, it does not follow from OMAC that we should be in doubt about whether we should intervene. For, despite our vast ignorance, we should not be in doubt about whether the expected value of intervention is greater than the expected value of nonintervention: we should think it is greater. Thus, says the friend of expected utility, we should not be in doubt about what we should do: we should intervene.

But *why* should we not be in doubt about whether the expected value of intervention is greater than the expected value of nonintervention? To answer that question, we need to answer two others. First, what general procedure should we follow to determine whether the expected value of an act is greater than the expected value of available alternative acts? Second, if we follow that procedure in Ashley's case, will it leave us in a position where we should not be in doubt about intervening?

In an important article, Fred Feldman contends that the nature of expected value itself recommends the following general procedure:

1. List all of the alternative actions available to us.

2. List all of the possible outcomes of the first alternative.

3. For each outcome of the first alternative, specify its value.

4. For each outcome of the first alternative, specify its probability on that alternative, given the information available to us.

5. For each outcome of the first alternative, multiply its value by its probability on that alternative.

6. Sum these products. This sum is the expected value of the first alternative.

7. Repeat steps 2–6 for each of the other alternatives. (Feldman [2006]; it's a must-read.)

Let's apply this procedure to Ashley's case.

Step 1 tells us to list the alternative actions available to us. What are they? At first blush, there are exactly two options: intervention and nonintervention. But that's a gross oversimplification. The fact is that there are a thousand (tens of thousands? millions? more?) ways in which we can intervene and many more ways in which we can fail to intervene. Each of them must be placed on our list. To the extent that we are in doubt about whether out list is complete, we should be in doubt about the results we arrive at.

Suppose we somehow identify a few of the most salient alternative actions. Step 2 tells us to list the possible outcomes of the first act on our list. Suppose the first act is firing a warning shot in the air to scare away the perpetrator. Recall that an outcome of an act is a total way the world might go if the act were performed. And note that the "might" in question is epistemic. We need to ask: how many total ways might the world go if we were to fire a warning shot, relative to the information at our disposal? There are millions of such ways, perhaps many, many more. We need to list each of them. To the extent that we should be in doubt about whether our list is complete, we should be in doubt about our results.

Suppose we somehow identify several of the most salient outcomes, say, a thousand of them. (To the extent that we lack a principled way to do this, more grounds for doubt arise.) The next two steps tell us that we need to assign numbers to those outcomes. Step 3 tells us to assign a number that represents the true value of each outcome. Step 4 tells us to assign a number that represents the probability of each outcome, given our firing a warning shot. (For each alternative act, the sum of the probabilities assigned to each outcome must equal exactly 1.) We haven't the foggiest idea what numbers to assign. We are awash in a sea of doubt.

Suppose we somehow assign the correct numbers. To arrive at the expected value of our first alternative action, we must multiply value and probability one thousand times, once for each outcome (step 5). Then we must add the products (step 6). By the time we finish this last step, Ashley's fate will have been long decided. Of course, even if, by some miracle, we arrive at this point in a second or two, we must now repeat the procedure for each of the salient alternative actions available to us, of which there are many (step 7). Our work has just begun. . . .

Perhaps friends of OMAC can avoid the epistemic fog surrounding expected utility by appealing to the Principle of Indifference which, for our purposes, can be put like this:

> *Indifference.* If we have no evidence favoring any of *n* mutually exclusive and jointly exhaustive possibilities, we should assign each a probability of $1/n$.

Indifference might be put to use in Ashley's case as follows. It is virtually certain that she will be saved if we intervene and it is virtually certain that she will not be saved if we do not intervene. Those are the foreseeable consequences of intervention and nonintervention. We are in the dark about the unforeseeable consequences of intervention and nonintervention, however. For example, we have no evidence to suppose that the unforeseeable consequences of nonintervention will not be much better than the unforeseeable consequences of intervention. This fact

drives the Agnostic's worry. The corrective is to remember that, by the same token, we have no evidence to suppose that the unforeseeable consequences of intervention will not be much better than the unforeseeable consequences of nonintervention. Thus, says the friend of Indifference, since we have no evidence favoring one of these two mutually exclusive and jointly exhaustive possibilities, we should assign each a probability of 1/2, in which case they cancel each other out. So we are left with the foreseeable consequences. On that score, there is no doubt about what we should do—we should intervene.

I have three concerns about the appeal to Indifference here. First, we have no good reason to believe Indifference. Our grounds for believing it are either a priori or empirical. I haven't the space to consider all a priori grounds that have been offered. Here's the most recent attempt I know of:

> Let's say that possibilities n1 and n2 are *evidentially symmetrical* for you if and only if you have no more evidence to think that n1 is the case than you have to think that n2 is the case, or vice versa. Now, when two possibilities are evidentially symmetrical for you, you should assign a probability to them that adequately reflects your evidence for them. Thus,

> *Evidential Symmetry.* If n1 and n2 are evidentially symmetrical for you, then you should assign exactly the same probability to n1 that you assign to n2.

An obvious corollary of this principle is this:

> *Indifference.* If you have no evidence favoring any of *n* mutually exclusive and jointly exhaustive possibilities, then you should assign each a probability of $1/n$. (I have gleaned this argument from White [forthcoming].)

What should we make of this argument?

I have two objections. First, . . . it is obvious that Indifference is *not* a corollary of Evidential Symmetry. For even if you should assign exactly the same probability to n1 that you assign to n2 when your evidence for them is symmetrical, it does not follow that you should assign $1/n$. You might well assign a vague or indeterminate probability, perhaps even the interval $[0,1]$ in some circumstances, to each of them. In fact, this way of representing the probability of possibilities under complete ignorance is a much more accurate representation of that cognitive condition than is assigning a sharp probability to each of them. Second, suppose n1 and n2 are evidentially symmetrical for you. Does it follow that you should assign each of them a probability? Of course not. You should assign no probability at all. A fortiori, you should not assign exactly the same probability, contrary to Evidential Symmetry.

Perhaps we can do better with empirical grounds for Indifference, at least insofar as it applies to our present concern. Suppose we have empirical grounds to think that where we find cases of massive causal ramification in the human sphere, the total good and bad consequences tend to cancel each other out in the long run. I concur with James Lenman's assessment of this suggestion:

> There are no cases of massive causal ramification of the kind to which identity-affecting actions are liable where we have empirical data adequate to any such conclusion, for the simple reason that, even if such ramification were easy to trace (in fact it is quite impossible), there are no such cases in which we have good grounds to suppose the ramification has yet come close to running its course. (Lenman [2000: 354].)

But one might object. We have empirical grounds to think that

> P. All *observed* cases of massive causal ramification are such that the good and the bad consequences tend to cancel each other out.

In that case, what would be wrong with a straightforward enumerative induction to the conclusion that

> C. *All* cases of massive causal ramification, including future cases, are such that the good and the bad consequences tend to cancel each other out?

With this conclusion in hand, we can reasonably ignore the unforeseeable consequences of intervention and nonintervention in Ashley's case and focus on the foreseeable consequences as a basis for reasonably believing we should intervene.

What's wrong with this inductive inference is that it is reasonable only if it is reasonable to suppose that the observed cases of massive causal ramification constitute a representative sample of the total population of massive causal ramifications. But is it reasonable to suppose this? If we had good reason to think that the observed cases were randomly selected from the total population, then we'd have good reason to suppose that they constitute a representative sample of the total population. But we *know* that's not the case: we know that the observed cases are *not* selected in such a way that gives every member of the total population of massive causal ramifications an equal chance of being in our sample. So why suppose they are representative of the total population? . . .

My second concern with the appeal to Indifference has to do with objections to Indifference itself. One is *Bertrand's Paradox*, a version of which is as follows. Imagine a factory that randomly produces square tiles of different lengths, ranging anywhere from 0 to 10 cm. What is the probability that the next tile to come out of the factory will have sides measuring 5 cm or less? The possible outcomes in this case correspond to all of the lengths from 0 cm to 10 cm—the next tile could have sides measuring 1 cm, or 4.5 cm, or 8 cm, or 9.87654321 cm, or. . . . There are many possibilities here but, on the face of it, half of these possibilities are ones in which the sides are 5 cm or less since 5 is halfway between 0 and 10. Since we have no evidence favoring any of these outcomes, Indifference tells us that each is equally likely, so *the probability that the next tile to come out of the factory will have sides measuring 5 cm or less is 1/2.* Here is a second question: What is the probability that the surface area of the next tile will be 25 cm^2 or less? Well, if all of the tiles are squares, and if the lengths range from 0 cm to 10 cm, then the surface areas will range from 0 cm² to 100 cm². The possible outcomes in this case correspond to all of the different surface areas—the next tile could have a surface area of 1 cm² or 26 cm² or 62 cm² or 99.999 cm². Again, there are many possibilities here but, on the face of it, a quarter of them are ones in which the surface area is 25 cm² or less, since 25 is a quarter of the way between 0 and 100. Since we have no evidence favoring any of these outcomes, Indifference tells us that each is equally likely, so *the probability that the next tile to come out of the factory will have a surface area of 25 cm² or less is 1/4.* Here is the problem: *The next tile to come out of the factory will have a surface area of 25 cm² or less if and only if that tile has a length of 5 cm or less.* So the probability that the surface area will be 25 cm² or less *just is* the probability that the length will be 5 cm or less. In other words, 1/4 = 1/2. Indifference leads to absurdity. . . .

Bertrand's Paradox and other objections don't highlight the main problem with Indifference, namely that it codifies a way to get detailed information out of complete ignorance. Better that we assign vague or indeterminate probabilities, even the interval [0,1] if need be, or that we refrain from assigning any probabilities at all. . . .

Perhaps friends of OMAC can ditch Indifference and argue as follows. Given the inscrutability of the distant future, in Ashley's case we have exactly as much reason to believe

A. The *unforeseeable* consequences of nonintervention outweigh the unforeseeable consequences of intervention

as we have to believe

B. The *unforeseeable* consequences of intervention outweigh the unforeseeable consequences of nonintervention.

Thus, we should—epistemically should—base our belief about what we should do on what reasons we have to believe

C. The foreseeable consequences of nonintervention outweigh the foreseeable consequences of intervention

and what reasons we have to believe

D. The foreseeable consequences of intervention outweigh the foreseeable consequences of nonintervention.

We have much more reason to believe (D) than we have to believe (C). Thus, we should *not* be in doubt about whether we should intervene given OMAC. Thus, OMAC is at home with premise (2) of the Moral Skepticism Objection.

On the face of it, this is a sensible line of thought. However, we can construct another argument for the opposite conclusion that, on the face of it, is equally sensible. Given that intervention and nonintervention have massive and inscrutable causal ramifications and given that the unforeseeable consequences swamp the foreseeable ones, in Ashley's case we have exactly as much reason to believe

E. The *total* consequences of nonintervention outweigh the total consequences of intervention

as we have to believe

F. The *total* consequences of intervention outweigh the total consequences of nonintervention.

Thus, we should—epistemically should—be in doubt about whether we should intervene given OMAC. So, OMAC is *not* at home with premise (2) of the Objection.

Which of the two arguments is more sensible? As expected, I give the nod to the second. Here's why. I grant that, given the inscrutability of the distant future, we have exactly as much reason to believe (A) as we do (B). But I deny that it follows that we should—epistemically should—base our belief about what we should do on what reasons we have to believe (C) and (D). For that follows only if we have *more* reason to believe (F) than we have to believe (E), despite the fact that intervention and nonintervention have massive and inscrutable causal ramifications and the unforeseeable consequences swamp the foreseeable ones. But given that intervention and nonintervention have massive and inscrutable causal ramifications and the unforeseeable consequences swamp the foreseeable ones, we do not have more reason to believe (F) than we have to believe (E). To suppose otherwise is like supposing that we have more reason to believe that the consequences of intervening to prevent the execution of Socrates outweigh the consequences of nonintervention than we have to believe that the consequences of not intervening to prevent the execution of Socrates outweigh the consequences of intervention. It is like supposing that we have more reason to believe that the consequences of intervening to prevent Brutus' assassination of Caesar outweigh the consequences of nonintervention than we have to believe that the consequences of not intervening to prevent the assassination of Caesar outweigh the consequences of intervention. We are in no position to suppose such things.

Much more might be said about all of these matters. Suffice to say, as I see things, OMAC posits right- and wrong-making features of an act that should leave us in doubt about its moral status.

OMAC is not alone on this score. Consider

Objective Rossianism (OR). An agent's act is permissible solely in virtue of the fact that it has no less on balance prima facie rightness than any option open to him; otherwise it is impermissible. (In order to deal with conflicting *prima facie* duties, Ross said that our duty *simpliciter* is that which has "the greatest balance of *prima facie* rightness"; see [Ross 1930: 41].)

Suppose that, as Ross said, one prima facie duty, the duty of Beneficence, is the duty to better other people, e.g. to help them achieve a greater degree of virtue, intelligence, pleasure, etc., and another is the duty of Non Maleficence, the duty not to injure others. Now, for any act, whether it constitutes bettering or injuring others depends on its total consequences. (I injure the child whose leg is destroyed by a mine I planted fifty years earlier. You benefit me when the advice you gave me thirty years ago pays off.) So whether, on some particular occasion, intervening to prevent suffering has more on balance prima facie rightness than nonintervention depends on the total consequences of both.

Or consider the moral imperative

Requirement Ro. Prevent suffering you can, unless *there is* better reason for you not to intervene.

Read Ro so that the total consequences of intervention and nonintervention might provide good reason not to intervene, even if we are ignorant of them. Then, whether or not on some particular occasion one's intervention violates Ro depends on the total consequences of intervention and nonintervention. Like OMAC, OR and Ro posit right- and wrong-making features of an act that should leave us in doubt about its moral status. Or so I have argued.

Let us say that any moral theory or principle that, like these three, posits right- and wrong-making features of an act that should leave us in doubt about its moral status is an instance of *Moral Inaccessibilism*, or *Inaccessibilism* for short. I contend that if we endorse an instance of Inaccessibilism, we should be in doubt about whether we should have intervened to prevent Ashley's suffering, i.e. we should reject premise (2) of the Moral Skepticism Objection.

III. TAKING CONSEQUENCES MUCH, *MUCH* LESS SERIOUSLY

Suppose we want to avoid the skeptical implications of Moral Inaccessibilism. In that case, we might convert OMAC into

Subjective Maximizing Act Consequentialism (SMAC). An agent's act is permissible solely in virtue of the fact that she does not believe that its total consequences are overall worse than those of any option open to her; otherwise it is impermissible.

And we might convert OR into

Subjective Rossianism (SR). An agent's act is permissible solely in virtue of the fact that she does not believe that it has less on balance prima facie rightness than that of any option open to her; otherwise it is impermissible. (Ross himself moved from something OR-ish, in Ross [1930], to something SR-ish, in Ross [1939], due to what he deemed to be the undesirable epistemic implications of the former.)

And we might convert Requirement Ro into the moral imperative

> Requirement Rs. Intervene to prevent horrific evil you can prevent, unless you believe there is better reason for you not to intervene.

SMAC implies that even if the total consequences of our intervening to prevent Ashley's suffering are worse than the consequences of nonintervention, we should intervene, provided it is not the case that we believe that the total consequences of intervention are overall worse than those of nonintervention. Similarly, SR implies that even if the on balance *prima facie* rightness of intervention is less than that of nonintervention, we should intervene, provided it is not the case that we believe that the on balance *prima facie* rightness of intervention is less than that of nonintervention. And Rs implies that even if there is better reason not to intervene than there is to intervene, we should intervene, provided it is not the case that we believe that there is better reason not to intervene.

Notice that, on these views, the right- and wrong-making features of an act are typically accessible to us since our beliefs are typically accessible to us; consequently, we should not be in doubt about its moral status. Let's call any view that, like these three, posits right- and wrong-making features of an act that should not leave us in doubt about its moral status an instance of *Moral Accessibilism*, or *Accessibilism* for short.

Accessibilism is relevant to the Moral Skepticism Objection. For suppose we rightly endorse Requirement Rs. (The arguments to follow can be made with SMAC and SR, *mutatis mutandis*.) In that case, we should accept premise (2) of the objection. After all, it is not the case that we believe

that there is better reason for us not to intervene than to intervene, and so the presumption in favor of intervention that is expressed by Rs is not overridden. However, we should reject premise (1). For, given Rs, there is no tension between saying we should not be in doubt about whether we should intervene, on the one hand, and saying we should be in doubt about whether there is some reason we don't know of that would justify someone else's nonintervention, on the other hand. That's because, given Rs, the fact that we should not be in doubt about whether we should intervene is grounded in the twin fact that we should prevent suffering we can prevent and it is not the case that we believe that there is better reason for us not to intervene. The fact that we should not be in doubt about whether we should intervene is not grounded in what anyone else believes or fails to believe. So even if we should be in doubt about whether some reason we don't know of would justify *God's* nonintervention, it does not follow that we should be in doubt about whether *we* should intervene. Thus, premise (1) of the Objection is false *given Requirement Rs*. . . .

So far I have argued that if our moral theories or principles are instances of Inaccessibilism, then we should reject premise (2) of the Objection, but if they are instances of Accessibilism, then we should reject premise (1). More specifically, I have argued that if we endorse OMAC, OR, or Ro, then we should reject premise (2), but if we endorse SMAC, SR, or Rs, then we should reject premise (1). No doubt it will have occurred to some readers that the moral theories and principles on which I have focused are not plausible enough to decide the matter. . . .

So what moral principles might we endorse so that . . . the Moral Skepticism Objection . . . will have [some] bite? . . . Excellent question! Here's what I would find helpful.

Specify your favored theory of the right- and wrong-making features of an act, or specify a moral principle that you think governs the prevention of horrific evil. If it contains terms of art like "all things considered reason," as in "we have an all things considered reason to prevent Ashley's suffering," or "all things considered duty" and "grounded in virtue" as in "we have an all things considered duty—grounded in virtue—to prevent Ashley's suffering," and the like, give a helpful and informative account of what they mean. Then do two things.

First, explain how it is that, on your theory or principles, we should not be in doubt about whether we should intervene to prevent Ashley's suffering. When you give your explanation, be sure to take into account the fact that most of what we do is either directly or indirectly identity-affecting, and thus that most of what we do has massive causal ramifications. If you deny this fact, explain why. If you don't deny it, explain how it is that, despite this fact, we should not be in doubt about whether we should intervene, given your theory or principle. If your explanation appeals to expected value, indifference, intuition, virtue, duties, or the tea leaves in your kitchen sink, explain why objections to your explanation have no force.

Second, explain how it is that, given your theory or principles, Agnosticism implies that we should be in doubt about whether we should intervene to prevent Ashley's suffering. And whatever you say on that score, make it plain why it is that your own theory or principles aren't really driving the doubt and Agnosticism is just coming along for the ride.

I have considered only six theories or principles in this paper, none of which are up to these two tasks, by my lights. My *tentative* hypothesis is that your theory or principles won't be up to them either. But I may well be wrong about that. . . .

REFERENCES

Alston, William (1991), "The Inductive Argument from Evil and the Human Cognitive Condition," *Philosophical Perspectives* 5, 29–67: collected in Howard-Snyder (1996b), 97–125.

———, (1996), "Some (Temporarily) Final Thoughts on Evidential Arguments from Evil," in Howard-Snyder (1996b), 311–32.

Bergmann, Michael (2001), "Skeptical Theism and Rowe's New Evidential Argument from Evil," *Noûs* 35: 278–96.

———, (2009), "Skeptical Theism and the Problem of Evil," in Thomas Flint and Michael Rea (eds.), *The Oxford Handbook of Philosophical Theology* (New York: Oxford University Press).

———, and Rea, Michael (2005), "In Defense of Skeptical Theism: A Reply to Almeida and Oppy," *Australasian Journal of Philosophy* 83: 241–51.

Feldman, Fred (2006), "Actual Utility, the Objection from Impracticality, and the Move to Expected Utility," *Philosophical Studies* 129: 49–79.

Hawthorne, James (2004), "Inductive Logic," in Edward N. Zalta (ed.), *The Stanford Encyclopedia of Philosophy*.

Howard-Snyder, Daniel (1996a), "The Argument from Inscrutable Evil," in Howard-Snyder (1996b).

———, (1996b), (ed.), *The Evidential Argument from Evil* (Bloomington: Indiana University Press).

Lenman, James (2000), "Consequentialism and Cluelessness," *Philosophy and Public Affairs* 29: 342–70.

Mason, Elinor (2004), "Consequentialism and the Principle of Indifference," *Utilitas* 16: 316–21.

Moore, G. E. (1903), *Principia Ethica* (Cambridge: Cambridge University Press).

Ross, W. D. (1930), *The Right and the Good* (Oxford: Oxford University Press).

———, 1939. *Foundations of Ethics* (Oxford: Clarendon Press).

Smart, J. C. C., and Williams, Bernard (1973), *Utilitarianism: For and Against* (Cambridge: Cambridge University Press).

White, Roger (forthcoming), "Evidential Symmetry and Mushy Credence," *Oxford Studies in Epistemology*, MS.

Wykstra, Stephen (1984), "The Humean Obstacle to Evidential Arguments from Suffering: On Avoiding the Evils of 'Appearance'," *International Journal for the Philosophy of Religion*, 16: 73–94.

———, (1996), "Rowe's Noseeum Argument from Evil," in Howard-Snyder (1996b), 126–50.

13

The Problem of Evil and the Desires of the Heart

ELEONORE STUMP

Eleonore Stump (1947–) is professor of philosophy at St. Louis University. She has written extensively in the areas of medieval philosophy, metaphysics, and philosophy of religion. In this article, she argues that traditional theodicies often fail to accord proper importance to the suffering that results from unsatisfied "desires of the heart." She maintains that, to the extent that they fail in this way, such theodicies are, at best, incomplete.

I. INTRODUCTION

The problem of evil is raised by the existence of suffering in the world. Can one hold consistently both that the world has such suffering in it and that it is governed by an omniscient, omnipotent, perfectly good God, as the major monotheisms claim? An affirmative answer to this question has often enough taken the form of a theodicy. A theodicy is an attempt to show that these claims are consistent by providing a morally sufficient reason for God to allow suffering. In the history of the discussions of the problem of evil, a great deal of effort has been expended on proposing and defending, or criticizing and attacking, theodicies and the putative morally sufficient reasons which theodicies propose.

Generally, a putative morally sufficient reason for God to allow suffering is centred on a supposed benefit which could not be gotten without the suffering and which outweighs it. And the benefit is most commonly thought of as some intrinsically valuable thing supposed to be essential to general human flourishing, such as the significant use of free will or virtuous character, either for human beings in general or for the sufferer in particular.[1]

So, for example, in his insightful reflections on the sort of sufferings represented by the afflictions of Job, the impressive tenth-century Jewish thinker Saadiah Gaon says,

> Now He that subjects the soul to its trials is none other than the Master of the universe, who is, of course, acquainted with all its doings. This testing of the soul [that is, the suffering of Job] has been compared to the assaying by means of fire of [lumps of metal] that have been referred to as gold or silver. It is thereby that the true nature of their composition is clearly established. For the original gold and silver remain, while the alloys that have been mingled with them are partly burned and partly take flight... The pure, clear souls that have been refined are thereupon exalted and ennobled.[2]

The same approach is common in contemporary times. So, for example, John Hick has proposed a

---

Reprinted from *Oxford Studies in Philosophy of Religion*, vol. 1 (2008), pp. 196–215, edited by Jonathan Kvanvig. Used by permission of Oxford University Press.

soul-making theodicy, which justifies suffering as building the character of the sufferer and thereby contributing to the flourishing of the sufferer.[3] Or, to take a very different example which nonetheless makes the same point, Richard Swinburne has argued that suffering contributes to the flourishing of sufferers because, among other things, a person's suffering makes him useful to others, and being useful to others is an important constituent of human well-being in general.[4]

Those who have attacked theodicies such as these have tended to focus on the theodicist's claims about the connections between the putative benefit and the suffering. Opponents of theodicy have argued that the proposed benefit could have been obtained without the suffering, for example, or that the suffering is not a morally acceptable means to that (or any other) benefit. But these attacks on theodicy share an assumption with the attempted theodicies themselves. Both the attacks and the attempted theodicies suppose that a person's generic human flourishing would be sufficient to justify God in allowing that a person's suffering if only the suffering and the flourishing were connected in the right way. In this paper, I want to call this assumption into question.

I will argue that the sufferings of unwilling innocents cannot be justified only in terms of the intrinsically valuable things which make for general human flourishing (however that flourishing is understood). I will argue that even if such flourishing is connected in the appropriate ways to the suffering in a person's life, intrinsically valuable things essential to flourishing are not by themselves sufficient to constitute a morally sufficient reason for God to allow human suffering. That is because human beings can set their hearts on things which are not necessary for such flourishing, and they suffer when they lose or fail to get what they set their hearts on.[5] That suffering also needs to be addressed in consideration of the problem of evil.

II. THE DESIRES OF THE HEART

The suffering to which I want to call attention can be thought of in terms of what the Psalmist calls "the desires of the heart."[6] When the Psalmist says, "Delight yourself in the Lord, and he will give you the desires of your heart,"[7] we all have some idea what the Psalmist is promising. We are clear, for example, that some abstract theological good which a person does not care much about does not count as one of the desires of that person's heart. Suffering also arises when a human being fails to get a desire of her heart or has and then loses a desire of her heart.

I do not know how to make the notion of a desire of the heart precise; but, clearly, we do have some intuitive grasp of it, and we commonly use the expression or others related to it in ordinary discourse. We say, for example, that a person is heartsick because he has lost his heart's desire. He is filled with heartache because his heart's desire is kept from him. He loses heart, because something he had put his heart into is taken from him. It would have been different for him if he had wanted it only half-heartedly; but since it was what he had at heart, he is likely to be heartsore a long time over the loss of it, unless, of course, he has a change of heart about it—and so on, and on.

Perhaps we could say that a person's heart's desire is a particular kind of commitment on her part to something—a person or a project—which matters greatly to her but which need not be essential to her flourishing, in the sense that human flourishing for her may be possible without it. So, for example, Coretta Scott King's life arguably exemplifies flourishing, on any ordinary measure of human flourishing and yet her husband's assassination was undoubtedly heartbreaking for her. If there is such a thing as a web of belief, with some beliefs peripheral and others central to a person's set of beliefs, maybe there is also a web of desire. A desire of a person's heart is a desire which is at or near the centre of the web of desire for her. If she loses what she wants when her desire is at or near the centre of the web, then other things which she had wanted begin to lose their ability to attract her because what she had most centrally wanted is gone. The web of desire starts to fall apart when the centre does not hold, we might say. That is why the ordinary good things of life, like food and work, fail to draw a person who has lost the desires of her heart. She is heartbroken, we say, and that is why she has no heart for anything else now.

If things essential to general human flourishing are intrinsically valuable for all human beings, then those things which are the desires of the heart can be thought of as the things which have the value they do for a particular person primarily because she has set her heart on them, like the value a child has for its parents, the value they have *for her* is derivative from her love of them, not the other way around. A loving father, trying to deal gently with his small daughter's childish tantrums, finally said to her with exasperated adult feeling, "It isn't reasonable to cry about these things!" Presumably, the father means that the things for which his little daughter was weeping did not have much value on the scale which measures the intrinsic value of good things essential to human flourishing; and, no doubt, he was right in that assessment. But there is another scale by which to measure, too, and that is the scale which measures the value a thing has for a particular person because of the love she has for it. The second scale cannot be reduced to the first. Clearly, we care not just about general human flourishing and the intrinsically valuable things essential to it. We also care about those things which are the desires of our hearts, and we suffer when we are denied our heart's desires. I would say that it is not reasonable to say to a weeping child that it is not reasonable for her to weep about the loss of something she had her heart set on.

Suffering which stems from a loss of the heart's desires is often enough compatible with flourishing.[8] As far as that goes, for any particular historical person picked as an exemplar of a flourishing life, it is certainly arguable that, at some time in her life, that person will have lost or failed to get something on which she had fixed her heart. Think, for example, not only of Coretta Scott King but also of Sojourner Truth, who was sold away from her parents at the age of nine, or Harriet Tubman, who suffered permanent neurological damage from the beatings she sustained in adolescence. If any human lives manifest flourishing, the lives of these women certainly do. Each of them is an exemplar of a highly admirable, meaningful life. Yet each of these women undoubtedly experienced heartbreak.

In fact, stern-minded thinkers in varying cultures, including some Stoics, Buddhists, and many

in the Christian tradition, have been fiercely committed to the position that human flourishing is independent of the vicissitudes of fortune. On their view, human flourishing ought to be understood in a way which makes it compatible even with such things as poverty, disease and disabilities, the death of loved ones, betrayal by intimate friends, estrangements from friends or family, and imprisonment. But it certainly seems as if each of these is sufficient to break the heart of a person who suffers them if the person is not antecedently in the grip of such a stern-minded attitude.

So, for example, in the history of the medieval Christian tradition, for example, human flourishing was commonly taken as a matter of a certain relationship with God, mediated by the indwelling of the Holy Spirit. On this view of flourishing, most of the evils human beings suffer are compatible with flourishing. That is because, as Christian confessional literature makes clear, a human person can feel that she is in such a relationship with God, even when she is afflicted with serious suffering of body or mind.

This sort of position is also common among the reflective in our own culture. In a moving passage reflecting on his long experience of caring for and living with the severely disabled, Jean Vanier says about the disabled and about himself, too,

> we can only accept ... [the] pain [in our lives] if we discover our true self beneath all the masks and realize that if we are broken, we are also more beautiful than we ever dared to suspect. When we realize our brokenness, we do not have to fall into depression ... Seeing our own brokenness and beauty allows us to recognize, hidden under the brokenness and self-centeredness of others, their beauty, their value, and their sacredness. This discovery is ... a blessed moment, a moment of grace, and a moment of enlightenment that comes in a meeting with the God of love, who reveals to us that we are beloved and so is everyone else.... We can start to live the pain of loss and accept anguish because a

new love and a new consciousness of self are being given to us.[9]

A particularly poignant example of such an attitude is given by John Hull in his memoir about his own blindness. After many pages of documenting the great suffering caused him by blindness, Hull summarizes his attitude towards his disability in this powerful passage:

> the thought keeps coming back to me ... Could there be a strange way in which blindness is a dark, paradoxical gift? Does it offer a way of life, a purification, an economy? Is it really like a kind of painful purging through a death? ... If blindness is a gift, it is not one that I would wish on anybody ... [But in the midst of the experience of music in church] as the whole place and my mind were filled with that wonderful music, I found myself saying, "I accept the gift. I accept the gift." I was filled with a profound sense of worship. I felt that I was in the very presence of God, that the giver of the gift had drawn near to me to inspect his handiwork. ... If I hardly dared approach him, he hardly dared approach me. ... He had, as it were, thrown his cloak of darkness around me from a distance, but had now drawn near to seek a kind of reassurance from me that everything was all right, that he had not misjudged the situation, that he did not have to stay. "It's all right," I was saying to him, "There's no need to wait. Go on, you can go now; everything's fine."[10]

Everything *is* fine, in some sense having to do with relationship to God, and so with flourishing, on this understanding of flourishing. I have no wish to undermine the appealing attitude exemplified in this powerful text. And yet something more needs to be said. The problem is that suffering is not confined to things which undermine a person's flourishing and keep him from being *fine*, in this deep sense of "fine." What is bad about the evils human beings suffer is not just that they can undermine a

person's flourishing, but also that they can keep her from having the desires of her heart, when the desires of her heart are for something which is not essential for general human flourishing. Suffering arises also from the loss of the desires of one's heart; and, in considerations of the problem of evil and proposed theodicies, this suffering needs to be addressed as well. This suffering also needs to be justified.

III. THE STERN-MINDED ATTITUDE

Stated so baldly, this last claim looks less open to question than it really is. We do not ordinarily suppose that a parent's goodness is impugned if the parent refuses to provide for the child anything at all which the child happens to set its heart on. But, as regards the problem of evil, what is at issue is apparently analogous, namely, God's allowing some human being to fail to have the desires of her heart when those desires are focused on something not essential to her flourishing. Why, someone might ask, should we suppose that a good God must provide whatever goods not necessary for her flourishing a human person has fixed her heart on?

Now it is certainly true that there can be very problematic instances of heart's desires. A person could set his heart on very evil things, for example, or a person might set his heart in random ways on trivial things or on a set of mutually incompossible things. And no doubt, there are other examples as well. In cases such as these, reasonable people are unlikely to suppose that some explanation is needed for why a good God would fail to give a person the desires of his heart. Even if we exclude such cases, however, there remain many instances in which a person sets his heart, in humanly understandable and appropriate ways, on something which is not essential to his flourishing and whose value for him is derivative of his love for it.[11] Surely, in that restricted class of cases, some justification is needed for God's allowing a person to suffer heartbreak.

But even this weaker claim will strike some people as false. Some people will object, for example, that human flourishing is a very great good, sufficient to outweigh suffering. For those who think of human flourishing as a relationship to God, it can seem an infinite good or a good too great to be commensurable with other goods; and this good is possible even when many other goods are lost or denied.[12] If God provides *this* good for a human being, then, an objector might claim, that is or ought to be enough for her. A person who does not find this greatest of all goods good enough, an objector might say, is like a person who wins the lottery but who is nonetheless unhappy because she did not get exactly what she wanted for Christmas.

In the history of Christianity in particular, there have been stern-minded thinkers who would not accept the claim that the suffering caused by any loss of the heart's desires requires justification. In effect, this stern-minded attitude is unwilling to assign a positive value to anything which is not essential to general human flourishing. For this reason, the stern-minded approach is, at best, unwilling to accord any value to the desires of the heart and, at worst, eager to extirpate the desires themselves. Such an attitude is persistent in the history of Christian thought from the Patristic period onwards.

In its Patristic form, it can be seen vividly in a story which Cassian tells about a monk named "Patermutus." It is worth quoting at length the heartrendingly horrible story which Cassian recounts with so much oblivious admiration:

> Patermutus's constant perseverance [in his request to be admitted into the monastery finally] induced [the monks] to receive him along with his little son, who was about eight years old.... To test [Patermutus] the more, and see if he would be more moved by family affection and the love of his own brood than by the obedience and mortification of Christ, which every monk should prefer to his love, [the monks] deliberately neglected the child, dressed him in rags ... and even subjected [the child] to cuffs and slaps, which ... the father saw some of them inflict on the innocent for no reason, so that [the father]

never saw [his son] without [the son's] cheeks being marked by the signs of tears. Although he saw the child being treated like this day after day before his eyes, the father's feelings remained firm and unmoving, for the love of Christ.... The superior of the monastery ... decided to test [the father's] strength of mind still further: one day when he noticed the child weeping, he pretended to be enraged at [the child], and ordered the father to pick up [his son] and throw him in the Nile. The father, as if the command had been given him by our Lord, at once ran and snatched up his son and carried him in his own arms to the river bank to throw him in. The deed would have been done ... had not some of the brethren been stationed in advance to watch the riverbank carefully; as the child was thrown they caught him.... Thus they prevented the command, performed as it was by the father's obedience and devotion, from having any effect.[13]

Cassian plainly prizes Patermutus's actions and attitude; but surely most of us will find it chilling and reprehensible. For my part, I would say that one can only wonder why the monks bothered to catch the child, if the father's willingness to kill the child was so praiseworthy in their eyes. Can it be morally praiseworthy to will an act whose performance is morally prohibited?

An attitude similar to Cassian's but less appalling can still be found more than a millenium later in some texts (but not others) of the work of Teresa of Avila, to take just one example from among a host of thinkers who could have been selected. Writing to her sister nuns, Teresa says,

> Oh, how desirable is ... [the] union with God's will! Happy the soul that has reached it. Such a soul will live tranquilly in this life, and in the next as well. Nothing in earthly events afflicts it unless it finds itself in some danger of losing God ...: neither sickness, nor poverty, nor death.... For this soul sees

well that the Lord knows what He is doing better than ... [the soul] knows what it is desiring.... But alas for us, how few there must be who reach [union with God's will!].... I tell you I am writing this with much pain upon seeing myself so far away [from union with God's will]—and all through my own fault.... Don't think the matter lies in my being so conformed to the will of God that if my father or brother dies I don't feel it, or that if there are trials or sicknesses I suffer them happily.[14]

Not feeling it when one's father dies, not weeping with grief over his death, is, in Teresa's view, a good spiritual condition which she is not yet willing to attribute to herself. Teresa is here echoing a tradition which finds its prime medieval exemplar in Augustine's *Confessions*. Augustine says that, at the death of his mother, by a powerful command of his will, he kept himself from weeping at her funeral, only to disgrace himself in his own eyes later by weeping copiously in private.[15]

In the same text from which I just quoted, Teresa emphasizes the importance of love of neighbour; but it is hard to see how love of neighbour coheres with the stern-minded attitude manifested by Teresa and Augustine in the face of the death (real or imagined) of a beloved parent. As I have argued elsewhere, it is the nature of love to desire the good of the beloved and union with him.[16] But the desire for the good of the beloved is frustrated if the beloved gets sick or dies. Or, if the stern-minded attitude is unwilling to concede that point, then this much is incontrovertible even on the stern-minded attitude: the desire for union with the beloved is frustrated when the beloved dies and so is absent. One way or another, then, the desires of love are frustrated when the beloved dies.

Consequently, there is something bad and lamentable, something worth tears, something whose loss brings affliction with it, about the death of any person whom one loves—one's father, or even one's neighbour, whom one is bound to love too, as Teresa thinks.

Unmoved tranquillity at the death of another person is thus incompatible with love of that person. To the extent to which one loves another person, one cannot be unmoved at his death. And so love of neighbour is in fact incompatible with the stern-minded attitude.

The stance Teresa wishes she might take towards her father's death, as she imagines it, can be usefully contrasted with Bernard of Clairvaux's reaction to the death of his brother. Commenting on his grief at that death, Bernard says to his religious community, "You, my sons, know how deep my sorrow is, how galling a wound it leaves."[17] And, addressing himself, he says, "Flow on, flow on, my tears.... Let my tears gush forth like fountains."[18] Reflecting on his own failure to repudiate his great sorrow over his brother's death, his failure, that is, to follow Augustine's model, Bernard says,

> It is but human and necessary that we respond to our friends with feeling, that we be happy in their company, disappointed in their absence. Social intercourse, especially between friends, cannot be purposeless: the reluctance to part and the yearning for each other when separated indicate how meaningful their mutual love must be when they are together.[19]

And Bernard is hardly the only figure in the Christian tradition who fails to accept and affirm Cassian's attitude. Aquinas is another.

There are isolated texts which might suggest to some readers that Aquinas himself is an adherent of Cassian's attitude. So, for example, in his commentary on Christ's line that he who loves his life will lose it, Aquinas reveals that he recognizes the concept of the desires of the heart; but, in this same passage, he also seems to suggest that such desires should be stamped out. He says,

> Everyone loves his own soul, but some love it *simpliciter* and some *secundum quid*. To love someone is to will the good for him; and so he who loves his soul wills the good for it. A person who wills for his soul

the good *simpliciter* also loves his soul *simpliciter*. But a person who wills some particular good for his soul loves his soul *secundum quid*. The goods for the soul *simpliciter* are those things by which the soul is good, namely, the highest good, which is God. And so he who wills for his soul the divine good, a spiritual good, loves his soul *simpliciter*. But he who wills for his soul earthly goods such as riches and honors, pleasures, and things of that sort, he loves his soul [only] *secundum quid* ... He who loves his soul *secundum quid* namely with regard to temporal goods, will lose it.[20]

And the implication seems to be that, for Aquinas, the person who does not want to lose his soul should extirpate from himself all desires for any good other than the highest good, which is, as Aquinas says, God.

But it is important to see that what is at issue for Aquinas in this passage is the desire for worldly things, that is for those goods, such as money or fame, which diminish when they are distributed. On Aquinas' scale of values, any good which diminishes when it is distributed is only a small good. When it comes to the desires of the heart for things which are earthly goods but great goods, such as the love of a particular person, Aquinas' attitude differs sharply from Cassian's. So, for example, in explaining why Christ told his disciples that he was going to the father in order to comfort them when they were sad at the prospect of being separated from him, Aquinas says,

> It is common among friends to be less sad over the absence of a friend when the friend is going to something which exalts him. That is why the Lord gives them this reason [for his leaving] in order to console them.[21]

Unlike Teresa's repudiation of grief at the prospect of losing her father, Aquinas is here, as in many other places, accepting the appropriateness of a person's grief at the loss of a loved person and validating the need for consolation for such grief.

So Aquinas is not to be ranked among the members of the stern-minded group, any more than Bernard is; and, of course, in other moods, when she is not self-consciously evaluating her own spiritual progress, Teresa herself sounds more like Bernard and Aquinas than like Cassian. As far as that goes, the Psalmist who authored Psalm 37 is not on Cassian's side. The Psalmist claims that God will give the desires of the heart to those who delight in the Lord; so the Psalmist is supposing that, for those who trust in God, God himself honours the desires of the heart. On this subject, then, the Christian tradition is of two minds. Not all its influential figures stand with Cassian; and, even among those who do, many are double-minded about it.

IV. A POSSIBLE CONFUSION

But, someone will surely object, isn't it a part of Christian doctrine that God allows the death of any person who dies? Does anyone die when God wills that that person live? So when a person dies, on Christian theology, isn't it the will of God that that person die? In what sense, then, could Teresa be united with God in will if she grieved over her father's death? How could she be united with God, as she explains she wants to be, if her will is frustrated in what God's will accepts or commands?

The position presupposed by the questions of this putative objector, in my view, rests on too simple an understanding of God's will and union with God's will.

To see why, assume that at death Teresa's father is united with God in heaven. Then the death which unites Teresa's father permanently with God has the opposite effect for Teresa: at least for the time being, it deprives Teresa of her father's presence and so keeps her from union with him, at least for the rest of Teresa's earthly life. For this reason, on the Christian doctrine Teresa accepts, love's desire for union with the beloved cannot be fulfilled in the same way for Teresa as for God. If Teresa's will is united with God's will in desiring union with a beloved person, then Teresa's will must also be frustrated at the very event, her father's dying, which fulfils God's will with respect to this desire.

Something analogous can be said about the other desire of love, for the good of the beloved. If Teresa desires the good of her father, she can only desire what her own mind sees as that good; but her mind's ability to see the good is obviously much smaller than God's. To the extent to which Teresa's will is united with God's will in desiring the good of the beloved, then Teresa will also desire for the beloved person things different from those desired by God, in virtue of Teresa's differing ability to see the good for the beloved person.

It is easy to become confused here because the phrase "the good" can be used either attributively or referentially.[22] In this context, "the good of the beloved" can be used either to refer to particular things which are conducive to the beloved's well-being; or it can be used opaquely, to refer to anything whatever, under the description *the good of the beloved*. A mother who is baffled by the quarrels among her adult children and clueless about how to bring about a just peace for them may say, despairingly, "I just want the good for everybody." She is then using the phrase "the good" attributively, with no idea of how to use it referentially.

If Teresa were tranquil over any affliction which happens to her father, because she thinks that in this tranquillity her will is united to God's will and that she is therefore willing the good for her father,[23] "the good" in this thought of hers is being used attributively, to designate *whatever* God thinks is good. But this cannot be the way "the good" is used in any thought of God's, without relativizing the good entirely to God's will. If we eschew such relativism, then it is not the case that anything God desires is good just because God desires it. And so it is also not true that God desires as the good of a beloved person *whatever* it is that God desires for her. When God desires the good for someone, then, God must desire it by desiring particular things as good for that person. Consequently, to say that God desires the good for a person is to use "the good" referentially.

For this reason, when, in an effort to will what God wills, Teresa desires *whatever* happens to her

father as the good for her father, she thereby actually *fails* to will what God wills. To be united with God in willing the good requires willing for the beloved particular things which are in fact the good for the beloved, and doing so requires recognizing those things which constitute that good.

At the death of Mao Tse-tung, one of the groups competing for power was called "the Whatever Faction," because the members of that group were committed to maintaining as true, and compulsory for all Chinese to believe, anything Mao said, whatever it was.[24] In trying to desire whatever happens as good because God wills it, a person is as it were trying to be part of a Whatever Faction for God. She is trying to maintain as good anything that happens, whatever it is, on the grounds that it is what God wills. By contrast, in his great lament over the death of his brother, Bernard of Clairvaux is willing to affirm both his passionate grief over the loss of his brother and his acceptance of God's allowing that death. Bernard says, "Shall I find fault with [God's] judgment because I wince from the pain?";[25] "I have no wish to repudiate the decrees of God, nor do I question that judgment by which each of us has received his due. . . ."[26] Bernard grieves over this particular death as a bad thing, even while he accepts that God's allowing this bad thing is a good thing.

Understanding the subtle but important difference in attitude between Teresa and Bernard on this score helps to elucidate the otherwise peculiar part of the book of Job in which God rebukes Job's comforters because they did not say of God the thing which is right, unlike God's servant Job, who did. What the comforters had said was that God is justified in allowing Job's suffering. Job, on the other hand, had complained bitterly that his suffering is unjust and that God should not have allowed it to happen. How is it that, in the story, God affirms Job's position and repudiates that of the comforters? The answer lies in seeing that the comforters took Job's suffering to be good just because, in their view, Job's suffering was willed by God. In effect, then, the comforters were (and wanted to be) part of the Whatever Faction of God. Job, by contrast, was intransigent in his refusal to be partisan in this way. And so, on the apparently paradoxical view of the book of Job, in opposing God, Job is more allied with God's will than are the comforters, who were taking God's part. That is why when in the story God comes to adjudicate, he sides with Job, who had opposed him, and not with the comforters, who were trying to be his partisans.

The apparent paradox here can be resolved by the scholastic distinction between God's antecedent and consequent will. On this distinction, whatever happens in the world happens only because it is in accordance with God's will, but that will is God's *consequent* will. God's consequent will, however, is to be distinguished from his antecedent will; and many of the things which happen in the world are not in accordance with God's *antecedent* will. Roughly put, God's *antecedent* will is what God would have willed if things in the world had been up to God alone. God's *consequent* will is what God in fact will, given what he knows that his creatures will. God's consequent will is his will for the greatest good available in the circumstances which are generated through creaturely free will.

To try to be in accord with God's will by taking as acceptable, as unworthy of sorrow, everything that happens is to confuse the consequent will of God with the antecedent will. It is to accept as intrinsically good even those things which God wills as good only secundum quid, that is, as the best available in the circumstances. But God does not will as intrinsically good everything he wills; what he wills in his consequent will, what is the best available in the circumstances, might be only the lesser of evils, not the intrinsically good.

And so to accept as good whatever happens on the grounds that it is God's will is the wrong way to try to be united with God's will. One can desire as intrinsically good what one sees for oneself is good in the circumstances, or one can desire[27] as intrinsically good whatever happens, on the grounds that it is God's will. But only the former desire can be in accordance with God's will, given that God's consequent will is not the same as his antecedent will. For the same reasons, only the former desire is conductive to union with God. Although it appears paradoxical, then, the closest a

human person may be able to come, in this life, to uniting her will with God's will may include her willing things (say, that a beloved person not die) which are opposed to God's (consequent) will.

It is also important to see in this connection that, in principle, there cannot be any competition between the love of God and the love of other persons. On the contrary, if one does not love one's neighbour, then one does not love God either. That is because to love God is to desire union with him; and union with God requires being united in will with him. But a person who does not love another, his father or brother, for example, cannot be united in will with a God who does love these people. So, in being tranquil and unmoved in the face of the death of a beloved father or mother, a person is not more united with God, or more in harmony with God's will, but less.

V. DENYING ONESELF

Something also needs to be said in this connection about the Christian doctrine mandating denial of the self. This much understanding of the two different ways in which one can try to will what God wills shows that there are also two correspondingly different interpretations of that doctrine.

Cassian and others who hold the stern-minded attitude manifest one such understanding. A person who shares Cassian's attitude will attempt to deny his self by, in effect, refusing to let his own mind and his own will exercise their characteristic functions. That is because a person who attempts to see as good whatever happens, on the grounds that whatever happens is willed by God, is trying to suppress, or trying to fail to acquire, his own understanding of the good. And a person who attempts to will as good whatever happens, on the same grounds, is trying to suppress the desires his own will forms, or trying not to acquire the desires his will would have formed if he were not in the grip of the stern-minded attitude. To attempt to deny the self in the stern-minded way is thus to try not to have a self at all. A woman who says sincerely to her father, "I want only what you want," and "whatever you think is good is good in my view, too," is a woman who is trying to be at one with her father by having no self of her own.

On the other hand, it is possible to let one's own faculties of intellect and will have their normal functioning and still deny oneself. This is a stance with which we are all familiar from our experiences of ordinary, daily life. Consider, for example, a mother with the stomach flu who creeps out of bed to care for her baby who also has the flu. When she leaves her bed to tend the baby, she is preferring to meet the baby's needs rather than her own. That is, she desires to stay in bed, but she also desires that the baby's needs take precedence over her own needs and desires. In her desire about the rank-ordering of desires, she does not cease to desire to stay in bed. She still has that desire; she just acts counter to it. This is to deny the self by first having a self to deny. Unlike the no-self position, this position is compatible with sorrow, and tears, for the things lost in the desires denied.

On reflection, it is clear that, contrary to first appearances, the no-self position is actually incompatible with the Christian injunction of self-denial. That is because one cannot crucify a self one does not have. To crucify one's self is to have desires and to be willing to act counter to them. An adherent to the Whatever Faction of God cannot deny his self, however, because he has constructed his desires in such a way that, whatever he wills, he does not will counter to his own desires. A person who is a partisan of the no-self position has a first-order desire for whatever it may be that is God's will, and he attempts to have no first-order desires which are in conflict with whatever it may be that is God's will. That is why (unlike the real Teresa, who was full of very human emotions) such a person would not weep if her father died. In theory, at any rate, whatever happens to her is in accordance with her first-order will and is therefore not a source of sorrow to her. In virtue of the fact that she has tried to extirpate from herself all desires except the one desire for whatever it may be that is God's will, such a person has no desires which are frustrated by whatever happens, as long as she herself remains committed to willing whatever God wills.[28]

The self-crucifying denier of the self, by contrast, has first-order desires for things his own intellect finds good, so that he is vulnerable to grief in the frustration of those desires. But he prefers his grief and frustration to the violation of God's will. In this sense, he also wills that God's will be done. His second-order desire is that God's desires take precedence over his own. When Christ says, "not my will but yours be done," he is not expressing the no-self position, because he is admitting that he has desires in conflict with God's desires. On the other hand, in virtue of preferring his pain to the violation of God's will, he is also willing that God's desires take precedence over his. This is the sense, then, in which he is willing that God's will be done.

VI. THE DESIRES OF THE HEART AND THE FLOURISHING OF A PERSON

So, for all these reasons, the stern-minded attitude is to be repudiated. Whatever its antiquity and ancestry, such influential thinkers as Bernard and Aquinas do not accept it. More importantly, it is an unpalatable position, even from the point of view of an ascetically minded Christianity. It underlies the repellent and lamentable mind-set exemplified in Cassian's story, and it is incompatible with the love of one's neighbour and consequently also with love of God. There are things worth desiring other than the intrinsically valuable things necessary for human flourishing, and the desires for these things should not be suppressed or stamped out. On the contrary, as Cassian's story makes plain, the attempt to extirpate any desires of the heart does not lead to human excellence, as Cassian thought it did, but to a kind of inhumanity willing to murder one's own child in the service of a confused and reprehensible attempt at self-denial.

There is an apparent paradox here, however. As I introduced the phrase, the desires of the heart are desires which are central to a person's web of desires but whose objects have the value they do for her because of her desire for them, not because of their connection to general human flourishing. On the face of it, then, losing the objects of such desires or giving up those desires themselves is compatible with general human flourishing for that person. But the rejection of the stern-minded attitude seems to imply that a person's flourishing requires that he have desires of the heart and that he strive to have what he desires. Consequently, it also seems to imply that it is essential to a person's flourishing that he have desires of the heart. But, then, if the desires of the heart are required for his flourishing, it seems that the objects of those desires are as well. And so it seems to follow, paradoxically, that it is essential to human flourishing that a person desire and seek to have things at least some of which are not necessary to human flourishing.

In recent work, Harry Frankfurt has argued that it is useful for a person to have final ends.[29] The central idea of his argument is the thought that a person with no final ends at all will have a life which lacks flourishing. And so final ends *are* useful as a means to an end, namely, human flourishing. The apparently paradoxical claim about the desires of the heart can be understood analogously. Human beings are constructed in such a way that they naturally set their hearts on things in addition to and different from intrinsically valuable things essential to general human flourishing. That is why confining a person's desires just to human flourishing has something inhuman about it. A person's flourishing therefore also requires that he care about and seek to have things besides those that are intrinsically valuable components of or means to human flourishing.[30] On Frankfurt's view, having a desire for something which is not a means to anything else is a means to a person's flourishing. On the view I have argued for here, having a desire for things which are not essential to flourishing and seeking to have those things is also necessary as a means to flourishing.

And so, although no particular thing valued as a desire of the heart is essential to a person's flourishing, human flourishing is not possible in the absence of the desires of the heart.

VII. CONCLUSION

For all these reasons, we can safely leave the objections of the stern-minded attitude to one side. It therefore remains the case that justification is also needed for suffering stemming from unfulfilled or frustrated desires of the heart. For this reason, theodicies which focus just on one or another variety of general human flourishing as the morally sufficient reason for God's allowing evil are, at best, incomplete. Even if we give a theodicy such as Hick's or Swinburne's everything it wants as regards the relation between suffering and flourishing, however flourishing is understood in their theodicies, there remains the problem of suffering stemming from the loss of the desires of one's heart.

Take the story of Job, for example. For the sake of argument, let it be the case, as Saadiah Gaon appears to hold in his excellent and impressive commentary, that Job's suffering is necessary to his ennobling and purification, morally acceptable as a means to these things, and outweighed by them, in the sense that (on some objective measure) Job's ennobling and purification are a greater good than his suffering is an evil. Even if this were entirely so, and even if it were right that ennobling and purification constituted consummate human flourishing, something more would be needed for theodicy in Job's case. Job might care about his children at least as much as about his own ennobling and purification; and he might be heartbroken at the loss of his children, even with the benefit to him of his ennobling and purification. Something also needs to be said about the moral justification for God's allowing such heartbreak.

Someone might object that if the benefit to Job really is connected to his suffering in the way I have just described, then nothing more is needed for theodicy, because the good given to Job through his suffering defeats the suffering. But this is to accord no value to the desires of Job's heart. It is, in effect, to say with regard to Job a much sterner version of what the loving but exasperated father said to his daughter: It is not reasonable to weep about these things. But, as I have been at pains to show, disregarding or downplaying the desires of the heart is itself unreasonable. Suffering is a function of what we care about, and we care not only about human flourishing; we care also about the things on which we have set our hearts. The suffering stemming from the loss of the heart's desires also needs to be redeemed. The benefit which outweighs the suffering for Job, as Saadiah Gaon sees it, outweighs that suffering only on the scale of values which measures the intrinsic worth of things essential to human flourishing in general. It does not outweigh it on the scale which measures things that have the value they do for a particular person only because he has set his heart on them.

That this is so helps to explain why so many people feel uneasy or disappointed at attempted solutions to the problem of evil which focus on some global good (for humanity in general—the significant use of free will, for example—as a morally sufficient reason for God to allow suffering. If a person's own flourishing is not sufficient to justify God in allowing her to be heartbroken, then, a fortiori, some component of or contribution to the flourishing of the human species considered as a whole cannot do so either.

And so the desires of the heart also need to be considered in connection with the problem of evil. For my part, I think it is possible to find a way to develop traditional theodicies to include satisfactory consideration of the problem posed by the desires of the heart;[31] but, clearly, that complicated and challenging task lies outside the scope of this paper.

REFERENCES

Adams, Marilyn, *Horrendous Evils and the Goodness of God* (Ithaca, NY: Cornell University Press, 1999).

Astell, Ann, *The Song of Songs in the Middle Ages* (Ithaca, NY: Cornell University Press, 1990).

Cassian, *The Monastic Institutes*, tr. Jerome Bertram (London: Saint Austin Press, 1999).

Frankfurt, Harry, "On the Usefulness of Final Ends," *Necessity, Volition, and Love* (Princeton, NJ: Princeton University Press, 1998).

Hick, John, *Evil and the God of Love* (New York: Harper and Row, 1966).

———, "God, Evil and Mystery," *Religious Studies* 3 (1968a): 539–46.

———, "The Problem of Evil in the First and Last Things," *Journal of Theological Studies* 19 (1968b): 591–602.

Hull, Jonathan, *Touching the Rock. An Experience of Blindness* (New York: Vintage Books, 1991).

MacFarquhar, Roderick, "The Succession to Mao and the End of Maoism," in *The Cambridge History of China*, vol. 15, *The People's Republic, pt.2: Revolutions within the Chinese Revolution: 1966–1982* (Cambridge: Cambridge University Press, 1991).

Saadiah Gaon, *The Book of Beliefs and Opinions*, tr. Samuel Rosenblatt (New Haven, CT: Yale University Press, 1948).

Stump, Elconore, "Love, By All Accounts," Proceedings and Addresses of The American Philosophical Association, Vol. 80, No. 2, November 2006.

———, *Wandering in Darkness: Narrative and the Problem of Suffering* (Oxford: Oxford University Press, forthcoming).

Swinburne, Richard, *Providence and the Problem of Evil* (Oxford: Oxford University Press, 1998).

Teresa of Avila, *The Interior Castle* (Mahwah, NJ: Paulist Press, 1979).

Vanier, Jean, *Becoming Human* (Mahwah, NJ: Paulist Press, 1998).

NOTES

For helpful comments on earlier drafts of this paper or on its contents, I am grateful to Jeffrey Brower, Frank Burch Brown, John Foley, John Kavanaugh, Scott MacDonald, Michael Murray, Michael Rea, Theodore Vitali, and anonymous reviewers for *Oxford Studies in Philosophy of Religion*.

1. There is a large, contentious philosophical literature on the nature of human flourishing or well-being,

and it is not part of my purpose to try to engage that literature here. For my purposes in this paper, I will understand flourishing to consist in just those things necessary in a person's life for that person's life to be admirable and meaningful.

2. Saadiah Gaon 1948: 246–7.

3. Hick 1966. For Hick's defence of his solutions against objections, see, for example, Hick 1968a: 539–46, and Hick 1968b: 591–602.

4. See Swinburne 1998.

5. In Adams 1999, Marilyn Adams makes a distinction which is at least related to the distinction I am after here. She says, "the value of a person's life may be assessed from the inside (in relation to that person's own goals, ideals, and choices) and from the outside (in relation to the aims, tastes, values, and preferences of others). . . . My notion is that for a person's life to be a great good to him/her on the whole, the external point of view (even if it is God's) is not sufficient" (p. 145).

6. The expression "the desire of the heart" is also ambiguous. It can mean either a particular kind of desire or else the thing which is desired in that way. When we say, "the desire of his heart was to be a great musician," the expression refers to a desire; when we say, "In losing her, he lost the desire of his heart," the expression refers to the thing desired. I will not try to sort out this ambiguity here; I will simply trust to the context to disambiguate the expression.

7. Ps. 37:4–5.

8. Except for conceptions of flourishing which make flourishing identical to the satisfaction of desires, but equating flourishing just with desire satisfaction is problematic enough that it can be left to one side here.

9. Vanier 1998: 158–9.

10. Hull 1991: 205–6.

11. Elsewhere I consider the complication of cases in which an apparently appropriate heart's desire is such that its fulfilment would undermine the flourishing of the person who has it. So, for example, the great English poet John Milton apparently had a heart's desire to be an administrator in the Puritan government of his time; but his government work kept him from writing poetry. All his greatest poetry was written after the fall of the Puritan regime. There are also cases in which a person sets his heart

on what he himself takes to be essential to his flourishing, when in fact he is mistaken on this score. Viktor Klemperer supposed that his flourishing was dependent on his writing a great study of eighteenth-century French literature, and he describes his own sense of the blight of his life in consequence of his inability to write a great book in his stunningly excellent diaries, published now to rave reviews. For consideration of complicated cases such as these, see my *Wandering in Darkness: Narrative and the Problem of Suffering* (Oxford, forthcoming).

12. For a persuasive statement of a case for such a view, see Adams 1998.

13. Cassian 1999: 55–6.

14. Teresa of Avila 1979: 98, 99, 100.

15. *Confessions* IX.12.

16. Stump 2006.

17. Cited in Astell 1990: 126.

18. Cited in Astell 1990: 130.

19. Cited in Astell 1990: 133.

20. *Super Evangelium S.Ioannis Lectura,* John 12: 24–5, Lectio IV.7, 1643–1644.

21. *Super Evangelium S.Ioannis Lectura,* John 14: 27–31, Lectio VIII.l, 1966.

22. "The commander of the armed forces" is used referentially when it refers to the particular person who is the President; it is used attributively when it refers to anyone who holds the office of commander without reference to a particular person who in fact currently holds the office.

23. It is important to put the point in terms of what *happens* to her father, rather than in terms of any state or condition of her father, since there are certainly things her father might do which cause Teresa a grief she would approve of having.

24. The official formula was "Whatever policy Chairman Mao decided upon, we shall resolutely defend; whatever directives Chairman Mao issued, we shall steadfastly obey." See MacFarquhar 1991: 372

25. Cited in Astell 1990: 133.

26. Cited in Astell 1990: 130.

27. Or try to accept—a distinction manifested by Teresa's own description of herself.

28. The last clause is a necessary caveat because, presumably, even an adherent to the position would

be distressed at finding sin in himself (and maybe even at finding sin in others), since sin cannot be considered in accordance with God's will.

29. Frankfurt 1998.

30. In this respect, the desires of the heart are to human flourishing what accidents are to a primary substance. Any particular accident is not necessary to a substance,

but it is necessary to a substance that it have accidents. Analogously, no particular desire of the heart is necessary for a person's flourishing, but it is necessary for her flourishing that she have desires of the heart.

31. I argue for this claim in detail in my *Wandering in Darkness. Narrative and the Problem of Suffering* (Oxford, forthcoming).

14

Horrendous Evils and the Goodness of God

MARILYN McCORD ADAMS

Marilyn McCord Adams (1943–) is Honorary Professor at the Australian Catholic University. She has held positions in philosophy and theology at Oxford University, Yale University, and the University of California, Los Angeles, and has written extensively on topics at the intersection of these disciplines. In this article, Adams argues that standard responses to the problem of evil fall short in their ability to deal with "horrendous evil." She then argues that God could defeat such evils only by somehow "integrating participation in horrendous evils into a person's relationship with God."

1. INTRODUCTION

Over the past thirty years, analytic philosophers of religion have defined "the problem of evil" in terms of the prima-facie difficulty in consistently maintaining

(1) God exists, and is omnipotent, omniscient, and perfectly good

and

(2) Evil exists.

In a crisp and classic article, "Evil and Omnipotence,"[1] J. L. Mackie emphasized that the problem

is not that (1) and (2) are logically inconsistent by themselves, but that they together with quasi-logical rules formulating attribute-analyses—such as

(P1) A perfectly good being would always eliminate evil so far as it could,

and

(P2) There are *no limits* to what an omnipotent being can do—

constitute an inconsistent premiss-set. He added, of course, that the inconsistency might be removed by substituting alternative and perhaps more subtle analyses, but cautioned that such replacements of

First published in *Proceedings of the Aristotelian Society*, Supplementary Vol. 63 (1989), pp. 297–310, with revisions and additional notes from the revised version in *The Problem of Evil*, ed. Robert Merrihew Adams and Marilyn McCord Adams (Oxford University Press, 1990), © The Aristotelian Society 1989. Reprinted by permission of the Aristotelian Society and Oxford University Press.

(P1) and (P2) would save "ordinary theism" from his charge of positive irrationality, only if true to its "essential requirements."[2]

In an earlier paper, "Problems of Evil: More Advice to Christian Philosophers,"[3] I underscored Mackie's point and took it a step further. In debates about whether the argument from evil can establish the irrationality of religious belief, care must be taken, both by the atheologians who deploy it and by the believers who defend against it, to ensure that the operative attribute-analyses accurately reflect that religion's understanding of divine power and goodness. It does the atheologian no good to argue for the falsity of Christianity on the ground that the existence of an omnipotent, omniscient, pleasure-maximizer is incompossible with a world such as ours, because Christians never believed God was a pleasure-maximizer anyway. But equally, the truth of Christianity would be inadequately defended by the observation that an omnipotent, omniscient egoist could have created a world with suffering creatures, because Christians insist that God loves other (created) persons than Himself. The extension of "evil" in (2) is likewise important. Since Mackie and his successors are out to show that "the several parts of the *essential* theological doctrine are inconsistent with *one another*,"[4] they can accomplish their aim only if they circumscribe the extension of "evil" as their religious opponents do. By the same token, it is not enough for Christian philosophers to explain how the power, knowledge, and goodness of God could coexist with some evils or other; a full account must exhibit the compossibility of divine perfection with evils in the amounts and of the kinds found in the actual world (and evaluated as such by Christian standards).

The moral of my earlier story might be summarized thus: where the internal coherence of a system of religious beliefs is at stake, successful arguments for its inconsistency must draw on premises (explicitly, or implicitly) internal to that system or obviously acceptable to its adherents; likewise for successful rebuttals or explanations of consistency. The thrust of my argument is to push both sides of the debate towards more detailed attention to and subtle understanding of the religious system in question.

As a Christian philosopher, I want to focus in this paper on the problem for the truth of Christianity raised by what I shall call "horrendous" evils. Although our world is riddled with them, the biblical record punctuated by them, and one of them—namely, the passion of Christ; according to Christian belief, the judicial murder of God by the people of God—is memorialized by the Church on its most solemn holiday (Good Friday) and in its central sacrament (the Eucharist), the problem of horrendous evils is largely skirted by standard treatments for the good reason that they are intractable by them. After showing why, I will draw on other Christian materials to sketch ways of meeting this, the deepest of religious problems.

2. DEFINING THE CATEGORY

For present purposes, I define "horrendous evils" as "evils the participation in (the doing or suffering of) which gives one reason prima facie to doubt whether one's life could (given their inclusion in it) be a great good to one on the whole."[5] Such reasonable doubt arises because it is so difficult humanly to conceive how such evils could be overcome. Borrowing Chisholm's contrast between *balancing off* (which occurs when the opposing values of *mutually exclusive* parts of a whole partially or totally cancel each other out) and *defeat* (which cannot occur by the mere addition to the whole of a new part of opposing value, but involves some "organic unity" among the values of parts and wholes, as when the positive aesthetic value of a whole painting defeats the ugliness of a small colour patch),[6] horrendous evils seem prima facie, not only to balance off but to engulf the positive value of a participant's life. Nevertheless, that very horrendous proportion, by which they threaten to rob a person's life of positive meaning, cries out not only to be engulfed, but to be made meaningful through positive and decisive defeat.

I understand this criterion to be objective, but relative to individuals. The example of habitual complainers, who know to make the worst of a good situation, shows individuals not to be incorrigible experts on what ills would defeat the positive value of their lives. Nevertheless, nature and experience endow people with different strengths; one bears easily what crushes another. And a major consideration in determining whether an individual's life is/has been a great good to him/her on the whole, is invariably and appropriately how it has seemed to him/her.[7]

I offer the following list of paradigmatic horrors: the rape of a woman and axing off of her arms, psychophysical torture whose ultimate goal is the disintegration of personality, betrayal of one's deepest loyalties, cannibalizing one's own offspring, child abuse of the sort described by Ivan Karamazov, child pornography, parental incest, slow death by starvation, participation in the Nazi death camps, the explosion of nuclear bombs over populated areas, having to choose which of one's children shall live and which be executed by terrorists, being the accidental and/or unwitting agent of the disfigurement or death of those one loves best. I regard these as *paradigmatic*, because I believe most people would find in the doing or suffering of them prima-facie reason to doubt the positive meaning of their lives.[8] Christian belief counts the crucifixion of Christ another: on the one hand, death by crucifixion seemed to defeat Jesus' Messianic vocation; for according to Jewish law, death by hanging from a tree made its victim ritually accursed, definitively excluded from the compass of God's people, *a fortiori* disqualified from being the Messiah. On the other hand, it represented the defeat of its perpetrators' leadership vocations, as those who were to prepare the people of God for the Messiah's coming, killed and ritually accursed the true Messiah, according to later theological understanding, God Himself.

3. THE IMPOTENCE OF STANDARD SOLUTIONS

For better and worse, the by now standard strategies for "solving" the problem of evil are powerless in the face of horrendous evils.

3.1. Seeking the Reason-Why

In his model article "Hume on Evil,"[9] Pike takes up Mackie's challenge, arguing that (P1) fails to reflect ordinary moral intuitions (more to the point, I would add, Christian beliefs), and traces the abiding sense of trouble to the hunch that an omnipotent, omniscient being could have no reason compatible with perfect goodness for permitting (bringing about) evils, because all legitimate excuses arise from ignorance or weakness. Solutions to the problem of evil have thus been sought in the form of counter-examples to this latter claim, i.e. logically possible reasons-why that would excuse even an omnipotent, omniscient God! The putative logically possible reasons offered have tended to be *generic* and *global*: generic in so far as some *general* reason is sought to cover all sorts of evils; global in so far as they seize upon some feature of the world as a whole. For example, philosophers have alleged that the desire to make a world with one of the following properties—"the best of all possible worlds,"[10] "a world more perfect than which is impossible," "a world exhibiting a perfect balance of retributive justice,"[11] "a world with as favorable a balance of (created) moral good over moral evil as God can weakly actualize"[12]—would constitute a reason compatible with perfect goodness for God's creating a world with evils in the amounts and of the kinds found in the actual world. Moreover, such general reasons are presented as so powerful as to do away with any need to catalogue types of evils one by one, and examine God's reason for permitting each in particular. Plantinga explicitly hopes that the problem of horrendous evils can thus be solved without being squarely confronted.[13]

3.2. The Insufficiency of Global Defeat

A pair of distinctions is in order here: (i) between two dimensions of divine goodness in relation to creation—namely, "producer of global goods" and "goodness to" or "love of individual created persons"; and (ii) between the overbalance/defeat of evil by good on the global scale, and the overbalance/defeat of evil by good within the context of an individual person's life.[14] Correspondingly, we may separate two problems of evil parallel to the two sorts of goodness mentioned in (i).

In effect, generic and global approaches are directed to the first problem: they defend divine goodness along the first (global) dimension by suggesting logically possible strategies for the global defeat of evils. But establishing God's excellence as a producer of global goods does not automatically solve the second problem, especially in a world containing horrendous evils. For God cannot be said to be good or loving to any created persons the positive meaning of whose lives He allows to be engulfed in and/or defeated by evils—that is, individuals within whose lives horrendous evils remain undefeated. Yet, the only way unsupplemented global and generic approaches could have to explain the latter, would be by applying their general reasons-why to particular cases of horrendous suffering.

Unfortunately, such an exercise fails to give satisfaction. Suppose for the sake of argument that horrendous evil could be included in maximally perfect world orders; its being partially constitutive of such an order would assign it that generic and global positive meaning. But would knowledge of such a fact defeat for a mother the prima-facie reason provided by her cannibalism of her own infant to wish that she had never been born? Again, the aim of perfect retributive balance confers meaning on evils imposed. But would knowledge that the torturer was being tortured give the victim who broke down and turned traitor under pressure any more reason to think his/her life worth while? Would it not merely multiply reasons for the torturer to doubt that his/her life could turn out to be a good to him/her on the whole? Could the truck-driver who accidentally runs over his beloved child find consolation in the idea that this middle-known[15] but unintended side-effect was part of the price God accepted for a world with the best balance of moral good over moral evil he could get?

Not only does the application to horrors of such generic and global reasons for divine permission of evils fail to solve the second problem of evil;

it makes it worse by adding *generic prima-facie* reasons to doubt whether human life would be a great good to individual human beings in possible worlds where such divine motives were operative. For, taken in isolation and made to bear the weight of the whole explanation, such reasons-why draw a picture of divine indifference or even hostility to the human plight. Would the fact that God permitted horrors because they were constitutive means to His end of global perfection, or that He tolerated them because He could obtain that global end anyway, make the participant's life more tolerable, more worth living for him/her? Given radical human vulnerability to horrendous evils, the ease with which humans participate in them, whether as victim or perpetrator, would not the thought that God visits horrors on anyone who caused them, simply because he/she deserves it, provide one more reason to expect human life to be a nightmare?

Those willing to split the two problems of evil apart might adopt a divide-and-conquer strategy, by simply denying divine goodness along the second dimension. For example, many Christians do not believe that God will ensure an overwhelmingly good life to each and every person He creates. Some say the decisive defeat of evil with good is promised only within the lives of the obedient, who enter by the narrow gate. Some speculate that the elect may be few. Many recognize that the sufferings of this present life are as nothing compared to the hell of eternal torment, designed to defeat goodness with horrors within the lives of the damned.

Such a road can be consistently travelled only at the heavy toll of admitting that human life in worlds such as ours is a bad bet. Imagine (adapting Rawls's device) persons in a pre-original position, considering possible worlds containing managers of differing power, wisdom, and character, and subjects of varying fates. The question they are to answer about each world is whether they would willingly enter it as a human being, from behind a veil of ignorance as to which position they would occupy. Reason would, I submit, dictate a negative verdict for worlds whose omniscient and omnipotent manager permits ante-mortem horrors that remain unde-feated within the context of the human participant's life; *a fortiori*, for worlds in which some or most humans suffer eternal torment.

3.3. Inaccessible Reasons

So far, I have argued that generic and global solutions are at best incomplete: however well their account of divine motivating reasons deals with the first problem of evil, the attempt to extend it to the second fails by making it worse. This verdict might seem prima facie tolerable to standard generic and global approaches and indicative of only a minor modification in their strategy: let the above-mentioned generic and global reasons cover divine permission of non-horrendous evils, and find other *reasons* compatible with perfect goodness *why* even an omnipotent, omniscient God would permit horrors.

In my judgement, such an approach is hope-less. As Plantinga[16] points out, where horrendous evils are concerned, not only do we not know God's *actual* reason for permitting them; we cannot even *conceive* of any plausible candidate sort of rea-son consistent with worthwhile lives for human participants in them.

4. THE HOW OF GOD'S VICTORY

Up to now, my discussion has given the reader cause to wonder whose side I am on anyway. For I have insisted, with rebels like Ivan Karamazov and John Stuart Mill, on spotlighting the problem hor-rendous evils pose. Yet, I have signalled my prefer-ence for a version of Christianity that insists on both dimensions of divine goodness, and maintains not only (*a*) that God will be good enough to cre-ated persons to make human life a good bet, but also (*b*) that each created person will have a life that is a great good to him/her on the whole. My cri-tique of standard approaches to the problem of evil thus seems to reinforce atheologian Mackie's ver-dict of "positive irrationality" for such a religious position.

4.1. Whys versus Hows

The inaccessibility of reasons-why seems especially decisive. For surely an all-wise and all-powerful God, who loved each created person enough (*a*) to defeat any experienced horrors within the context of the participant's life, and (*b*) to give each created person a life that is a great good to him/her on the whole, would not permit such persons to suffer horrors for no reason.[17] Does not our inability even to conceive of plausible candidate reasons suffice to make belief in such a God positively irrational in a world containing horrors? In my judgement, it does not.

To be sure, motivating reasons come in several varieties relative to our conceptual grasp: There are (i) reasons of the sort we can readily understand when we are informed of them (e.g. the mother who permits her child to undergo painful heart sur-gery because it is the only humanly possible way to save its life). Moreover, there are (ii) reasons we would be cognitively, emotionally, and spiritually equipped to grasp if only we had a larger memory or wider attention span (analogy: I may be able to memorize small town street plans; memorizing the road networks of the entire country is a task requir-ing more of the same, in the way that proving Gödel's theorem is not). Some generic and global approaches insinuate that divine permission of evils has motivating reasons of this sort. Finally, there are (iii) reasons that we are cognitively, emotionally, and/or spiritually too immature to fathom (the way a two-year-old child is incapable of understanding its mother's reasons for permitting the surgery). I agree with Plantinga that our ignorance of divine reasons for permitting horrendous evils is not of types (i) or (ii), but of type (iii).

Nevertheless, if there are varieties of ignorance, there are also varieties of reassurance.[18] The two-year-old heart patient is convinced of its mother's love, not by her cognitively inaccessible reasons, but by her intimate care and presence through its painful experience. The story of Job suggests some-thing similar is true with human participation in horrendous suffering: God does not give Job His reasons-why, and implies that Job isn't smart enough to grasp them; rather Job is lectured on the extent of divine power, and sees God's goodness face to face! Likewise, I suggest, to exhibit the logical compossibility of both dimensions of divine goodness with horrendous suffering, it is not necessary to find logically possible reasons *why* God might permit them. It is enough to show *how* God can be good enough to created persons despite their participation in horrors—by defeating them within the context of the individual's life and by giving that individual a life that is a great good to him/her on the whole.

4.2. What Sort of Valuables?

In my opinion, the reasonableness of Christianity can be maintained in the face of horrendous evils only by drawing on resources of religious value theory. For one way for God to be *good to* created persons is by relating them appropriately to relevant and great goods. But philosophical and religious theories differ importantly on what valuables they admit into their ontology. Some maintain that "what you see is what you get," but nevertheless admit a wide range of valuables, from sensory pleasures, the beauty of nature and cultural artefacts, the joys of creativity, to loving personal intimacy. Others posit a transcendent good (e.g. the Form of the Good in Platonism, or God, the Supremely Valuable Object, in Christianity). In the spirit of Ivan Karamazov, I am convinced that the depth of horrific evil cannot be accurately estimated without recognizing it to be incommensurate with any package of merely non-transcendent goods and so unable to be balanced off, much less defeated, thereby.

Where the *internal* coherence of Christianity is the issue, however, it is fair to appeal to its own store of valuables. From a Christian point of view God is a being a greater than which cannot be conceived, a good incommensurate with both created goods and temporal evils. Likewise, the good of beatific, face-to-face intimacy with God is simply incommensurate with any merely non-transcendent goods or ills a person might experience. Thus, the good of beatific face-to-face intimacy with

God would *engulf* (in a sense analogous to Chisholmian balancing off) even the horrendous evils humans experience in this present life here below, and overcome any prima-facie reasons the individual had to doubt whether his/her life would or could be worth living.

4.3. Personal Meaning, Horrors Defeated

Engulfing personal horrors within the context of the participant's life would vouchsafe to that individual a life that was a great good to him/her on the whole. I am still inclined to think it would guarantee that immeasurable divine goodness to any person thus benefited. But there is good theological reason for Christians to believe that God would go further, beyond engulfment to defeat. For it is the nature of persons to look for meaning, both in their lives and in the world. Divine respect for and commitment to created personhood would drive God to make all those sufferings which threaten to destroy the positive meaning of a person's life meaningful through positive defeat.[19]

How could God do it? So far as I can see, only by integrating participation in horrendous evils into a person's relationship with God. Possible dimensions of integration are charted by Christian soteriology. I pause here to sketch three:[20] (i) First, because God in Christ participated in horrendous evil through His passion and death, human experience of horrors can be a means of *identifying* with Christ, either through *sympathetic* identification (in which each person suffers his/her own pains, but their similarity enables each to know what it is like for the other) or through *mystical* identification (in which the created person is supposed literally to experience a share of Christ's pain[21]). (ii) Julian of Norwich's description of heavenly welcome suggests the possible defeat of horrendous evil through divine gratitude. According to Julian, before the elect have a chance to thank God for all He has done for them, God will say, "Thank you for all your suffering, the suffering of your youth." She says that the creature's experience of divine gratitude will bring such full and unending joy as could not be merited by the whole sea of human pain and suffering throughout the ages.[22] (iii) A third idea identifies temporal suffering itself with a vision into the inner life of God, and can be developed several ways. Perhaps, contrary to medieval theology, God is not impassible, but rather has matched capacities for joy and for suffering. Perhaps, as the Heidelberg catechism suggests, God responds to human sin and the sufferings of Christ with an agony beyond human conception.[23] Alternatively, the inner life of God may be, strictly speaking and in and of itself, beyond both joy and sorrow. But, just as (according to Rudolf Otto) humans experience divine presence now as *tremendum* (with deep dread and anxiety), now as *fascinans* (with ineffable attraction), so perhaps our deepest suffering as much as our highest joys may themselves be direct visions into the inner life of God, imperfect but somehow less obscure in proportion to their intensity. And if a face-to-face vision of God is a good for humans incommensurate with any non-transcendent goods or ills, so any vision of God (including horrendous suffering) would have a good aspect in so far as it is a vision of God (even if it has an evil aspect in so far as it is horrendous suffering). For the most part, horrors are not recognized as experiences of God (any more than the city slicker recognizes his visual image of a brown patch as a vision of Beulah the cow in the distance). But, Christian mysticism might claim, at least from the post-mortem perspective of the beatific vision, such sufferings will be seen for what they were, and retrospectively no one will wish away any intimate encounters with God from his/her life-history in this world. The created person's experience of the beatific vision together with his/her knowledge that intimate divine presence stretched back over his/her ante-mortem life and reached down into the depths of his/her worst suffering, would provide retrospective comfort independent of comprehension of the reasons-why akin to the two-year-old's assurance of its mother's love. Taking this third approach. Christians would not need to commit themselves about what in any event we do not know: namely, whether we will (like the two-year-old) ever grow up enough to understand the reasons why God permits our participation in

horrendous evils. For by contrast with the best of earthly mothers, such divine intimacy is an incommensurate good and would cancel out for the creature any need to know why.

5. CONCLUSION

The worst evils demand to be defeated by the best goods. Horrendous evils can be overcome only by the goodness of God. Relative to human nature, participation in horrendous evils and loving intimacy with God are alike disproportionate: for the former threatens to engulf the good in an individual human life with evil, while the latter guarantees the reverse engulfment of evil by good. Relative to one another, there is also disproportion, because the good that God *is*, and intimate relationship with Him, is incommensurate with created goods and evils alike. Because intimacy with God so outscales relations (good or bad) with any creatures, integration into the human person's relationship with God confers significant meaning and positive value even on horrendous suffering. This result coheres with basic Christian intuition: that the powers of darkness are stronger than humans, but they are no match for God!

Standard generic and global solutions have for the most part tried to operate within the territory common to believer and unbeliever, within the confines of religion-neutral value theory. Many discussions reflect the hope that substitute attribute-analyses, candidate reasons-why, and/or defeaters could issue out of values shared by believers and unbelievers alike. And some virtually make this a requirement on an adequate solution. Mackie knew better how to distinguish the many charges that may be levelled against religion. Just as philosophers may or may not find the existence of God plausible, so they may be variously attracted or repelled by Christian values of grace and redemptive sacrifice. But agreement on truth-value is not necessary to consensus on internal consistency. My contention has been that it is not only legitimate, but, given horrendous evils, necessary for Christians to dip into their richer store of valuables to exhibit the consistency of (1) and (2).[24] I would go one step further: assuming the pragmatic and/or moral (I would prefer to say, broadly speaking, religious) importance of believing that (one's own) human life is worth living, the ability of Christianity to exhibit how this could be so despite human vulnerability to horrendous evil, constitutes a pragmatic/moral/religious consideration in its favour, relative to value schemes that do not.

To me, the most troublesome weakness in what I have said lies in the area of conceptual under-development. The contention that God suffered in Christ or that one person can experience another's pain requires detailed analysis and articulation in metaphysics and philosophy of mind. I have shouldered some of this burden elsewhere,[25] but its full discharge is well beyond the scope of this paper.

NOTES

In the development of these ideas, I am indebted to the members of our Fall 1987 seminar on the problem of evil at UCLA—especially to Robert Merrihew Adams (its co-leader) and to Keith De Rose, William Fitzpatrick, and Houston Smit. I am also grateful to the Very Rcvd. Jon Hart Olson for many conversations in mystical theology.

1. J. L. Mackie, "Evil and Omnipotence," *Mind*, 64 (1955) [Chapter 1 in this collection]; repr. in Nelson Pike (ed.), *God and Evil* (Englewood Cliffs, NJ: Prentice-Hall, 1964), 46–60.

2. Ibid. 47 [pp. 26–7, 37 above].

3. Marilyn McCord Adams, "Problems of Evil: More Advice to Christian Philosophers," *Faith and Philosophy* (Apr. 1988), 121–43.

4. Mackie, "Evil and Omnipotence," pp. 46–7 [p. 25 above], (emphasis mine).

5. Stewart Sutherland (in his comment "Horrendous Evils and the Goodness of God—II," *Proceedings of the Aristotelian Society*, suppl. vol. 63 (1989), 311–23; esp. 311) takes my criterion to be somehow "first-person." This was not my intention. My definition may be made more explicit as follows: an evil *e* is horrendous if and only if participation in *e* by person *p* gives everyone prima-facie reason to doubt whether *p*'s life can, given *p*'s participation in *e*, be a great good to *p* on the whole.

6. Roderick Chisholm, "The Defeat of Good and Evil" [Chapter III in this collection].

7. Cf. Malcolm's astonishment at Wittgenstein's dying exclamation that he had had a wonderful life, *Ludwig Wittgenstein: A Memoir* (London: Oxford University Press, 1962), 100.

8. Once again, more explicitly, most people would agree that a person *p*'s doing or suffering of them constitutes prima-facie reason to doubt whether *p*'s life can be, given such participation, a great good to *p* on the whole.

9. "Hume on Evil," *Philosophical Review*, 72 (1963), 180–97 [Chapter II in this collection]; reprinted in Pike (ed.), *God and Evil*, p. 88 [pp. 40–1 above].

10. Following Leibniz, Pike draws on this feature as part of what I have called his Epistemic Defence ("Problems of Evil: More Advice to Christian Philosophers," pp. 124–5).

11. Augustine, *On Free Choice of Will*, iii. 93–102, implies that there is a maximum value for created worlds, and a plurality of worlds that meet it. All of these contain rational free creatures; evils are foreseen but unintended side-effects of their creation. No matter what they choose, however, God can order their choices into a maximally perfect universe by establishing an order of retributive justice.

12. Plantinga takes this line in numerous discussions, in the course of answering Mackie's objection to the Free Will Defence, that God should have made sinless free creatures. Plantinga insists that, given incompatibilist freedom in creatures, God cannot strongly actualize any world He wants. It is logically possible that a world with evils in the amounts and of the kinds found in this world is the best that He could do, Plantinga argues, given His aim of getting some moral goodness in the world.

13. Alvin Plantinga, "Self-Profile," in James E. Tomberlin and Peter van Inwagen (eds.). *Profiles:*

Alvin Plantinga (Dordrecht, Boston, Mass., and Lancaster, Pa.: Reidel, 1985), 38.

14. I owe the second of these distinctions to a remark by Keith De Rose in our Fall 1987 seminar on the problem of evil at UCLA.

15. Middle knowledge, or knowledge of what is "in between" the actual and the possible, is the sort of knowledge of what a free creature *would do* in every situation in which that creature could possibly find himself. Following Luis de Molina and Francisco Suarez, Alvin Plantinga ascribes such knowledge to God, prior in the order of explanation to God's decision about which free creatures to actualize (in *The Nature of Necessity* (Oxford: Clarendon Press, 1974), pp. 164–93 [Chapter V in this collection]). Robert Merrihew Adams challenges this idea in his article "Middle Knowledge and the Problem of Evil," *American Philosophical Quarterly*, 14 (1977) [Chapter VI in this collection]; repr. in *The Virtue of Faith* (New York: Oxford University Press, 1987), 77–93.

16. Alvin Plantinga, "Self-Profile," pp. 34–5.

17. This point was made by William Fitzpatrick in our Fall 1987 seminar on the problem of evil at UCLA.

18. Contrary to what Sutherland suggests ("Horrendous Evils," pp. 314–15), so far as the compossibility problem is concerned, I intend no illicit shift from reason to emotion. My point is that intimacy with a loving other is a good, participation in which can defeat evils, and so provide everyone with reason to think a person's life can be a great good to his/her on the whole, despite his/her participation in evils.

19. Note, once again, contrary to what Sutherland suggests ("Horrendous Evils," pp. 321–3) "horrendous evil *e* is defeated" entails *none* of the following propositions: "*e* was not horrendous," "*e* was not unjust," "*e* was not so bad after all." Nor does my suggestion that even horrendous evils can be defeated by a great enough (because incommensurate and uncreated) good, in any way impugn the reliability of our moral intuitions about injustice, cold-bloodedness, or horror. The judgement that participation in *e* constitutes

prima-facie reason to believe that *p*'s life is ruined, stands and remains a daunting measure of *e*'s horror.

20. In my paper "Redemptive Suffering: A Christian Solution to the Problem of Evil," in Robert Audi and William J. Wainwright (eds.). *Rationality, Religious Belief, and Moral Commitment: New Essays in Philosophy of Religion* (Cornell University Pres., 1986), 248–67, I sketch how horrendous suffering can be meaningful by being made a vehicle of divine redemption for victim, perpetrator, and onlooker, and thus an occasion of the victim's collaboration with God. In "Separation and Reversal in Luke-Acts," in Thomas Morris (ed.), *Philosophy and the Christian Faith* (Notre Dame, Ind.: Notre Dame University Press, 1988), 92–117, I attempted to chart the redemptive plot-line whereby horrendous sufferings are made meaningful by being woven into the divine redemptive plot. My considered opinion is that such collaboration would be too strenuous for the human condition were it not to be supplemented by a more explicit and beatific divine intimacy.

21. For example, Julian of Norwich tells us that she prayed for and received the latter (*Revelations of Divine Love*, ch. 17). Mother Theresa of Calcutta seems to construe Matthew 25: 31–46 to mean that the poorest and the least *are* Christ, and that their sufferings *are* Christ's (Malcolm Muggeridge, *Something Beautiful for God* [New York; Harper & Row, 1960], 72–5).

22. *Revelations of Divine Love*, ch. 14. I am grateful to Houston Smit for recognizing this scenario of Julian's as a case of Chisholmian defeat.

23. Cf. Plantinga, "Self-Profile," p. 36.

24. I develop this point at some length in "Problems of Evil: More Advice to Christian Philosophers," pp. 127–35.

25. For example in "The Metaphysics of the Incarnation in Some Fourteenth Century Franciscans," in William A. Frank and Girard J. Etzkorn (eds.), *Essays Honoring Allan B. Walter* (St. Bonaventure, NY: The Franciscan Institute, 1985), 21–57.

15

Suffering as Religious Experience

LAURA WADDELL EKSTROM

Laura Waddell Ekstrom (1966–) is professor of philosophy at the College of William and Mary, specializing primarily in ethics and agency theory. In this article, Ekstrom argues that some instances of suffering might reasonably be viewed as religious experiences that serve as a means of intimacy with God. Thus, whereas atheologians typically take suffering as evidence against the existence of God, Ekstrom argues that it might in fact be a route to knowledge of God.

INTRODUCTION

Works of literature, accounts of human history, and the events of everyday life confront us directly with the reality of pain and suffering. Some of us of a melancholy (some might say morbid) disposition are overcome with worry over this reality. Light-hearted neighbors and friends perplex us. How do they carry on so, trimming their yards and enjoying the weather, all the while maintaining faith in a perfect and provident Lord of the universe? Is it out of callousness, shallowness, blessedness, or wisdom? Have they any dark nights of the soul or anguish over the cries and shed blood of their fellow creatures? The worry leads some of us to academic study of the problem of evil. But our answers are incomplete and fail fully to satisfy. O God, where are you through the violent violation of a woman? Why tarry when a child falls feverish and is ripped from life too soon? Why still your hand through war, betrayal, and pain?

Yet through our own suffering, confusion and bitterness may take a startling turn. Job's heartrending cries of injustice against the Almighty become the breathtaking utterance, "My ears had heard of you but now my eyes have seen you."[1] In his suffering, Job reports, he has met God. God has shown himself, made himself known to the sufferer. The philosopher Nicholas Wolterstorff gives something of a similar account in his report of a vision of God. As we strain to discern an explanation for divine permission of suffering, "instead of hearing an answer," Wolterstorff writes, "we catch sight of God himself scraped and torn." He attests: "Through the prism of my tears I have seen a suffering God."[2] God is seen, God is known, in suffering.

The aim of this paper is to explore the idea of suffering as a kind of religious experience. It is argued by David Hume, William Rowe, and Paul Draper, among others, that pain and suffering constitute evidence against the existence of God.[3] But perhaps at least some such instances of pain and suffering are, rather, avenues to knowledge of God. Many individuals, Wolterstorff and Job among them, report that the times during which they have suffered the most deeply are the occasions of the most vivid of whatever glimpses they have been given into the character of God. The experiences are marked, that is, by intimacy with the divine. Is not precisely this the mark of (at least one

Reprinted from Peter van Inwagen, ed., *Christian Faith and the Problem of Evil* (Grand Rapids, MI: Wm. B. Eerdmans, 2009), pp. 95–110. Used by permission of Wm. B. Eerdmans.

important type of) religious experience? And is not suffering as a means to intimacy with God exactly what one would expect of a God who, on Christian scripture and tradition, took on human form and suffered along with and for the world?[4]

Understanding some instances of human suffering as means to intimacy with the divine makes available a line of partial theodicy distinct from the traditional soul-making, punishment, and free will theodicies. I call it the *divine intimacy theodicy*. The theodicy is suggested to an extent in the work of such contemporary philosophers as Marilyn Adams, Nicholas Wolterstorff, and Eleonore Stump, as well as in the writings of many Christian mystics of the medieval and later periods, including, for instance, Therese of Lisieux (1873–1897).[5] Why would the divine agent permit instances of evil? Perhaps a reply applicable to some instances of personal suffering is this: in order to provide occasions in which we can perceive God, understand him to some degree, know him, even meet him directly. In this essay I explore the plausibility of this line of thought.[6]

THE NATURE OF RELIGIOUS EXPERIENCE

Religious experience is variously characterized. Rudolf Otto (1869–1937) describes it as experience in which the soul is "held speechless, trembles inwardly to the farthest fiber of its being," as it faces something so forceful and overwhelming that one feels oneself to be "dust and ashes as against majesty." The experience is one of "fear and trembling" but also of "wonderfulness and rapture."[7] The Christian mystic Teresa of Avila (1515–1582) reports an experience in which the mystic is

> conscious of having been most delectably wounded.... [The soul] complains to its Spouse with words of love, and even cries aloud, being unable to help itself, for it realizes that he is present but will not manifest himself in such a way as to allow it to enjoy him, and this is a great grief, though a sweet and delectable one.... So powerful is the

effect of this upon the soul that it becomes consumed with desire, yet cannot think what to ask, so clearly conscious is it of the presence of God.[8]

John of the Cross (1542–1591) describes experience in which the understanding of the soul "is now moved and informed by ... the supernatural light of God, and has been changed into the divine, for its understanding and that of God are now both one."[9]

One way of understanding religious experience is on analogy with sensory experience of the physical world. One might say that religious experience is experience of the divine by way of some perceptual faculties, perhaps including a special spiritual faculty or a *sensus divinitatus*. So as not to beg any questions concerning the veridicality of the experience, religious experience might be defined more cautiously as experience that the agent *takes to be* of the divine: experience perceived by the perceiver as acquaintance or intimacy with God. William Alston, for instance, understands religious experience as "(putative) direct awareness of God."[10]

I propose to understand the category of religious experience rather broadly. I consider the term "religious experience" to apply appropriately to at least the following three types of experience. First, a religious experience may be an experience in which it seems to one that one perceives God. Examples include a vision of divinity, a sense of God's presence during prayer or worship, and a feeling of God's nearness and comfort. Such experiences are regularly had by some theists. But an atheist may have them as well, as in Paul's experience on the road to Damascus.

Second, the category of religious experience includes experiences *like* those of God—experiences of the same sort as God's own experiences. In the Christian tradition, we could describe religious experience of the second sort as experience like that of one of the three persons comprising God. Or perhaps, so as not to beg any questions, we should describe the second type of religious experience as experience like what God would experience were God to exist with a nature as depicted by Christian scripture and tradition.

Third, an experience counts as a religious experience if it brings to consciousness the issue of God's nature and existence and makes vivid one's own attitude regarding this issue. Religious experiences of the third sort may include, for example, experience showing us ugly, horrifying or frightening aspects of the world; experience of our own capacity for evil; and experience of our frailty. Such experiences tend to bring to mind questions concerning the existence of God, as well as questions concerning the goodness, power, and knowledge of God. Religious experiences of the third type also include experiences carrying a sense of awe or wonder, such as witnessing the birth of a child or feeling moved by the beauty of a natural scene: the vista from a mountaintop or a seashore, for example.

Each of these types of experience has a legitimate claim to being religious in character. Consider an atheist who was raised in a religious family. She might sensibly describe her observations of pervasive poverty and disease during a visit to India as a *religious experience*: the experience raised vividly for her the problem of evil and occasioned her realization that she had become an atheist. A theist's sense of the majestic presence of God during worship is religious experience of a different (the first) sort: it is experience in which one is putatively aware of God. Further, insofar as it makes sense to describe experience like an eagle's (say, soaring above the rooftops) as *avian experience*, and insofar as it makes sense to describe experiences of running, jumping, and playing with toys *childhood experience*, so too there seems room for counting experiences similar to those of the divine being—if there is any—*religious experience*.

WHY COUNT SUFFERING AS RELIGIOUS EXPERIENCE?

Is it plausible to suppose that some instances of suffering qualify as religious experiences as characterized above? Testimonial evidence supports the claim that instances of suffering are sometimes instances of religious experience of the first type: experience in which it seems to the perceiver that he or she is

aware of the presence of God. Consider, as one example, the divine vision recounted by Julian of Norwich in the midst of suffering a severe illness for which she had received last rites: "At once I saw the red blood trickling down under the garland, hot, fresh, and plentiful, just as it did at the time of his passion when the crown of thorns was pressed on to the blessed head of God-and-Man.... And I had a strong, deep, conviction that it was he himself,"[11] She reports of the divine being: "I saw that he is to us everything which is good and comforting for our help. He is our clothing, who wraps and enfolds us for love, embraces us and shelters us, surrounds us for his love."[12] Many individuals in sorrow and pain have reported a vision of the divine or a feeling of God's nearness and comfort in their distress.

It is likewise reasonable to consider some occasions of suffering as religious experiences of the third type: experiences that vividly raise fundamental religious questions and illuminate one's commitments regarding them. One's becoming the victim of a crime, for instance, or suffering a debilitating physical injury, commonly brings to one's mind the question of God's existence and nature. The experience of hardship is often a sort of testing experience in which one "shows one's true colors," demonstrating one's deepest commitments. Suffering is a religious experience of the third sort in driving us to seek God or in causing doubt, reinforcing unbelief, or in generating questions concerning God's nature and existence.

I would like to focus more attention on the notion that some instances of suffering qualify as religious experience of the second type: experiences *like* those of God.

Suppose that, as on traditional Christian doctrine, God created persons in order for them to love and to be intimate with him and to glorify him forever. Suppose that persons were once in a state of intimacy with God, but that we rebelled by choice, with the consequence that we suffer physical and emotional pain, as well as the spiritual pain of being out of harmony with the Creator. Suppose that God enacted a plan for reestablishing our harmony with him involving his taking on human form and suffering rejection, torture, and execution.

From the perspective of one who adopts this account, some human suffering may be viewed, in fact, as a kind of privilege, in that it allows us to share in some of the experiences of God and thus gives us a window into understanding his nature. Some instances of suffering are avenues for intimacy, oneness, with God. One cannot love what one does not know, and one means of knowing someone is to have experience like hers. Naturally we feel affinity toward and grow to understand and to cherish other persons with experiences similar to our own. These include educational, career, and family experiences, but also experiences of illness and adversity. A person whose experiences are quite different from one's own is difficult for one to come deeply to understand and fully to appreciate. Shared experiences facilitate dialogue in providing something in common about which to converse, and they make possible understanding that is beyond words, communicated perhaps with understanding looks or gestures. The parent of an ill newborn knows something about the other parents in the emergency room without their exchanging any words. Lovers become intimate through sharing experiences. Victims of a similar sort of oppression or injustice understand each other in a way that outsiders to their experience cannot.

For the Christian, then, instances of suffering can be occasions for identification with the person of Jesus Christ. Intimacy with Christ gained through suffering provides deeper appreciation of his passion.[13] I understand the notion of *identification with Christ* in a sympathetic rather than a mystical sense: the claim is not that the sufferer bears Christ's *actual* sufferings, as, first, it is unclear what the point of that bearing would be and, second, the mystical view would seem to require quite peculiar views concerning pain. Rather, I mean to suggest that the sufferer may sympathetically identify with Christ in sharing similar experience, as any other two persons identify with each other in the loose sense that they connect with, appreciate, or understand each other better when they share experiences of the same type or similar types.

Several objections immediately arise. The first is that this aspect of the theodicy is so thoroughgoingly

Christian. Since I accept the truth of orthodox Christian doctrine, this objection is from my perspective otiose. But to widen the appeal of the theodicy, we can set aside reference to the person of Christ and understand suffering as experience like that of God, like that of the divine being, if we join Wolterstorff and others in affirming, against tradition, that God is not impassible but is, rather, a God who suffers. Suppose, for instance, that God grieves over human sin. Then in feeling deep sorrow over the neglect and abuse of children, and in having regret and disapproval over the poverty and arrogance in our world, a person may have experience *like* God's and so may have a glimpse into the divine nature. An individual's own sorrow and suffering may, then, be a means to understanding and having intimacy with the divine being.

DIVINE PASSIBILITY

On the traditional conception of the divine nature, God is not affected by anything and so cannot suffer.[14] The doctrine of impassibility is defended primarily by appeal to philosophical considerations, including reflection on the natures of perfection, immutability, and transcendence. But the doctrine of divine impassibility has been recently criticized by a number of philosophers, including Alvin Plantinga, Charles Hartshore, Charles Taliaferro, Kelly James Clark, Nicholas Wolterstorff, and Richard Swinburne. Like Wolterstorff's avowal of a suffering God, Plantinga, for instance, affirms the existence of a God who "enters into and shares our suffering." Plantinga writes: "Some theologians claim that God cannot suffer. I believe they are wrong. God's capacity for suffering, I believe, is proportional to his greatness; it exceeds our capacity for suffering in the same measure as his capacity for knowledge exceeds ours."[15]

Of the considerations in favor of rejecting divine impassibility, the most salient from my perspective are the scriptural evidence and the natures of goodness and love. Many biblical passages depict God as experiencing emotions that entail suffering. Consider the following: "The LORD was grieved that he had made man on the earth, and his heart was filled with pain" (Gen. 6:6). "I have seen these people, the LORD said to Moses, and they are a stiff-necked people. Now leave me alone so that my anger may burn against them and that I may destroy them" (Exod. 32:9–10). The writer of Psalm 78 describes how the Israelites "grieved [God] ... they vexed the Holy One of Israel" (41–42) and speaks of God's "wrath, indignation and hostility" (49). Consider, as well: "Praise be to the Lord, to God our Savior, who daily bears our burdens" (Ps. 68:19).

Impassibilists dismiss such passages as mere anthropomorphism. Commenting on Genesis 6:6, for example, John Calvin writes:

> Since we cannot comprehend [God] as he is, it is necessary that, for our sake, he should, in a certain sense, transform himself.... Certainly God is not sorrowful or sad; but remains forever like himself in his celestial and happy repose; yet because it could not otherwise be known how great is God's hatred and detestation of sin, therefore the spirit accommodates himself to our capacity.... God was so offended by the atrocious wickedness of men, [he speaks] as if they had wounded his heart with mortal grief.[16]

According to Calvin, God permits biblical writers to use figures of speech about himself in accommodation to humanity's limited capacities of understanding. Given interpretive differences, the impassibility issue cannot be settled, of course, simply by citing biblical material. Nonetheless, a passibilist conception of God, it must be admitted, fits most naturally with the scriptural account of God's activities and involvement with human beings. The impassibilist must explain away or reinterpret numerous passages that, on their face, suggest that God is affected by and suffers over his creation.

On the traditional conception of the divine agent, God is not only omnipotent and omniscient, but also wholly good and perfectly loving. A number of philosophers, including Wolterstorff and Taliaferro, have registered their rejection of the Greek-influenced medieval conception of divine

love as non-suffering benevolence. The argument is that apathy, unperturbed emotional indifference to the plight of humanity, is incompatible with God's love of humanity.

Here is why the incompatibility claim seems right. Suppose that we understand love, rather uncontroversially, as consisting in or at least essentially involving concern for the well-being or flourishing of a beloved object. This understanding of love applies equally to love of a cause or of an ideal or of a person, but I am concerned particularly with love of persons. In his recent work on love, Harry Frankfurt adds that the lover's concern for the beloved is disinterested, in the sense that the good of the beloved is desired by the lover for its own sake rather than for the sake of promoting any other interests.[17] Frankfurt emphasizes that lovers are not merely concerned for the interests of their beloveds; further, they *identify* the interests of the beloveds as their own.[18] And he argues that if the lover "comes to believe that his beloved is not flourishing, then it is unavoidable that this causes him harm."[19] Lack of flourishing in the beloved, by the nature of love, causes harm in the lover.

Of course, it could be claimed that this account applies only to instances of human love and not to divine love. But the move appears *ad hoc*. If love of someone consists in or essentially involves concern for her well-being, then it involves valuing, or having concerned approval for, her flourishing and disvaluing, or having concerned disapproval for, her harm. To say that I love my daughter, yet that I experience no sorrow, grief, or passion of any kind at her pain or disgrace, stretches the concept of love beyond comprehensibility. Furthermore, since one can love something only insofar as one is acquainted with it, it would seem that God cannot love us fully without knowing us fully. But our being fully known requires acquaintance on the part of the knower with our suffering and with the evil in our world.[20] Thus, reflection on the nature of love supports the conception of a God who suffers.

Further support for the passibility of God comes from the consideration of the nature of goodness. A morally good being grieves over evil. In a recent book offering an extended defense of the traditional doctrine of divine impassibility,[21] Richard Creel argues in part that it serves no *purpose* to attribute suffering to God, as God may act out of love and justice without being sorrowful. But to the contrary, we question the goodness of an agent who acts correctly towards victims of crime or disease, yet wholly without sorrow or empathy for the persons served. Passibilism, Creel argues, makes God worthy of our pity rather than our worship. But a great moral character, one worthy of worship, shows itself great in part by its sorrow, what it sorrows over and to what degree. Noble sorrow at witnessing a tragic occurrence is a good. Hence it would seem that God's goodness and love include sorrow, as well as joy, over the world. This sorrow is arguably not a defect, but a strength or an asset, a part of being supremely good.

Taliaferro understands divine sorrow as "concerned disapproval." "God disapproves of our cruelty and malice," he writes, "God cares about our failures, and this concerned disapproval may rightly be counted as an instance of sorrow."[22] Consider, for instance, Miriam's rape. Taliaferro writes: "Part of what it means to be sorrowful here is that you do disapprove of it, the harming of someone who matters to you, and you disapprove of this profoundly. Any tenable notion of the goodness of the God of Christian theism must include the supposition that God exercises profound, concerned disapproval of creaturely ills."[23] It does seem reasonable to suppose that the God who is love, the God who is perfectly good, is deeply concerned for persons and suffers profound sorrow over their sins and afflictions. It is facile to presume oneself too sophisticated to go in for such supposed "sentimentalism." Proponents of the divine impassibility doctrine must defend it further against substantive religious and moral reasons for concluding that God suffers.

OBJECTIONS: PATHOLOGY, CRUELTY, AND INEFFICACY

In this section, I consider four central objections to a divine intimacy theodicy. The first, which I will address only briefly, comes from the direction of one unconvinced of the passibility of God. I have suggested that there is reason to think that God does suffer, provided by scripture and by reflection on the natures of goodness and love. But should the considerations in favor of the attribute of impassibility prove in the end more powerful, the divine intimacy theodicy is not thereby defeated. If suffering cannot be religious experience in the sense of being experience like that of God himself, it can qualify still as religious experience of the first and third sorts, and thus it can be justified as a means to intimacy with the divine. Furthermore, should traditional impassibilism survive recent attacks. Christian theism can yet make sense of suffering as experience shared with the person of Jesus Christ and so can count some occasions of suffering as avenues to intimacy with God through sympathetic identification with Christ.

A second and potentially more damaging objection is this: To view suffering as religious experience is evidence of a personality disturbance or psychological disorder. That is, it seems to indicate not right thinking but pathology that a person would glory in suffering or see spiritual dimensions to pain. The objection gains force from considering the physical conditions of the lives of some Christian mystics of the medieval and later periods who viewed suffering in such a manner. For instance, the Cistercian nun Beatrice of Nazareth (1200–1268), the author of *The Seven Manners of Love*, is reported to have deprived herself of food, worn uncomfortable garments, scourged herself, and slept on thorns.[24] Other religious figures may strike us as melodramatic and distressingly passive in their welcoming attitudes toward suffering. Consider the remarks of Therese of Lisieux concerning the onset of symptoms of the tuberculosis that took her life at the age of twenty-four:

Oh! how sweet this memory really is! After remaining at the Tomb until midnight, I returned to our cell, but I had scarcely laid my head upon the pillow when I felt something like a bubbling stream mounting to my lips. I didn't know what it was, but I thought that perhaps I was going to die and my soul was flooded with joy. However, as our lamp was extinguished, I told myself I would have to wait until the morning to be certain of my good fortune, for it seemed to me that it was blood I had coughed up. The morning was not long in coming; upon awakening, I thought immediately of the joyful thing that I had to learn, and so I went over to the window. I was able to see that I was not mistaken. Ah! my soul was filled with a great consolation; I was interiorly persuaded that Jesus, on the anniversary of his own death, wanted to have me hear his first call. It was like a sweet and distant murmur that announced the Bridegroom's arrival.[25]

Therese welcomes the blood in her cough as the answer to her prayer that God consume her with his love, that God carry her to him quickly, and that she be allowed to share in the suffering of Christ. She declares in her "Act of Oblation to Merciful Love":

I thank you, O my God! for all the graces you have granted me, especially the grace of making me pass through the crucible of suffering. It is with joy I shall contemplate you on the last day carrying the scepter of your cross. Since you deigned to give me a share in this very precious cross, I hope in heaven to resemble you and to see shining in my glorified body the sacred stigmata of your passion.[26]

In light of such passages, it may strike one as at best wishful thinking and, worse, indicative of a psychiatric condition, to believe that God is with one or is providing one intimacy with himself through suffering.

But of course those who report experience of supernatural phenomena are notoriously subject to the charge of being delusional. And certainly adopting the proposed partial theodicy need not lead one to self-mutilation or to other eccentric or damaging behaviors. The view under consideration is perfectly consistent with a mandate to *alleviate*

suffering so far as possible and with a mandate not to self-impose pain. Furthermore, which views indicate spiritual insight and which indicate a condition in need of medical or psychological treatment is a matter of opinion. As it stands, the objection from pathology amounts to no more than the claim that it seems to the objector that the proposed view is crazy or, in other words, false. Without any further positive reasons to doubt the sanity of the proponent of the divine intimacy theodicy, other than that she believes the view, the objection is dismissible.

The objector might respond by pointing to such factors as social isolation, inadequate sleep, poor nutrition, and lack of medical care in the lives of some religious mystics. These circumstances, it may be argued, indicate that the view of suffering as religious experience is pathological and not reasonable. Yet surely these considerations are inconclusive. Recall C. D. Broad's remark that a person "might need to be slightly 'cracked' in order to have some peep-holes into the super-sensible world."[27] Difficult living conditions might in fact facilitate spiritual insight. Furthermore, a charge of insanity against every adherent to a divine intimacy theodicy is grandiose.

A third objection is an objection from cruelty. Why would a loving God create such a cruel way of our getting to know him? Why would suffering as a *means* to knowing God be preferable to direct divine self-revelation? Since permitting suffering is a cruel way of fostering intimacy, the objection goes, the perfect being would not be justified in this permission and so the account of suffering as religious experience fails as a partial theodicy.

It is surely troubling to conceive of God as declaring to created beings in a tone of sinister delight, "Suffer, and then I will let you know me," as if enduring a crucible of suffering were a passkey. But this image inaccurately reflects the divine intimacy theodicy. A perfect being does not, of course, delight over suffering, but rather causes or allows it when it is necessary to bringing about a greater good or preventing a worse evil. And the suggestion I am exploring is that, perhaps, some occasions of suffering are necessary for certain individuals' coming to love of and intimacy with God. The objector may counter that some persons experience God in moments of great joy and beauty. Yet this may be true while it is also true that other persons' paths to God are paths through suffering. And it may be that the good thereby achieved could not be achieved in any other way: namely, the profound good of appreciation for and intimacy with a loving and suffering God.

The objector might be troubled with the question of why God would not simply show himself at all times, to everyone. Here the right line of response may be that for God to directly, constantly, and obviously manifest his presence would be coercive.[28] Perhaps God's remaining somewhat hidden protects our freedom, preserving our independence of thought and action. The rationale behind divine hiddenness may be something like this: I (the divine agent) will not intervene in the natural course of events to prevent your difficulties and your suffering, in part because perhaps then you will appreciate the ways in which I have loved and provided for you all along; perhaps you will freely come to recognize that acting wholly by your own lights is unsuccessful and that you need my help; perhaps you will be rid of some of your arrogance and will recognize your limitations. Suffering, that is, may be for some persons the most effective non-coercive means to achieving the end of love of and intimacy with God. Additionally, it may be that it is impossible fully to know God without personally experiencing suffering, because God himself suffers. If God is passible in emotion, then there is something that a person could not know about God if she did not suffer, one aspect of God's being that would remain entirely mysterious.

The fourth and final objection I will consider is this: a common reaction to suffering is not a sense of intimacy with the divine but rather confusion and rejection of God's existence. Suffering is easily interpreted as evidence that God does not exist or does not care about the sufferer. Hence, many cases of suffering, particularly those of non-theists, cannot plausibly be construed as religious experience.

In response, first, the divine intimacy theodicy is not designed to apply to all cases of suffering.

Second, from the fact that some persons reject the existence of God on the basis of suffering, it does not follow that some occasions of suffering do not provide an *opportunity* for intimacy with God. We can choose, it seems, the manner in which we respond to suffering, including which types of attitudes we adopt in the midst of it. The thesis at issue is not that meaning *is* always found in suffering by everyone who suffers, but rather that a certain kind of meaning *can* be found in suffering, through divine intimacy.

Suffering might be religious experience without the sufferer recognizing it as such. This claim seems unproblematic, since a person can have an experience of a certain type without ever recognizing it as an experience of that type. Consider the following examples. First, suppose that Keith thinks that he is devising a novel line of reasoning. But in fact he is remembering a conversation in which someone else recounted a certain line of thought. Keith is having a memory experience, but he does not, and need not ever, recognize it as such. Second, suppose that Sandra begins thinking about chance and providence. Although she need not ever recognize the experience as such, she may be having a telepathic experience of the thoughts of Peter, who is across the room. Third, imagine a husband who begins to have indigestion, headaches, and back pain during the pregnancy of his wife. He consults his doctor, who finds his symptoms mysterious. He is, perhaps, having an empathic experience without realizing it. The concept of a religious experience, unrecognized as such, appears cogent.

CONCLUSION

A full justificatory account of suffering may be unattainable for us. I have simply sketched here and begun to explore the suggestion that one justifying reason for certain instances of suffering is that those occasions constitute religious experiences. Some cases of suffering may be viewed as kinds of experience that can bring a person closer to God, such that the good either in or resulting from them is intimacy with the divine agent.

The account of suffering as religious experience may have use not only as a partial theodicy, but also as a method for the theist for dealing with the existential problem of evil. That is, one way of enduring unchangeable occasions of pain and suffering may be to adopt an attitude of acceptance and, oddly, enjoyment in identifying with God. Consider how this might work, in particular, for a Christian theist. One in the midst of dealing with a deep betrayal of loyalty, for instance, might call to mind the thought, "As I have been rejected, Christ was rejected even by his close friend, Peter," and take comfort in the sympathetic identification. Likewise, although perhaps Christ never experienced precisely the particular physical pain from which one suffers, the sufferer is in part able to appreciate something about the person of Christ that perhaps not all others fully can: the sacrifice of his passion.[29]

NOTES

1. Job 42:5.

2. Nicholas Wolterstorff, *Lament for a Son* (Grand Rapids: Eerdmans Publishing Co., 1987), pp. 80–81.

3. David Hume, *Dialogues Concerning Natural Religion*, ed. Richard Popkin (Indianapolis: Hackett, 1980); William Rowe, "The Problem of Evil and Some Varieties of Atheism," *American Philosophical Quarterly* 16 (1979): 335–41; Paul Draper, "Pain and Pleasure: An Evidential Problem for Theists," *Noûs* 23 (1989).

4. According to orthodox Christian tradition, the person of Jesus Christ suffered for us, yet God the Father is not capable of suffering.

5. Marilyn McCord Adams, "Redemptive Suffering: A Christian Solution to the Problem of Evil," *in Rationality, Religious Belief, and Moral Commitment*, ed. Robert Audi and William J. Wainwright (Ithaca, N.Y.: Cornell University Press, 1986), and "Horrendous Evils and the Goodness of God," *Proceedings of the Aristotelian Society*, supplementary vol. 63 (1989), pp. 297–310; Wolterstorff, *Lament for a Son*, and "Suffering Love," in *Philosophy and the Christian Faith*, ed. Thomas V. Morris (Notre Dame, Ind.: University of Notre Dame Press, 1988); Eleonore Stump, *Faith and the Problem of Evil: The Stob Lectures, 1998–99* (Grand Rapids: The Stob Lectures Endowment, 1999), and "The Mirror of Evil," in *God and the Philosophers*, ed. Thomas V. Morris (New York: Oxford University Press, 1994), pp. 235–47, and "The Problem of Evil," *Faith and Philosophy* 2:4 (1985): 392–418.

6. The divine intimacy theodicy most likely has some measure of plausibility only when applied to human suffering and not to the suffering of non-human animals. Nonetheless, the matter is open in the absence of conclusive information concerning the capacities of members of other species.

7. Rudolf Otto, *The Idea of the Holy* (London: Oxford University Press, 1936), pp. 17–26, 31–33.

8. *The Interior Castle*, trans. and ed. E. Allison Peers (Garden City, N.Y.: Doubleday Image, 1961), pp. 135–36.

9. *The Living Flame of Love*, trans. and ed. E. Allison Peers (Garden City, N.Y.: Doubleday Image, 1962), p. 78.

10. William Alston, *Perceiving God: The Epistemology of Religious Experience* (Ithaca, N.Y.: Cornell University Press, 1991), p. 35.

11. Julian of Norwich, *Revelations of Divine Love* (New York: Penguin Books, 1984), p. 66.

12. Julian of Norwich, Long Text 5, quoted in *Enduring Grace: Living Portraits of Seven Women Mystics* (New York: HarperCollins, 1993), p. 88.

13. Marilyn McCord Adams similarly suggests that instances of suffering, even horrendous ones, might be made *meaningful* by being integrated into the sufferer's relationship with God through identification with Christ, understood either as sympathetic identification (in which each person suffers her own pain, enabling her to understand something of Christ's suffering) or as mystical identification (in which the human sufferer literally experiences a share of Christ's pain). Alternately, Adams suggests, meaningfulness may derive from suffering serving as a vision into the inner life of God, either because God is not impassible, or because the sheer intensity of the experience gives

one a glimpse of what it is like to be beyond joy and sorrow. She proposes, as well, that sufferings might be made meaningful through defeat by divine gratitude which, when expressed by God in the afterlife, gives one full and unending joy. "Horrendous Evils and the Goodness of God," *Proceedings of the Aristotelian Society*, supplementary vol. 63 (1989), pp. 297–310; reprinted in *The Problem of Evil*, ed. Marilyn McCord Adams and Robert Merrihew Adams (New York: Oxford University Press, 1990), pp. 209–21.

14. The Westminster Confession of Faith (II.1) states: "There is but one ... true God, who is infinite in being and perfection, a most pure spirit, invisible, without body, parts, or passions. ..."

15. "Self-Profile," in *Alvin Plantinga*, ed. James E. Tomberlin and Peter van Inwagen (Dordrecht: D. Reidel, 1985), p. 36.

16. *Calvin's Commentaries*, vol. 1, trans, and ed. John Owen (Grand Rapids: Baker Book House, 1979), p. 249.

17. Harry Frankfurt, "On Caring," in *Necessity, Volition, and Love* (Cambridge: Cambridge University Press, 1999), p. 165.

18. Frankfurt, "On Caring," p. 168.

19. Frankfurt, "On Caring," p. 170.

20. Cf. Nicholas Wolterstorff, "Suffering Love," in *Philosophy and the Christian Faith*, ed. Thomas V. Morris (Notre Dame, Ind.: University of Notre Dame Press, 1988), p. 223.

21. Richard E. Creel, *Divine Impassibility* (Cambridge: Cambridge University Press, 1986).

22. Charles Taliaferro, "The Passibility of God," *Religious Studies*, vol. 25: 220.

23. Taliaferro, "Passibility," p. 220.

24. *Women Mystics in Medieval Europe*, ed. Emilie Zum Brunn and Georgette Epiney-Burgard, trans. Sheila Hughes (New York: Paragon House, 1989), p. 72.

25. *Story of a Soul: The Autobiography of St. Therese of Lisieux*, trans. John Clarke O.C.D. (Washington, D.C.: ICS Publications, 1996), pp. 210–11.

26. *Story of a Soul*, p. 277.

27. C. D. Broad, "Arguments for the Existence of God. II," *Journal of Theological Studies* 40 (1939): 164.

28. Michael J. Murray, "Coercion and the Hiddenness of God," *American Philosophical Quarterly* 30 (1993): 27–38.

29. I am grateful to Michael Murray and Kelly James Clark for comments on an earlier version of this essay.

16

Deus Absconditus

MICHAEL J. MURRAY

Michael J. Murray (1963–) is currently the Executive Vice President of the John Templeton Foundation. Previously he was professor of philosophy at Franklin and Marshall College. He works primarily in the fields of philosophy of religion and history of modern philosophy. In this article he offers

Reprinted from *Divine Hiddenness: New Essays*, ed. by Daniel Howard-Snyder and Paul K. Moser. Copyright © 2002 Cambridge University Press.

a critique of J. L. Schellenberg's argument from divine hiddenness to atheism, defending the conclusion that divine hiddenness is often necessary for allowing God's creatures to retain the freedom that is required for soul-making.

> Awake, O Lord! Why do you sleep?
> Rouse yourself! Do not reject us forever.
> Why do you hide your face?
>
> Psalm 44:23-4

It is no surprise to discover that few (if any) have found the existence of God to be an obvious fact about the world. At least this is so in the sense in which we normally use the word "obvious," as when we say that it is *obvious* that the World Trade Center weighs more than a deck of cards or that it is *obvious* that Van Gogh is a better painter than I. Despite St. Paul's claim that God's eternal power and divine nature "have been clearly seen, being understood from what has been made" (Romans 1:20), few (if any) think that such is as "clearly seen" as the book you now hold in your hand.

This fact has raised troubles of at least two sorts for the theist. First, it leads the theist to wonder why God postpones that time at which, according to Christian tradition, we will see God "face to face." Since, at that time, God *will* be as clearly seen as the book you now hold in your hand, what accounts for the delay? Why is there this period of the earthly life where God's reality is less than obvious? Second, the theist has to confront the fact that God's hiddenness seems to lead a number of people to reject God's existence outright and thus to be a contributing cause to what the traditional theist would regard as a great evil: unbelief. For some, the route to atheism is indeed found in the fact that there is, in the famous words of Bertrand Russell, "not enough evidence." But more recently, some have argued that the hiddenness of God provides positive, in fact decisive, evidence in favor of atheism. J. L. Schellenberg, in a recent work, argues that if the God of Western theism exists he would provide evidence of this fact sufficient to render reasonable unbelief impossible. Since, however, such evidence is not forthcoming, such a God does not exist.

Theists in the Judeo-Christian tradition have often argued that the hiddenness of God finds its explanation in the Fall and subsequent Curse. Sometimes the passage immediately following the one from St. Paul's epistle to the Romans cited above is taken as evidence that hiddenness should be explained in just this way, at least for the Christian, since Paul there goes on to claim that "For although they knew God, they neither glorified Him as God nor gave thanks to Him, but their thinking became futile and their foolish hearts were darkened" (Romans 1:21). Yet, while the Fall may play some part in explaining the hiddenness of God, the Judeo-Christian theist would be hard pressed to lay the full explanation for hiddenness here. The reason is simply that the Judeo-Christian Scriptures seem to teach that even prior to the Curse, there is a measure of divine hiddenness already. Even in Genesis 3, one finds that Adam and Eve think that they can somehow escape the presence of God by hiding from God in the garden (Genesis 3:8-10). Although it is Adam and Eve that do the hiding here, still the presence of God, while still obvious to them in a certain sense, is escapable in a way it seems not to be when one looks at descriptions of the beatified state as described, for example, in Revelation 22:1-5. In what follows I will offer an account of divine hiddenness that attempts to allay the two types of concerns raised above.

I. DIVINE HIDDENNESS AND "MORALLY SIGNIFICANT FREEDOM"

In an earlier essay I argued that at least one of the reasons that God must remain hidden is that failing to do so would lead to a loss of morally significant freedom on the part of creatures.[1] The reason, in brief, is that making us powerfully aware of the truth of God's existence would suffice to coerce (at least many of) us into behaving in accordance with God's moral commands. Such awareness can lead to this simply because God's presence would provide us with overpowering incentives which would make choosing the good ineluctable for us.

I will flesh out this account in some detail below, but before doing so, let's take notice of the overall strategy being pursued here. Theists have often argued that morally significant freedom is a good (indeed, a very good) thing. Thus, in creating the world, God would seek to establish conditions that would permit the existence of such freedom. A variety of such conditions are necessary, but among them is that there not be overwhelmingly powerful incentives present in the environment which consistently coerce or otherwise force creatures to follow a particular course of action.

Theists have, at least of late, lain a great deal of explanatory weight on the need to preserve creaturely freedom. Here I will attempt to lay the explanation of divine hiddenness there. Others have sought to lay the explanation for all (or at least much) of the evil that the world contains there as well. In such cases, the argument is roughly that morally significant freedom is an intrinsic good, and that though evil is a necessary consequence of allowing creatures to have freedom of such a sort, the intrinsic goodness of freedom outweighs evils liabilities.[2] The evil in question might not only be of the (moral) sort that we read about in the headlines of the newspaper, but of the (epistemic) sort in view in this essay, namely, the unbelief of great numbers of people due to the lack of evidence entailed by God's hiddenness.

But there is something odd about laying all this freight at freedom's doorstep; and it is an oddity that seems to be too little noticed by analytic Christian philosophers. We can begin to see what is odd by first noticing that it is not the intrinsic goodness of libertarian freedom *simpliciter* that is at issue here. For if it were, it seems that libertarian freedom simply could not do the work it has been given to do in these accounts. The reason for this is that there seems to be no reason why God could not create a world with libertarian free beings who are incapable of doing evil. If human minds were created in such a way that they were not, say, even capable of deliberating about evil courses of action, it might

still be the case that multiple courses of action would be open to them given the history of the world and the laws of nature. No doubt, this would restrict the kinds of behavior that such creatures could engage in (assuming that it must be possible for one to deliberate about a course of action for one to be able to freely choose it). But God surely restricts the sorts of activities we can choose to undertake in all sorts of ways by not only limiting the kinds of things we can think about (by, say, limiting the sorts of cognitive equipment we have), but even by limiting the kinds of things we are physically capable of accomplishing (by limiting the sorts of bodily equipment we have). It is hard to see why similar constraints could not simply preclude deliberation about evil courses of action, while stopping short of full blown determinism. If this is right, libertarian freedom *simpliciter* cannot explain or justify the existence of evil.

It is, then, libertarian freedom *to choose between good and evil courses of action* that is important here. And the theist might argue that this is just what was meant by "morally significant freedom" in the first place. Without the ability to choose freely between good and evil courses of action, freedom would have no moral significance and thus would not be an intrinsic good.[3] What is odd about this story, however, is just how rare this supposed intrinsic good is among rational beings on the Christian scheme of things. For if we consider the sorts of rational beings Christians admit to being aware of, it seems that only one type of being has freedom of this sort, and beings of this type possess it only for an infinitesimally small span of their existence. Traditional Christian theology holds that neither God, angels, nor demons have such freedom, and that of human beings, neither beatified nor damned have it either. Thus, freedom of this sort is found only among human beings during that narrow span of their existence spent in the earthly life.

All of this seems to argue that morally significant freedom of the sort described above might not be best regarded as the intrinsic good many have claimed it to be. If it is such a good, it would be odd, to say the least, that neither God, angels, nor the beatified possess it.

We might, however, look at the worth of morally significant freedom in creatures in another way. Reflecting on the rarity of such freedom as it is described above leads to the question: Why does God allow creatures to pass through this earthly phase of existence in the first place? Since all rational creatures will end up either perfected in the beatific vision, choosing good forever, or separated from God, choosing evil forever, why have them pass through this prior stage during which they stand poised between these two extremes?

When posed this way, I think an answer readily suggests itself, namely, that the function of this earthly life, a time during which we are capable of making free choices between morally good and evil courses of action, is to have the opportunity to develop morally significant characters. Developing characters which have moral significance requires that they be chosen and cultivated by their bearers. And this can only be done if creatures are first given the sort of morally significant freedom we have been discussing heretofore. Philosophers have taken to calling this sort of character development "soul-making," following the phrase coined by John Hick.[4] Thus, we might say that the function of the earthly life on this view is soul-making, and that a necessary condition for soul-making is morally significant libertarian freedom. Libertarian freedom alone simply will not do here since the point of character development is that one has the opportunity to choose to do *good* or *evil*, and by so choosing to become either a lover and imitator of God, or one who "worships and serves the creature rather than the creator."[5]

Thus, even if we have reason to doubt the *intrinsic* worth of morally significant freedom, there is good reason to think that it has significant *instrumental* value as a necessary condition for rational creatures engaging in soul-making. Of course, possessing the capacity for morally significant soul-making is not sufficient. In addition, external constraints on the agent must not preclude the possibility of the agent at least frequently being able to choose freely between good and evil courses of action. What I was claiming above is that among those conditions is the absence of circumstances which provide overwhelming incentives for creatures

to choose only good or only evil. For if the moral environment contained such incentives, the creature with the capacity to choose freely would be precluded from exercising that ability and thus blocked from engaging in the sort of soul-making that makes freedom (and the earthly life) valuable in the first place.

The result of all this is that God must remain hidden to a certain extent to prevent precluding incentives from being introduced. Here then we find an answer to the first concern regarding hiddenness. At least one reason why we do not see God face to face from the beginning is that to do so would be to lose the ability to develop morally significant characters. According to the Christian scriptures, God calls his creatures to be "imitators" of him.[6] But to do this in a way that yields moral significance requires that character be to some extent self-wrought.[7] And soul-making of this sort requires divine hiddenness, at least for a time.

As mentioned above, J. L. Schellenberg has offered an argument for atheism on the basis of divine hiddenness. Along the way, Schellenberg critiques a variety of accounts of hiddenness a theist might offer, including a soul-making account of the sort sketched above. In what follows I will develop this account in more detail against the background of and in response to this critique of Schellenberg's.

II. SCHELLENBERG'S CRITIQUE OF THE SOUL-MAKING RESPONSE

In his wonderfully provocative book, *Divine Hiddenness and Human Reason,* J. L. Schellenberg has presented an extended argument that the extent to which evidence for the existence God is not forthcoming, in conjunction with certain other plausible assumptions, entails the truth of atheism. This argument, which I will call "The Atheist Argument," is presented by Schellenberg as follows:

(1) If there is a God, he is perfectly loving.

(2) If a perfectly loving God exists, reasonable nonbelief does not occur.

(3) Reasonable nonbelief does occur.

(4) No perfectly loving God exists.

(5) There is no God.[8]

After an extended presentation and defense of the argument and its premises in the first half of the book, Schellenberg goes on, in the second half, to discuss various responses theists might lodge against its premises. Specifically, he focuses on theistic critiques of premise (2) since, he argues, only this premise of the argument is open to question. In this section I will examine Schellenberg's critique of the soul-making account and argue that his critique ultimately fails. As a result, the theist has plausible grounds for rejecting (2) and thus for rejecting The Atheist Argument.

Preliminary Considerations

Because Schellenberg recognizes that most theists will want to take issue with (2), he begins his survey of potential theistic responses by discussing what it is that the theist must show in order to defeat the premise. He contends that,

> (2) is false if and only if there is a state of affairs in the actual world which it would be logically impossible for God to bring about without permitting the occurrence of at least one instance of reasonable non-belief, for the sake of which God would be willing to sacrifice the good of belief and all it entails.[9]

As noted above, the second half of the book is devoted to explaining and critiquing various theistic attempts to provide accounts which attack (2) in just the way Schellenberg suggests. The first such attempt roughly mirrors the account described at the end of Section I. On this view, the state of affairs that God wants to actualize which logically requires him to permit some instances of reasonable unbelief consists of (i) creatures who have the capacity for acting freely and (ii) a world suitably constituted for the exercise of that freedom. On this view, if God were to make his existence evident to too great an extent, an extent that would

rule out reasonable non-belief, we would all become powerfully aware of the importance of not only believing in His existence but also obeying His will. Yet such a powerful awareness of God's existence and moral will would suffice to overwhelm the freedom of the creature in a way that would preclude further morally significant free actions by the creature. Because it would be utterly obvious to us that God, the one responsible for temporal happiness as well as eternal bliss or damnation, exists and wills that we act in certain ways, we would be compelled to believe and act accordingly. As a result, God must keep His existence veiled to a certain extent in order to insure that this sort of overwhelming does not occur.

To know whether or not such a claim is plausible, we first need to know whether God's revealing himself in the way Schellenberg thinks he would (and in fact *must* given the fact that God is a perfectly loving being) could lead to such a result.

It is noteworthy that Schellenberg has only argued that God's loving nature entails that God would make his *existence* known to creatures in such a way that reasonable unbelief is not possible. Schellenberg makes no claims about whether or not God's loving nature would also require that God make known the existence of other facts that might be necessary for human beings to be able to attain ultimate human fulfillment. In one sense, this minimalist strategy helps Schellenberg, since one might think that if God simply made his *existence* clearly known, there is no reason to think that this would introduce any incentives that might serve to derail human freedom. Bare knowledge that God exists simply doesn't seem to have any immediate practical import.

One might, of course, agree that God would make his existence plainly known, but might further argue that God's loving nature further entails that other facts would be made known as well. Many theists claim that ultimate human fulfillment requires not only belief in God, but a number of other beliefs about what it takes to be rightly related to God as well. If loving entails seeking the well-being of the beloved, God would surely seek to make the necessary information for human fulfillment available. As a result, I will assume for the moment (as I think all parties in the dispute must) that, all other things being equal, God's love would lead him to make us aware not merely of his bare existence, but also of all of the other truths needed to obtain our complete temporal and eternal happiness. Surely such a revelation would carry significant practical import. Nonetheless, for those who want to stick to Schellenberg's more minimalist strategy, I will return to address that view shortly.

III. THE SOUL-MAKING RESPONSE TO (2)

Given my more robust notion of what divine love entails, we can see why there might be good reason for God to remain hidden on the soul-making account. At the end of Section I I noted that introduction of powerful motives to choose either only good or only evil would preclude the possibility of soul-making. Instead, the environment needs to be such that there are, at least in a number of cases, incentives to choose to do good and incentives to choose to do evil, such that neither incentive induces desires that overwhelm all competing desires.

Yet surely a probabilifying demonstration or revelation of God's existence and plan for human well-being as described above would introduce just such incentives. If God were to reveal Himself and His will in the way required to eliminate reasonable nonbelief, any desire that we might have to believe or act in ways contrary to that which has been revealed would be overwhelmed. Our fear of punishment, or at least our fear of the prospect of missing out on a very great good, would compel us to believe the things that God has revealed and to act in accordance with them. But in doing this, God would have removed the ability for self-determination since there are no longer good and evil courses of action between which creatures could freely and deliberately choose. Thus we would all be compelled to choose in accordance with the divine will and would all thereby become conformed to the divine image.

However, a character wrought in this fashion would not be one for which we are responsible since it does not derive from morally significant choosing. It has instead been forced upon us. Richard Swinburne, defending a position regarding divine hiddenness summarizes these considerations in the following paragraph, also quoted by Schellenberg:

> The existence of God would be for [human beings] an item of evident common knowledge. Knowing that there was a God, men would know that their most secret thoughts and actions were known to God; and knowing that he was just, they would expect for their bad actions and thoughts whatever punishment was just.... In such a world men would have little temptation to do wrong—it would be the mark of both prudence and reason to do what was virtuous. Yet a man only has a genuine choice of destiny if he has reasons for pursuing either good or evil courses of action.[10]

Schellenberg emphasizes that on this view, desires for evil would not cease to exist were we to be given such a revelation, it is just that powerful new desires would be introduced, e.g., the desire to avoid punishment, with a strength that overwhelms contrary desires and renders them "inefficacious." He cites coercion as a similar case in which the introduction of a new desire renders all competing desires inefficacious. I may desire, says Schellenberg, to go to the university bookstore to buy a copy of a newly released book. Yet, if some crazy ideologue, bent on keeping scholars from being exposed to the ideas in the book, threatens me with serious physical harm if I go to the bookstore, I won't go. My desire to go is still present, but this desire has been overwhelmed by a newly introduced desire, the desire to avoid the serious physical harm.

Schellenberg thus summarizes the soul-making case against (2) of the Atheist Argument as follows:

(16) In the situation in question [that is, where God reveals himself in such powerful fashion

that reasonable unbelief is rendered impossible], persons would have strong prudential reasons for not doing wrong.

(17) Because of the strength of these reasons, it would require little in the way of an act of will to do what is right—there is little temptation to do wrong, contrary desires would be overcome.

(18) Where there is little temptation to do wrong, persons lack a genuine choice of destiny.

(19) Therefore, in the situation in question no one would have a choice of destiny.[11]

IV. INCENTIVES, COERCION, AND ''SOUL-MAKING''

The remainder of this chapter in Schellenberg's book is occupied with an assessment of (16) through (19). Here Schellenberg contends that there are good reasons to reject both (16) and (17). Before looking at his criticisms of these premises however, it will prove worthwhile to try to fill in a few more details in this argument. How exactly, one might wonder, would probabilifying knowledge of God's existence and will for human creatures influence our desires? What does it take for desires to be sufficiently strong to overwhelm competing desires? How does this overwhelming prevent our ability to engage in self-determination exactly? Answering these questions will help us both to understand the force of Schellenberg's critique of (16) and (17) and to see what, if anything, can be said in reply.

Recall that on the soul-making account the trouble that arises in a world in which God is not to some extent hidden is that incentives are introduced which serve to *coerce* otherwise free creatures, in ways which render them incapable of soul-making. Thus, if God were to make himself plainly evident to us in the ways described above, we would find ourselves confronted with what would amount to threats (if God were to reveal disobedience as subject to punishment) or offers (if God were to

reveal obedience as a source of temporal and eternal well-being) that would suffice to coerce human behavior.[12] In what follows I will speak generally about the ways in which God's revealing himself in perspicuous fashion can introduce "incentives" which can "overwhelm" competing desires. One can think of such incentives as consisting of either threats or offers, though I will frequently use examples drawn from cases of coercion via threats.

It should be obvious that not just any incentives will suffice to overwhelm our desires for contrary courses of action. The incentive must be sufficiently strong that it outweighs the desires I have for those things which are inconsistent with acting in accordance with it. Let's say that a desired course of action, A_1, renders competing desired courses of action, A_2-A_n, *ineligible* when A_1 is sufficiently compelling that it makes it impossible for me reasonably to choose A_2-A_n over A_1.[13] We can then say that an individual, P, is *coerced* to do some act, A, by a threat when a desire is induced by a threat, which desire is sufficiently compelling that it renders every other course of action except A ineligible for P.[14]

This next leads us to wonder what it is that makes desires induced by threats "sufficiently compelling." One might think that the only relevant variable is the *strength* of the threat, i.e., the degree to which the state of affairs that the threatener is promising to bring about (if the conditions of the threat are not met) are disutile for the threatened in comparison with the disutility of performing the act commanded by the threatener. Thus if a stranger threatens to call me a ninny if I fail to hand over my money to her, this threat would not compel me in the least since I am not a bit concerned about being called a name by this stranger and I would like to keep my money. On the other hand, if someone threatens to shoot me in the leg if I fail to give her my money, I would surely give her the money since I care a great deal about my bodily integrity, far more than keeping the few dollars I carry with me.

However, a moment's reflection should make it clear that threat strength alone does not determine whether or not a desire induced by a threat is sufficiently compelling to coerce me. To see why this is so, compare the following two cases. In the first case, a maximum security prison assigns one guard to each prisoner and gives the guards orders to shoot all who attempt to escape. Here the threat strength is very high. Thus, one can suppose that prisoners in such a situation would find all courses of action which include an attempted escape ineligible. In the second case, prisoners are again being watched by guards who have orders to shoot any who attempt to escape. However, in this case, there are only two guards on duty for the entire prison at anyone time, and they are perched high in a tower. While the threat strength is identical for prisoners in both prisons, it seems clear that prisoners in the latter case might find an escape attempt eligible. The reason for this difference, presumably, is that the prisoners in the second case might believe that the probability that the threat could be successfully carried out is quite low. The guards, the prisoner might reason, might be too busy watching other prisoners to notice an attempted escape, or they might miss when shooting from such a great distance. In any case, the prisoner's belief that the threat cannot be successfully carried out significantly mitigates the compelling force of the desire induced by the threat. Thus, in addition to threat strength, another factor, which I call *threat imminence,* is relevant. We can define threat imminence as the degree to which the threatened believes the consequences of the threat will be successfully carried out if the terms of the threat are not met.

But notice that there is more than one way that threats can be imminent or distant as I have characterized imminence. While the sort of imminence described above, which I will call *probabilistic imminence,* is one species of imminence, there are at least two others. First, there is *temporal imminence.* When the threatened understands that there will be a significant lapse between the time that he fails to meet the conditions of the threat and the time that the threat is carried out, the desire induced by the threat is less compelling than when the consequences will follow immediately upon the failure to meet the conditions. Thus, if someone was to threaten to give me a powerful shock that would

hospitalize me for two weeks if I failed to hand over my money immediately, this situation would be more compelling than one in which a threatener threatened to poke me with a delayed-reaction cattle prod which would cause me to receive the same shocking sensation fifty years hence, if I failed to hand over my money now. Even though the threat strength is the same, and even though I might have an equal degree of certainty that the threat will be carried out in both cases, I am less compelled by the threat in the latter case than I am in the former.

The final species of threat imminence is *epistemic imminence.* We might say that epistemic imminence is the degree to which the disutility of the threatened consequence is *epistemically forceful* to the threatened. To illustrate the role of epistemic imminence consider the fact that massive advertising campaigns against smoking, drug use, and drinking and driving have been successful in reducing the incidence of these behaviors. In all three cases, no one believes that the purpose of such advertisements is to convey information to the target audience that members of that audience do not already have. Instead, the goal is to make the disutility of engaging in that behavior more epistemically powerful. By repeatedly showing accident scenes strewn with dead or mangled bodies, people become more powerfully aware of how dangerous drinking and driving is.

Yet even these two factors, threat strength and threat imminence, are not sufficient to determine the degree to which threat-induced desires are compelling. This should be clear from the fact that two individuals, in circumstances where threat strength and threat imminence are identical for each, might feel differently about the eligibility of their alternatives. Two prisoners might find themselves under threats of identical strength and imminence and yet one might feel that an escape attempt is still eligible while another may not. One might simply feel that a probability of .5 that he will be shot is a risk too great to bear, whereas the other might think that the same probability makes for a "good bet." This factor, which I will call *threat-indifference,* is the third factor determining the strength of the compelling force of a threat. Some individuals are simply more threat-indifferent than others. Threat-indifference can be described in two ways. One might say that threat-indifference is the degree to which one finds pleasure in taking the risks posed by failing to abide by conditions of a threat. It might also be described as a sense of indifference to one's own well-being in the face of a threat. However we characterize this trait, it is surely relevant since something like it is needed to explain why, when two individuals are in the same circumstances, one is coerced while the other is not.

In sum, there are at least three factors which determine the degree to which a threat-induced desire is compelling: threat strength, threat imminence, and threat-indifference. The degree to which the desire compels me to act in accordance with the threat is directly proportional to the first two and inversely proportional to the third.

V. AN ASSESSMENT OF SCHELLENBERG'S CRITIQUE OF (16) AND (17)

With this in mind, let us return to Schellenberg's critique of (16) and (17) and see to what extent they are successful. Schellenberg raises two problems for (16) and I will treat each in turn. First, he charges that the only way in which probabilifying revelations of God's existence and moral will could provide strong prudential reasons for not doing wrong, is if the knowledge acquired as a result of this revelation were *certain*.

> The situation referred to [by Swinburne] is ... one in which humans know for *certain* that there is a God and in which whatever reasons humans take themselves to have for doing good actions they consider themselves *certainly* to have. A situation in which the evidence available is [merely] sufficient for belief ... is, however, not of this sort.... In any case, given evidence [merely] sufficient for belief instead of proof, one who is under the influence of

desires for what is "correctly believed to be evil" is likely to seize upon the margin of possible error: believing, but not certain of God's existence, or of punishment, she may well move, through self-deception, from the belief that God exists and will punish bad actions to [other beliefs which deny at least one of the two conjuncts].... If self-deception *is* still open to individuals, then clearly they are still in a position to yield to bad desires and so retain a genuine choice of destiny.[15]

Schellenberg holds here that unless we know with *certainty* that a threatener (God in this case) exists and will carry out the threat, we cannot be coerced, since it is always open to us to deceive ourselves about the truth of propositions we know less than certainly. As a result, it is false that these probabilifying revelations would suffice to provide the recipient of the revelation with strong prudential reasons for not doing evil (and correspondingly, with overwhelming incentives), since one can always reappropriate ones beliefs in such a way as to eliminate these strong prudential reasons.

But is this true? We might recast Schellenberg's point as the claim that probabilistic threat imminence must be maximal if a threat is to be sufficient to coerce. But clearly that is false. Consider a case in which someone comes up behind me late at night in Manhattan, sticks a small cylindrical object in my back, and demands that I hand over my money or be shot. I do not know with *certainty* that this threat can be carried out. There is some non-zero probability that, even if this mugger has a gun, he also has an overridingly strong aversion to shooting people. Furthermore, there is some non-zero probability that the cylinder I feel in my back is not a gun but a carrot. One might suppose there is even some non-zero probability that someone has surgically inserted a bullet-proof vest under my skin in my infancy that would, in this case, prevent me from being harmed by this mugger. And yet, while all of these things have some non-zero probability, none of these things matter in the least. Even if I thought there was only a .5 probability that the mugger would carry through on his threat, *I* would be coerced into handing over the money.

And something similar holds in the case under discussion here. Even if I do not know with certainty that God exists or that He will bring temporal and/or eternal punishments on me if I fail to believe or act in certain ways, I can still be coerced into acting or believing in those ways. This is not to deny that if probabilistic threat imminence falls below a certain point that I will not be coerced by the threat. Still, the sort of probabilifying revelation that critics of theism such as Schellenberg have in mind would insure that probabilistic threat imminence would remain above this threshold.

However, Schellenberg has one further problem with (16), a problem which also amounts to his only substantive critique of (17). He seems to think that even if the probabilistic imminence problem is soluble, there is an additional problem concerning temporal imminence that is not. The recipient of the clear and evident revelation will believe, he claims, that the punishments attending failure to believe or act in a certain way will be either temporal, eternal, or both. That is, the divine retribution may be meted out immediately, or it may be postponed to the after-life (in hell, say), or both. However, if punishments are *only* eternal, and, he claims, our experience surely teaches us that this, if anything, is the case,[16] we again find that threats of such punishment would fail to produce strong prudential reasons for not doing wrong, against (16). Furthermore, Schellenberg contends, in his only significant argument against (17), that even if such strong prudential reasons were to arise, they could easily be ignored or shoved willfully into the background of our deliberation. As a result, it is false that the desires to do evil would be overwhelmed:

> Human beings, it seems, might very well conceive of God as justly lenient in the moment of desire, and of punishment as, at worst, an afterlife affair, and hence find themselves in a situation of temptation [to engage in evil] after all.... As soon as punishment is pushed off into the future,

rendered less immediate and concrete, the force of any desires I may have to *avoid* punishment is reduced.... If punishment is seen as something in the future, its deterrent effect must be greatly reduced ... I suggest therefore, that it is only if an individual believes that God's policy of punishment implies that a failure to do good actions will in the *here and now* result in bodily harm or loss of life, that the motivating effect of his belief can plausibly be viewed as great.[17]

No doubt what Schellenberg is pointing to here is the role of temporal imminence in coercion. Greater temporal imminence translates into greater compelling force of the threat.

The adequacy of this criticism depends on how we answer two questions. First, is Schellenberg correct in his contention that the recipient of these probabilifying revelations would come to believe that the punishment for wrong-doing was ultimately to be meted out in eternity alone? If not, then his argument that one would not be coerced by such revelation due to the great temporal distance between performing the evil action and the punishment inflicted for it fails. Second, is it true that if punishment were to be meted out solely in eternity the temporal distance between performing the bad action and receiving the punishment would be great enough to mitigate the force of the threat and leave the creature free for soul-making? If so, then despite the fact that the "threat" will not be carried out until later, the creature will still be left with multiple eligible courses of action, and these will be sufficient to allow him or her to engage in soul-making.

It seems to me that the answer to the first question is certainly no and the answer to the second question is probably also no. Schellenberg argues that even if we were to believe, initially, that punishments for wrongdoing would be forthcoming immediately after an evil act is committed, experience would cure us of this error. Looking at others, or ourselves, it is obvious that there are a number of evils that we "get away with." And this may seem enough to make his point. But is it? Even if there are some evil acts for which we receive no temporal punishment (that we know of), all the theist must hold is that *on some occasions* we believe that evil-doing is met with temporal punishments. That alone can provide sufficient probabilistic imminence to yield coercion. Consider again the case of the mugger discussed above. Let's say that I know that during the recent rise in muggings, police have determined that only half of the muggers in fact have guns, guns which they inevitably use if the victim resists. The other half try to mug victims using mere water pistols. It does not at all seem implausible that this knowledge would make me any less coerced when a mugger approaches me and asks for my money. What this shows is that even if we agree with Schellenberg that experience shows us that negative temporal consequences do not *inevitably* follow our evil acts, our belief that such negative consequences *sometimes* follow evil acts can suffice for coercion.[18]

Furthermore, while it is admittedly true that reducing temporal imminence reduces the compelling force of a threat, it seems unlikely that pushing the threat of punishment for wrong-doing off into the afterlife in this case will suffice for mitigating its coercive force. The first reason for this is that, at least on the traditional Christian view, the punishment described in eternity is so great in magnitude and duration, viz., maximal and eternal, that the temporal distance suggested by the average human life span seems unlikely to mitigate the coercive force of the threat to any great degree. This reply gains even more force when one realizes that, while one's life span may be some seventy or so years, a given life might continue only for a few more minutes or hours. As a result, it is unreasonable to assume that the coercive force of the threat is mitigated by the fact that the punishment will not be realized for some number of years since, for all we know, it might be realized in the twinkling of an eye. We might liken the recipient of this probabilifying revelation to a victim of an extortion attempt who is told, "If you fail to carry out the plan, we will kill you. You never know when—maybe when you least expect it. But sometime, one of us will hunt you down and finish you off." The victim here might assume that it will take them a long time

to track him down and so he might refuse to comply. But since the recipient of this threat is unsure how long it will take for the threateners to find him, it is likely that a threat of this sort would nonetheless be coercive, and that is all we really need here. If many people, or even some people, would find a threat of this sort coercive, and the threat implied by the "clear and evident revelation" Schellenberg describes is of this sort, this seems to provide God with good reason for remaining hidden.[19]

At the end of Section II I noted that Schellenberg's official line of argument is that God's love entails that God would make his existence known to creatures. There I argued further that similar considerations should lead us to think that God's love equally entails that God would also reveal to creatures facts relevant to their achieving human flourishing, especially when those facts are accessible only via revelation. Let's call these two positions respectively the weaker and the stronger positions (weaker not being used pejoratively here, but merely to indicate that Schellenberg makes weaker claims concerning what God's love entails about what God would reveal about himself).

Note that while Schellenberg commits himself only to the weaker position, he is, as the discussion in this section makes clear, more than willing to dispute with those who hold the stronger view.[20] Throughout this section we have seen since not everyone will have this high degree of threat indifference, we should not expect revelations of high epistemic imminence to be the norm. This gives the theist good reason for denying that God would produce grand scale theophanies complete with parting clouds, lightening bolts and thunder claps, where God proclaims His existence, etc. to all of the worlds inhabitants. The variability of threat indifference across human beings just would not permit *this* sort of business. Still God might make His existence evident to everyone in more subtle ways, ways that mitigate the *epistemic imminence* of the threat involved and thus mitigate the coercive force of the attending threat.

There is, however, an important response available to the defender of the argument from hiddenness at this point.[21] At most, the argument

I give above shows that we should not expect grand public theophanies to be common. But that does not prevent God from making his existence known to creatures by way of private religious experience. In fact, a glance at the recent literature in philosophy of religion would lead one to think that this is the way religious believers in fact come into cognitive contact with God in the first place. Wouldn't it at least be reasonable to expect that God would make his existence as evident to each creature as it could be via religious experience, tailoring the epistemic imminence to the threat indifference of each creature so as not to coerce him or her? Nothing said above seems to preclude this. And yet, the defender of the argument from hiddenness could claim, this expectation is frustrated as well. For surely, each individual is not the recipient of this sort of religious experience.

This is an interesting and important response, one that deserves a more extensive treatment than I can give it here. A complete response would require a separate essay, I will only attempt to sketch an outline of a response here.[22]

To respond to the "private revelation" view in detail, we would first have to know a bit more about how its advocate understands religious experience. While much of this is contested territory, I propose that we regard religious experience, like sensory experience, as beginning with a perceiver coming to be in a state of directly perceiving some state of affairs, a state which provides the perceiver with *grounds* for coming to hold certain dispositional or occurrent beliefs. But being in possession of the grounds and forming beliefs on those grounds are two distinct perceptual moments. Even in ordinary cases of sensory experience, we are in possession of grounds which are sufficient to lead suitably disposed perceivers to form a variety of beliefs. The process of forming beliefs upon being in possession of certain perceptual grounds is one which is in turn dependent on other dispositions had by the perceiver. And there is little doubt that at least some of these dispositions are under the perceiver's direct or indirect voluntary control.

Thus I can train myself to form true beliefs about the species of plant I am perceiving by

forming dispositions that lead me to have certain beliefs when I come to be in possession of certain grounds (these might be visual, tactile, or olfactory sensory grounds). In doing so I have indirect voluntary control over my belief-forming capacities. Likewise I can exercise direct voluntary control over belief-forming dispositions when I, for example, will myself to be more attentive to my surroundings. When I am told that I need to be careful of poisonous snakes in an area where I am hiking, I can voluntarily heighten my awareness, making me more apt to form beliefs about the presence of snakes than I would be if I were oblivious to the danger.

In the case of religious experience, God can provide the perceiver with certain religious experiential grounds, but whether those grounds will suffice to form true beliefs, or any beliefs at all, will depend in at least some measure on whether or not the perceiver has disposed himself to rightly forming beliefs on the basis of those grounds. It is a significant part of the Christian story of the Fall that one place where we would expect creatures to be especially self-deceived is with respect to whether or not one is properly disposed to form beliefs on the basis of religious experiential grounds. As a result, one should be especially wary when advocates of the "private revelation" view contend that it is obvious that not everyone is the recipient of clear religious experiences.

Schellenberg's final point is an attack on (18). This premise holds that "where there is little temptation to do wrong, persons lack a genuine choice of destiny." Schellenberg points out this is false since even in a world in which there is no temptation to do evil, one is still able to choose between merely doing the obligatory and doing the supererogatory. And this alone should be sufficient for soul-making.

Schellenberg argues here, as others have against this sort of theodicy, that evil is not in fact a necessary condition for soul-making. Is Schellenberg right that the distinction between obligatory and supererogatory acts pulls the rug out from under (18) and, by extension, we might assume, soul-making theodicies in general. I hold that it does not, at least for the Christian theist, because I am inclined to think that the Christian should not endorse the distinction between obligatory and supererogatory acts. One might reasonably hold that the ethical import of Christ's teaching had as a consequence that the supererogatory is, for the Christian, obligatory!

> But I tell you, do not resist an evil person. If someone strikes you on the right cheek, turn to him the other also. And if someone wants to sue you and take your tunic, let him have your cloak as well. If someone forces you to go one mile, go with him two miles.[23]

While this view has some strange consequences, there are not as many such consequences as one might think. However, further discussion or defense of this view would require a separate treatment.

VII. CONCLUSIONS

From this we can conclude that the argument set forth in (16) – (19) stands. Schellenberg's attacks on (16) through (18) seem to fail once we take into account those factors that determine the way in which incentives give rise to coercion. I have argued that the coercive force of a threat is determined by three factors: threat strength, threat imminence, and threat indifference. Further, threat imminence comes in three species, probabilistic, temporal, and epistemic. Schellenberg has set forth two serious challenges to the argument proposed by the soul-making account. First, he has argued that the probabilistic and temporal imminence of a threat attending a probabilifying revelation of God's existence and moral will for His creatures would sufficiently mitigate the force of the induced desire that it allows freedom of a sort sufficient to engage in soul-making. I have argued that by looking at parallel cases of coercion we have good reason to deny this claim. Second, Schellenberg attempts to show that there are actual cases in which free creatures who believe they have been the recipients of probabilifying revelation are still free in the sense required for soul-making. I have argued that the theist should expect that there would be some such probabilifying revelations but that, given the wide variability of threat indifference across individuals, such revelations would be and are rare.

Notice then that this response to Schellenberg makes for a strong case that divine hiddenness is, in most cases, the only way to go if God hopes to preserve the ability of free creatures to engage in soul-making. On the traditional Christian view, at any rate, the strength of the threat for failure to believe and/or obey is fixed: There will be severe negative consequences—some temporal, others eternal. I have argued furthermore that probabilistic and temporal imminence cannot be attenuated in such a way as to eliminate the coerciveness of such a probabilifying revelation. Finally, a good case can be made that creaturely threat indifference also cannot be mitigated, by God anyway, since it appears to be a character trait that we, in some measure, freely cultivate. To fix this feature of our character would be to interfere in our self-determination in just the way this account argues God ought not. As a result, the only remaining factor that can be attenuated is epistemic imminence, i.e., divine hiddenness, and this, it seems, is what God has done.

NOTES

1. "Coercion and the Hiddenness of God," *American Philosophical Quarterly,* Vol. 30, Number 1, pp. 27–38.

2. Although such evil is necessary here only in the sense that there is no world God can actualize which contains free creatures who do not go wrong (at least without a significant loss of overall goodness in the created world).

3. Nothing I have said here actually sustains such a strong conclusion. However, those theists who

propose libertarian freedom as an intrinsic good often cite its relation to moral good to ground its worth. Here I am arguing that there is no such intrinsic relation.

4. See his *Evil and the God of Love* (New York: Harper and Row, 1966 and 1977), pp. 255–61 and 318–36.

5. One might argue that this view on the purpose of the earthly life is summed up in the following passage from the second epistle of St. Peter: "Grace and peace be multiplied to you in the knowledge of God and of Jesus our Lord; seeing that His divine power has granted to us everything pertaining to life and godliness, through the true knowledge of Him who called us by His own glory and excellence. For by these He has granted to us His precious and magnificent promises, so that by them you may become partakers of the divine nature, having escaped the corruption that is in the world by lust. (11 Peter. 1::2–4)

6. Ephesians.5:1

7. Some Christian readers might fear that an account of this sort positively precludes the role of grace in salvation and sanctification, making it Pelagian *in excelsis*. I have responded to this charge in more detail in my "Heaven and Hell," in *Reason for the Hope Within,* Michael Murray (ed.) (Grand Rapids: William B. Eerdmans, 1998), pp. 298–9. But there is no reason on the view developed here for denying that grace is a necessary condition for soul-making. It cannot, however, be the case that such grace is intrinsically sufficient.

8. J. L. Schellenberg, *Divine Hiddenness and Human Reason* (Ithaca: Cornell University Press, 1993), p. 83.

9. Ibid., pp. 85–6.

10. Ibid., pp. 117–18.

11. Ibid., p. 121.

12. The question of whether or not offers can be coercive is widely disputed in the literature and cannot be addressed here. I have elsewhere argued that offers can be coercive, see, "Are Coerced Acts Free," David Dudrick and Michael Murray, *American Philosophical Quarterly,* Vol. 32, no. 2, p. 116.

13. One must, of course, define exactly what it means to be unable rationally to choose some course of action. I discuss this in detail in "Are Coerced Acts

Free?" pp. 116–19. Roughly, the idea is this. Each of us has a certain threshold such that if (i) a threat carries a grave enough consequence and (ii) the act required of the threatened by the threatener, P, is not, relative to the threat, sufficiently grave, then I am unable to deliberately choose to do anything other than P. So, for example, if one threatens to shoot me if I fail to touch my nose, I *cannot,* all other things being equal, choose to do other than touch my nose. Surely other factors might be added to the case that *would* make it possible for me to choose to do something other than touch my nose. For example, we might add that if I touch my nose I will suffer excruciating pain for eternity. Or we might add that I believe I have a bullet-proof vest on. But barring such additions to the case, I contend that *I* simply cannot choose to do other than touch my nose. To put it more strongly, no possible world continuous with a world segment up to that time, as described, contains me performing any free and deliberate action other than touching my nose.

14. The account of coercion here is vastly oversimplified. Unless a good deal is built into the notion of what counts as a threat, this definition will entail that I am coerced any time one course of action is vastly preferred by me over its competitors. Surely such an account fails to capture what is distinctive about coercion. A fully fleshed out account of coercion can be found in "Are Coerced Acts Free?" Op.cit.

15. *Divine Hiddenness and Human Reason,* pp. 121–4.

16. Schellenberg says this explicitly, "Even if the expectation of [temporal] punishment ... were prevalent in some quarters at first, upon further experience and reflection the understanding of humans might be expected to mature and deepen ... to the point where such views were universally rejected. Further, those who (unreasonably) expected severe punishment to follow each bad action would soon note that those who did not have this expectation, and so occasionally fell into temptation and did bad actions, were not immediately severely punished." *Divine Hiddenness and Human Reason,* p. 125.

17. Ibid., p. 124.

18. Of course, inevitable negative consequences alone are not sufficient for coercion. High threat strength,

probabilistic and epistemic imminence, and low threat-indifference must be present as well.

19. Schellenberg next presents a fallback position that the theist might retreat to in light of his criticisms discussed above. However, since I have argued these earlier criticisms fail, there seems little reason to discuss this weaker attempt to defend (16) and (17) which he proposes. His discussion of this fallback position is found at, Ibid., pp. 126–8.

20. Ibid., pp. 129–30.

21. In conversation, Schellenberg has indicated to me that he thinks this is the right response, and the one that gets to the heart of the argument from hiddenness. He also discusses this sort of position briefly at the close of section I in the essay in this volume.

22. I provide another response to this view in my "Coercion and the Hiddenness of God," section V.

23. Matthew 5:39-41.

17

Divine Hiddenness, Divine Silence

MICHAEL REA

Michael Rea (1968–) is professor of philosophy at the University of Notre Dame, and co-editor of the present volume. His research focuses primarily on metaphysics and philosophical theology. In this article, he explains why divine silence poses a serious intellectual obstacle to belief in God, and then goes on to consider ways of overcoming that obstacle. After considering several ways in which divine silence might actually be beneficial to human beings, he argues that perhaps silence is nothing more or less than God's preferred mode of interaction with creatures like us. Perhaps God simply desires communion rather than overt communication with human beings, and perhaps God has provided ways for us to experience God's presence richly even amidst the silence.

Several years ago, and a short while after her death, some of the private writings of Mother Teresa were published under the title *Come Be My Light*. The journal entries were shocking—not because they disclosed hidden sins or scandals, but because they revealed something far more troubling. They painted a picture of a woman celebrated for her faith and devotion to God but wracked by pain and doubt for lack of the felt presence of God in her life—a woman who sought God with tears and cried out for years for some small taste of the divine, for some tiny assurance in her soul of God's love and presence in her life, but, like so many of the rest of us, received nothing but silence in response. In one of the most poignant passages of the book, she writes:

> Lord, my God, who am I that You should forsake me? The child of your love—and now become as the most hated one— the one You have thrown away as

Published for the first time in the sixth edition of *Philosophy of Religion: An Anthology*, edited by Louis Pojman and Michael Rea (Cengage Learning, 2010). © 2010 by Michael Rea.

unwanted-unloved. I call, I cling, I want—and there is no One to answer—no One on Whom I can cling—no, No One.—Alone. The darkness is so dark ... The loneliness of the heart that wants love is unbearable.—Where is my faith?—even deep down, right in, there is nothing but emptiness & darkness.—My God—how painful is this unknown pain. It pains without ceasing ... I am told God loves me—and yet the reality of darkness & coldness & emptiness is so great that nothing touches my soul.... The whole time smiling—Sisters & people pass such remarks.—They think my faith, trust & love are filling my very being & that the intimacy with God and union to His will must be absorbing my heart.—Could they but know—and how my cheerfulness is the cloak by which I cover the emptiness & misery.—What are You doing My God to one so small?[1]

What indeed? What are we to make of the silence of God?

Divine silence—or, as many think of it, divine hiddenness—is the source of one of the two most important and widely discussed objections to belief in God. It is also, I venture to say, one of the most important sources of doubt and spiritual distress for religious believers. Mother Teresa eventually reconciled herself to a certain extent with God's hiddenness, but (moving all the way to the other edge of the continuum) Friedrich Nietzsche saw it as just one more reason to sneer at religious belief. He writes:

A god who is all-knowing and all-powerful and who does not even make sure his creatures understand his intention—could that be a god of goodness? Who allows countless doubts and uncertainties to persist, for thousands of years, as though the salvation of mankind were unaffected by them, or who, on the other hand, holds out the prospect of frightful consequences if any mistake is made as to the nature of truth? Would he not be a cruel god if he possessed the truth and could behold mankind miserably tormenting itself over that truth?—But perhaps he is a god of goodness notwithstanding and merely *could* express himself more clearly! Did he perhaps lack the intelligence to do so? Or the eloquence? So much the worse! For then he was perhaps also in error as to that which he calls his "truth," and is himself not so very far from being the "poor deluded devil"![2]

It's pretty clear that Nietzsche thinks that the existence of an all good, all powerful God is outright incompatible with our experience of divine hiddenness. But why? In the next section of this article, I will try briefly to answer this question. That is, I will try briefly to get clear on exactly what the problem of divine hiddenness is supposed to be. (Only briefly, though, because I think we all have at least a basic grasp of what the worry is.) After that, I'll spend the remainder of the article discussing three strategies for dealing with the problem.

THE PROBLEM OF DIVINE HIDDENNESS

The problem of divine hiddenness starts with the supposition that *God exists*. There is no problem (for adults) about the hiddenness of Santa Claus, or of unicorns, or leprechauns, or the like. We simply don't believe in these sorts of things. The problem of divine hiddenness arises under the supposition—genuine, or "for the sake of argument"—that God exists. The problem gains traction because our concept of God is the concept of a being that we *ought* to encounter—*tangibly and vividly*, it would seem—at some point in our lives. Again, there is no real problem of the hiddenness of abstract objects. Nobody says, "Well, if there are such things, why don't they show themselves once in a while?" They're just not that sort of thing. God, however, is supposed to be the sort of being who *would* show up once in awhile. But almost none of us ever really see God, hear God, touch God, or encounter God in any other palpable way. Even those who say that God speaks to them in prayer don't usually mean that they hear voices—or have any other experience apart from the felt conviction that some particular idea they've had is, in some sense, "from the Lord." That, in a nutshell, is the problem.

Why do we think that we ought to encounter God? Simple: Our concept of God is the concept of a perfectly rational, perfectly wise being who loves us like a perfect parent. A being like that would want to have a relationship with us; and we all know that, in order to have a relationship with someone, you have to communicate with him or her. This is why the junior high approach to romance does not work. You know how this goes: Boy sees girl; boy likes girl; and . . . boy takes every possible measure to prevent this fact from becoming known to girl. If people never grew out of this sort of immaturity, the human race would die out. So it's a safe bet that a perfectly *rational* God wouldn't take this approach in trying to relate to us. So it stands to reason that God would show up in our lives once in a while.

More seriously: The theistic religions are in full agreement about the fact that it is *bad for us* to spend our lives without a relationship with God. We all know that, all else being equal, it is bad for a child to grow up without a father or a mother, or to believe—for *good* reasons or bad—that her father or mother doesn't love her. We all know that good parents go out of their way to talk to their children, to reassure them of their love, to be present in vivid and tangible ways—ways that the child can understand and benefit from at whatever stage of life she's at—and so on. Good parents don't lock themselves in a room day after day, waiting for their children to acquire the wherewithal to seek them out. Good parents don't expect that their children will discover their love for them simply by way of inference from the orderliness of the living room and the presence of fun toys in the basement. Good parents go out of their way to say, "I love you," and to hold their children and to comfort them when they're sad. How much more, then, should

we expect the same from a being who (we're told) loves us *like a perfect parent?* If my daughter were crying out for my presence in the way that Mother Teresa cried out for God's, I would move heaven and earth if I could to be there for her. If my son were in despair because he thought that he had irreparably disappointed me, I would hold his hand and tell him that that's not true. How could I not? And yet I'm selfish, imperfect, lacking in resources, and short on wisdom, only human. How much more then should we expect God to respond to such cries?

Of course, I don't mean to suggest that God would be bound to respond in some *very particular way* to us when we cry out for his presence. Nor, I should think, would God be bound to respond *every single time*. Good parents sometimes turn a deaf ear to their children's cries, and often for the child's good; they sometimes leave their children with babysitters (even when it's not strictly necessary), ignoring vehement protests; and so on. So what kind of encounter with God am I saying that we ought to expect?

Well, it's hard to say exactly. But you might think that, at a minimum we ought to expect at least one of the following to be the case:

- *Our evidence should be conclusive:* It shouldn't be the case that one can be fully aware of the available evidence of God's existence and at the same time rationally believe that God does not exist.

or

- *Experience of God's love and presence should be widely available:* It shouldn't be the case that, in general, people never (or only very rarely) have experiences that seem to be experiences of the love or presence of God.

And yet both of these things that seem like they *shouldn't* be the case *are* the case. It is exactly this that I have in mind when I say that God is *hidden* or *silent*, and when I say that we don't encounter God often in palpable ways: Our evidence is inconclusive; religious experience—of the interesting and unambiguous sort—is rare. And it's really hard to see any good reason why God might leave matters this way.

So it looks like we have only three options: (a) We identify some mistake in our reasoning thus far; (b) we find some believable, good reason why God might remain hidden; or (c) we concede that there is no God. There is really no other way forward.

If you're interested in identifying a mistake in the reasoning, it helps to have the premises of the argument carefully laid out and numbered. Like so:

1. Suppose that God exists—that is, suppose that there is a perfectly powerful, perfectly wise being who loves us like a perfect parent.

2. God is mostly hidden from people: Our evidence is inconclusive; religious experience of the interesting and unambiguous sort is rare.

3. There is no good reason for God to remain hidden.

4. If God is mostly hidden and there is no good reason for God to remain hidden, then one of the following is true:

   a. God exists but, like a **negligent father**, does not love us enough to make himself known.

   b. God exists but, like an **inept lover**, lacks the wisdom to appreciate the importance or proper way of revealing himself to us.

   c. God exists but is **too weak** to reveal himself in the ways that he should in order to secure his relational goals.

5. Premises (1)–(4) are inconsistent.

6. Therefore: God does not exist.

This will be our official statement of the problem of divine hiddenness.[3]

DEALING WITH THE PROBLEM

The advantage to articulating a problem in the way that I just have—with numbered premises and inferences signaled with "therefore's"—is that it gives us a pretty systematic way of addressing the problem. If premises (1–4) *really are inconsistent* (and

I think they are, since our concept of God rules out 4a–4c), then one of them is false. The trick then is to ask about each one, "Is this premise true or false? And if it is false, why is it false?" In the next few minutes, I'll suggest some reasons for thinking that premises (2) and (3) might be false. My own sympathies lie with those who reject premise (3). But I'll start with some thoughts about premise (2).

Conclusive Evidence?

In St. Paul's epistle to the Romans, Paul writes:

> The wrath of God is being revealed from heaven against all the godlessness and wickedness of men who suppress the truth by their wickedness, since what may be known about God is plain to them, because God has made it plain to them. For since the creation of the world God's invisible qualities—his eternal power and divine nature—have been clearly seen, being understood from what has been made, so that men are without excuse. For although they knew God, they neither glorified him as God nor gave thanks to him, but their thinking became futile and their foolish hearts were darkened.[4]

Does it sound like St. Paul would agree with the claim that God is mostly hidden? No. On Paul's view, as some people read it, there is no reasonable Non-belief: Non-belief is due to sin. Or, a bit more softly, what passes for non-belief is really a kind of self-deception. Being an atheist is sort of like being an alcoholic in denial: You want so badly not to see the truth that you suppress it and convince yourself that things are how you want them to be.

This is an offensive doctrine. But I think that it has to be taken seriously. Self-deception is a real phenomenon; and there is nothing at all implausible about the idea that people would prefer—indeed, would want very badly—for there to be no God. One of my colleagues once pointed out that most sensible people would recoil in horror upon hearing that a person of great power and influence had taken a special interest in them and had very definite, detailed, and not-easily-implemented views about how they ought to live their lives. Along the same lines, eminent philosopher Thomas Nagel, in a now famous chapter entitled "Naturalism and the Fear of Religion," writes:

> I want atheism to be true and am made uneasy by the fact that some of the most intelligent and well-informed people I know are religious believers. It is not just that I do not believe in God, and, naturally, hope that I'm right in my belief. It's that I hope there is no God! I do not want there to be a God; I do not want the universe to be like that....
>
> My guess is that this cosmic authority problem is not a rare condition and that it is responsible for much of the scientism and reductionism of our time.[5]

So is it really so crazy to think—*on the supposition that there is a God, remember*—that many people would be in the grip of this kind of self-deception? No. To be sure, the view implies that a great many people—including many whom we regard as otherwise very wise and intelligent—suffer from a kind of deep-seated irrationality. But I don't think we should shrink from this sort of claim on principle. After all, atheists say that sort of thing about theists all the time.

Still, this is a hard doctrine, and it has some real problems as a general explanation of the phenomenon of divine hiddenness. Remember, even believers struggle with God's hiddenness. Many people seem to be utterly broken by divine silence in the midst of their own suffering or the suffering of others, or simply by the ongoing and unsatisfied longing for the presence of God. I've seen more than one friend break down in tears over this sort of thing. And remember Mother Teresa. Moreover, many people are atheists or agnostics despite years of what at least *seems* to them to be honest seeking after God. Is it possible that all of these people are radically self-deceived? Sure. But then we must ask why a compassionate God would allow such pervasive and destructive self-deception to go unchecked.

Every day drug, alcohol, and sex addicts, people with eating disorders and abusive personalities, and many others as well are made to face up to their own self-deception and admit to themselves and others what they very badly want to hide. Often—maybe mostly—they're made to do this by someone who simply confronts them vividly one way or another with the truth. Why wouldn't God do that for us? This question calls out for an answer as much as the original question of why God would remain hidden calls out for an answer. So denying that second premise seems to me to be just a way of relocating the problem—sort of like pushing around a bulge under the carpet instead of stomping it out entirely. And it seems that the only sensible answer is: God must have some very good reason.

Good Reason?

So now we come to the third premise: Maybe God does have a good reason for remaining hidden. But what could such a reason be? Here I want to consider two different *kinds* of response. One response says that he does it for *our* sake. Many philosophers think that, in general, God could be justified in permitting suffering of innocents only if the innocents themselves benefit.[6] The idea is that a perfectly loving being wouldn't make *me* suffer for the benefit of someone else. And even folks who think that God could allow some people to suffer for the benefit of others typically think that, at the very least, there would have to be some benefit to *human beings generally* in order for God to be justified in permitting the evils that come from his remaining hidden. The other sort of response denies this: God has reasons, but his reasons are his own and have nothing directly to do with benefiting us (which is why we often can't *see* any benefit to us in God's hiddenness). I'll take each in turn.

So first, what might be some of the ways in which *we* (humans generally) could benefit from divine hiddenness? Here I'll consider two suggestions.

First, one might think that hiddenness is necessary for preserving the *freedom and integrity* of our own responses to God.

Some folks suggest that if God were to show himself openly, we would effectively be coerced into submission. I have kids, and they each in their own ways sometimes try to manipulate and bully the other one. I want them to *freely* choose not to do this—which means I often don't appear in the doorway when I hear that the conditions for manipulation and bullying are growing ripe. If I appear in the doorway, they'll be on their guard; their freedom to grow will be, in a certain way, undermined.

That's one way of pitching the idea that divine hiddenness might help to preserve our freedom. But here's another: Suppose Bill Gates were to go back on the dating scene. Wouldn't it be natural for him to want to be with someone who would love him for himself rather than for his resources? Yet wouldn't it also be natural for him to worry that even the most virtuous of prospective dating partners would find it difficult to avoid having her judgment clouded by the prospect of living in unimaginable wealth? The worry wouldn't be that there would be anything coercive about his impressive circumstances; rather, it's that a certain kind of genuineness in a person's response to him is made vastly more difficult by those circumstances. But, of course, Bill Gates's impressiveness pales in comparison with God's; and, unlike Gates, God's resources and intrinsic nature are so incredibly impressive as to be not only overwhelmingly and unimaginably beautiful but also overwhelmingly and unimaginably *terrifying*. Viewed in this light, it is easy to suppose that God *must* hide from us if he wants to allow us to develop the right sort of non-self-interested love for him.

Note too that if this is God's motivation, divine hiddenness is as much for our benefit as God's. Which brings me to the second, but related, "benefit to us" strategy for understanding divine hiddenness. Perhaps God's hiddenness is good for our souls. Perhaps it helps to produce virtues in us that we wouldn't otherwise acquire. Maybe it teaches us to seek God, to hunger and thirst after him, to not take him for granted. Much in the scriptures suggests that this is what God wants for us. The psalmist writes, "As a deer longs for

flowing streams, so my soul longs for you, O God," (Ps. 42:1, NRSV) and the idea seems clearly to be that we *all* should long after God in this way. Likewise, at one point in the Gospels Jesus gives thanks to God for hiding certain things from those who are not seeking him; and he admonishes us to ask, *seek*, and *knock* (Mt. 11:25; Mt. 7:7). God wants us to be seekers after him, and what better way to cultivate that disposition than to hide?

Or maybe divine hiddenness teaches us that God cannot be manipulated by us—that God is not at our beck and call. We cannot summon God by performing the right sorts of incantations; God is maximally free, maximally authoritative, and will be manipulated by no one. This too might be a lesson that is good for us to learn, and so it, too, might be among the purposes of divine hiddenness.

The Personality of God?

Or maybe . . . just maybe . . . although divine hiddenness often *does* have these salutary effects, and others, that still is not their point at all.

The last suggestion I'd like to consider is one that sees divine hiddenness not as something that God does to produce some great good for us, but rather as something that God engages in for his own reasons, independently of (though not in violation of) our good. Throughout this talk I have sometimes used the term divine *silence* to refer to the phenomenon of hiddenness. I think that that's a more fruitful way of thinking of God's mode of interaction with us. And what I want to suggest is that perhaps divine silence is nothing more or less than an expression of God's personality.

Remember our problem: We experience divine silence and, under the assumption that God exists, we ask, "*What's his problem? Doesn't he love me? Doesn't he care? Doesn't he understand that you have to talk to people to relate to them? What kind of father is he?*" The objections implied by these rhetorical questions are altogether natural, but they are flawed. They are flawed in just the same way in which complaints about the behavior of human persons are often flawed: They depend on a particular interpretation of behavior that can in fact be interpreted in a number of different ways, depending upon what assumptions we make about the person's beliefs, desires, motives, dispositions, and overall personality.

Someone from your school doesn't greet you in the hallway. Have you hurt her feelings? Does she think you're a fool and not want to be seen talking to you? Does she think so poorly of herself that she thinks *you* wouldn't want to be seen talking to her? Is she depressed and having a bad day? As a matter of fact, she's the class genius—beautiful mind sort of genius—and she's always off in her own world, introverted and totally preoccupied. Does that affect your interpretation of her behavior?

You're on a first date. After a while you notice that you've been doing almost all the talking. You start asking questions to draw her out, but her answers are brief, and the silences in between grow longer and longer. You spend the entire ride home without saying a word. Does she hate you? Does she find you boring? Have you offended her? Or is she just rude? As it happens, she just arrived in the United States and was raised with the view that if you *really* want to win a man over, you should be quiet and let him do all the talking. Does that information affect your interpretation?

My point? Interpreting silence requires a lot of information about what sort of person you're dealing with—about the person's cultural background, about what sorts of social norms he or she is likely to recognize and respect, about his or her views about what various kinds of behavior (both verbal and not) communicate to others, about his or her general "style" of interacting with other people, about what's going on in his or her life, and so on. But if this is what it takes to interpret the behavior of an ordinary human person, imagine how difficult it must be to interpret the behavior of an invisible and transcendent *divine* person.

Seen in this light, the suggestion that divine silence *in and of itself* somehow indicates disinterest or lack of love and concern on God's part is absurd. God is as alien and "wholly other" from us as it is possible for another person to be. So isn't it almost ridiculous to think that we would have any idea what divine silence would indicate? To assume that divine silence indicates a lack of concern for us involves quite a lot of unwarranted assumptions about the degree to which divine modes of interaction would likely resemble 21st-century human modes of interaction.

Granted, divine silence *would* indicate a lack of concern for rational creatures if we had good reason to think that God had provided no way for us to find him or to experience his presence in the midst of his silence. This would indicate a lack of concern because it would indicate that God is *trying* to prevent us from finding him, or at least doing nothing to help, and thus bringing about something that is both intrinsically very bad for us and totally beyond our control. But as far as I can tell, we don't have good reason for thinking that God has left us without *any* way of finding him or experiencing his presence.

I think that we have a tendency to assume that we can experience God's presence only if we tangibly *perceive* something—a voice, a vision, an ache in our stomachs or our heads, a tingly feeling of some sort. But experiencing the presence of a person sometimes involves none of this. Sometimes it is just a matter of the person *being* present, together with our believing that she is present and taking a certain attitude toward her presence. Consider: You're studying in the library. You look up and you see a reflection in the window: The girl you've been in love with all year but never had the courage to ask out has entered the library behind you. Without seeing you, she turns down the aisle of books adjacent to yours—just a single stack of shelves separates you—and takes up a seat. She's out of your view, but is there any doubt that you'll experience her presence? And you would, even apart from the initial glimpse that alerted you to her presence—all you'd need to experience it—to *genuinely experience it*—is the true conviction that she's right there on the other side of those books, together with a certain kind of attention and attitude toward that conviction.

In her book *A Wind in the Door*, Madeline L'Engle makes this point very nicely by way of the distinction between communication and communion:

> "Hey, Meg! [says Calvin] Communication implies sound. Communion doesn't." He sent her a brief image of walking silently through the woods, the two of them alone together, their feet almost noiseless on the rusty carpet of pine needles. They walked without speaking, without touching, and yet they were as close as it is possible for two human beings to be.... Mr. Jenkins had never had that kind of communion with another human being, a communion so rich and full that silence speaks more powerfully than words."[7]

And, of course, silent communion is not the only way to experience a person unseen. Think of times when you relay a story about an encounter with another person and, after a bit of effort, you falter and say, "Well, you just had to be there." What you communicate, I think, is that your words have failed at their goal—the goal of *putting us there, of mediating to us an experience of a person we don't see and maybe have never met*. Sometimes we do fail in that way, but often we succeed. When you say "You just had to be there," nobody ever says, "Well, of course! You *always* have to be there; you simply can't convey an experience like that in words!" *Stories about other persons can mediate their presence to us—they can give us a taste of what it is like to be in the presence of the person, sort of like memories give us a taste of what it is like to be in the presence of the remembered event, even when we 're not*. Again, though, it matters that we *believe* that the person reporting the events in question is reporting events involving *real persons*. When we do, we can be transported and get at least a bit of what it's like to be around the person we're being told about. And this, it seems, is what biblical narrative—and, to a certain extent, the liturgies of the church—can do for us when we approach them with eyes of faith.[8]

My claim, then, is that divine silence might just be an expression of God's preferred mode of interaction, and that we need not experience his silence as *absence*—especially if we see Biblical narratives

and liturgies as things that in some sense mediate the presence of God to us, if we live out our lives in the conviction that God is ever present with us, and if we seek something more like *communion* with God rather than just communication.

The pressing question, however, is what to do with the fact that God's silence is *painful* for us. Many believers experience crippling doubt, overwhelming sadness, and ultimate loss of faith as a result of ongoing silence from their heavenly Father. On the assumption that God exists and that a loving relationship with God is a great good, it would appear that many people have been positively damaged by divine silence. Isn't it just this that leads us to take divine silence as evidence of God's lack of concern? Perhaps silence is just an expression of God's personality, but then, the objector might say, God's personality is just that of an unloving and inattentive parent.

The problem with this objection is that it completely ignores the fact that sometimes our being pained by another person's behavior is *our* problem rather than theirs—due to our own dysfunctional attitudes and ways of relating to others, our own epistemic or moral vices, our own immaturity, and the like. In such cases, it is our responsibility to find a way out of our suffering rather than the other person's responsibility to stop behaving in the ways that cause us pain. And maybe this is how it is with divine silence, too. Maybe our suffering in the face of divine silence is unreasonable, due more to our own immaturity or dysfunction than to any lack of kindness on God's part. Maybe it is a result of our own untrusting, uncharitable interpretations of divine silence, or an inappropriate refusal to accept God for who God is and to accept God's preferences about when and in what ways to communicate with us. And maybe there are ways of experiencing the world that are fully available to us, if only we would strive for maturity in the ways that we ought to, that would allow us to be content with or even to appreciate the silence of God in the midst of our joys and sufferings. Coping with divine silence, then, would just be a matter of finding these more positive ways of experiencing it.

It helps, in this vein, to be reminded of a fact about God and a fact about ordinary human relationships. The fact about God is that the most enigmatic, eccentric, and complicated people we might ever encounter in literature or in real life are, by comparison with God, utterly familiar and mundane. The fact about human relationships is that experiencing the silence of another person can, in the right context and seen in the right way, be an incredibly rich way of experiencing the *person*—all the more so with a person who is sufficiently beyond you in intellect, wisdom, and virtue. A wise and virtuous person who is utterly beyond you intellectually and silently leads you on a journey that might teach you a lot more about herself and about other things on your journey than she would if she tried to tell you all of the things that she wants to teach you. In such a case, objecting to the silence, interpreting it as an offence, or wishing that the person would just talk to you rather than make you figure things out for yourself might just be childish—an immature refusal to tolerate legitimate differences among persons and to be charitable in the way that you interpret another's behavior. And there is no reason to think that the person would owe it to you to cater to these objections—even if her decision to be silent was arrived at not for the sake of your greater good, but simply because *that's who she is, and that's how she prefers to communicate with people like you.*

You might be tempted to object that, on this view, God is like a father who neglects his children, leaving them bereft and unloved while he sits in stony silence thinking "I just gotta be me." But to object like this is to fail to take seriously the idea that God might have a genuine, robust personality and that it might be *deeply good* for God to live out his own personality. One odd feature of much contemporary philosophy of religion is that it seems to portray God as having a "personality" that is almost entirely empty, allowing his behavior to be almost exhaustively determined by facts about how it would be best *for others* for an omnipotent being to behave. But why should we think of God like this? God is supposed to be a person not only of unsurpassable love and goodness but of unsurpassable beauty. Could God really be *that* sort of person if he's nothing more than a cosmic, others-oriented, utility-maximizing machine? On that way of thinking, God—the being who is supposed to be a person *par excellence*—ends up having no real *self*. So, as I see it, silence of the sort we experience from God might just flow out of who God is, *and it might be deeply good for God to live out his personality*. If that's right, and if our suffering in the face of divine silence is indeed unreasonable, the result of immaturity or other dysfunctions that we can and should overcome anyway, then I see no reason why even perfect love would require God to desist from his preferred mode of interaction in order to alleviate our suffering.

On the view that I am developing, then, it is not true that divine silence serves no *greater good*. Rather, it serves the good that comes of the most perfect and beautiful person in the universe expressing himself in the way that he sees fit. This is good on its own terms, and it is justified if—as theists generally believe—God has provided ways (not our preferred ways, but ways nonetheless) of finding and experiencing his presence despite his silence. And if, as I have suggested, there are ways of experiencing divine silence that we would find non-burdensome or even beautiful, and if God's persisting in his silence provides opportunities for us to grow in maturity or in our ability to relate to others, then divine silence might even be good for us.[9]

NOTES

1. Mother Teresa, *Come Be My Light: The Private Writings of the Saint of Calcutta,* edited with commentary by Brian Kolodiejchuk, New York: Doubleday, 2007, pp. 186–87.

2. *Daybreak*, trans R. J. Holingdale, Cambridge: Cambridge University Press, 1982, pp. 89–90.

3. The most widely discussed articulation of the problem of divine hiddenness is J. L. Schellenberg's

Divine Hiddenness and Human Reason (Ithaca, NY: Cambridge University Press). *Divine Hiddenness: New Essays,* edited by Daniel Howard-Snyder and Paul K. Moser (Cambridge: Cambridge University Press, 2002) is another important volume which includes both further articulations of the problem as well as a variety of responses. All but the last of the responses that I present in the section entitled "Dealing with the Problem" are represented and defended in some detail in that volume. Finally, see also Ted Poston and Trent Dougherty, "Divine Hiddenness and the Nature of Belief," *Religious Studies* 43 (2007): 183–98, and my "Narrative, Liturgy, and the Hiddenness of God," pp. 76–96, in *Metaphysics and God: Essays in Honor of Eleonore Stump*, edited by Kevin Timpe (New York: Routledge, 2009).

4. Rom. 1:18–21; New Revised Standard Version Bible, copyright 1989, Division of Christian Education of the National Council of the Churches of Christ in the United States of America.

5. *The Last Word*, Oxford: Oxford University Press 2009; pp. 130–131.

6. See, e.g., Eleonore Stump, "The Problem of Evil," *Faith and Philosophy* 2 (1985): 393–423, and "Providence and the Problem of Evil," pp. 51–91 in *Christian Philosophy*, edited by Thomas P. Flint (Notre Dame, IN: University of Notre Dame Press, 1990). For critical discussion of this principle, along with references to other philosophers who endorse it, see Jeff Jordan, "Divine Love and Human Suffering," *International Journal for Philosophy of Religion* 56 (2004): 169–78.

7. *A Wind in the Door*, New York: Farrar, Straus, and Giroux, 1973, p. 171.

8. I develop this idea in more detail in "Narrative, Liturgy, and the Hiddenness of God." The idea takes inspiration from recent work by Eleonore Stump—especially her *Wandering in Darkness* (Oxford: Oxford University Press, 2010).

9. This essay has been given as a talk aimed at undergraduate and non-academic audiences on several occasions, most recently at Wake Forest University and Bethel College, South Bend.

Index

A

Accessibilism, 109
Actions
    consequences, 102–103
        approximation, 103–104
    good/evil, choice, 144
    identification, 104–105
    right-making/wrong-making
        features, 103
Adam
    fall, 11
    viewpoint, 71
Adams, Marilyn McCord, 72–73, 124, 134
Additional premises, 76
Agnostic
    assumptions, 98–101
    defining, 37
    doubt, 99
    perspective, 99–100
Agnosticism
    implication, 110
    preliminaries, 98–102
    versions, 97–98
        implication, 98
Agnostic thesis (AT), 97–98
Allen, Diogenes, 47
Analogy Argument, 62–65
    inductiveness, 67–68
    objections, 68
    success, 65–68
Animal suffering, evil (evidence), 38
Antecedent/consequent will, scholastic
        distinction, 119
Ante-mortem life, 130
Anthropomorphism, perseverance, 8
Antiperkinsus (Arminius), 14

Atheism
    arguments, 42
    indifferent atheism, 42
    justification, 61
    rational support, 40
Atheist, defining, 37
Atheist Argument, 145–146
    soul-making, impact, 147–148
Atheologian, claim, 80
Augustinian theodicy, 71

B

Beatrice of Nazareth, 138
Becoming Divine (Jantzen), 28
Beecher, Henry Ward, 45
Beneficence, duty, 108
Benevolence
    derivative value, 33
    increase, 34
Bernard of Clairvaux, 116, 120
Bertrand's Paradox, 106–107
Best, selection, 11, 15–16
Biological order, natural selection, 54
Bios, 95
Blessed fault (felix culpa), 4, 11
Blind process, 52
Books, examination, 86–87
Broad, C.D., 139
Brothers Karamazov, The (Dostoevsky), 4,
        58
    excerpt, 17–22
Bryan, William Jennings, 45

C

Calvin, John, 137
Cannibalism, 127

Cassian, 115
Cato, protest, 7
Causal determinism, freedom
        (incompatibility), 83
Causal necessity/possibility, 75
Causal ramification, 103, 106
Causal systems, sensitivity, 103
Children
    beating, 19
    torture, 18, 20
    unspoken kind words, 26
Children of God, creation, 93
Christ
    identification, 136
    love, 115
    mortification, 115
    passion, 125
Christianity
    falsity, 125
    internal coherence, 129
    stern-minded thinkers, 115
    truth, horrendous evils, 125
Cicero, fortune, 7
Circassians, crimes, 18
City of God, 12
Clark, Kelly James, 136
Clear and evident revelation, 152
Come Be My Light (Mother Teresa), 156
Conceptual Argument, 68–70
Conditional syllogism, 11
Confessions (Augustine), 116
Consequences
    cancellation, 106
    consideration, 102–108
        reduction, 108–110
    negative consequences, 152

Consequent/antecedent will, scholastic distinction, 119
Consequent will, result, 13–14
Creationism. *See* Special creationism
Creator, harmony, 135–136
Creel, Richard, 138
Critique of Pure Reason (Kant), 80

D

Darwin, Charles, 45, 49
Darwinian evolution, 46
Darwinism, likelihood, 51–52
Death, tranquility, 116
Deity, moral attributes, 8
Descartes, Rene, 76
Desires of the heart. *See* Heart
Determination, necessitation (contrast), 13
Deus absconditus, 142
    incentives/coercion, 148–150
Devil, human creation, 18
Direct attack, 41
Disability, attitude, 114
Disabled, viewpoints, 113–114
Divine, issue, 59–60
Divine agent, conception, 137
Divine benevolence, support (method), 9
Divine goodness, denial, 127
Divine hiddenness, 61, 143–145, 154, 156
    analogy argument, 62–65
    basis, 145
    circumstances, 63
    conceptual argument, 68–70
    freedom, preservation, 161
    problem, 27, 157–159
        interactions, 159–164
Divine Hiddenness and Human Reason (Schellenberg), 28, 73, 145
Divine indifference, 127
Divine intimacy theodicy, 134
    cruelty, 138–140
    design, 140
    inefficacy, 138–140
    objections, 138–140
    pathology, 138–140
Divine Mediator, 12
Divine passibility, 136–138
    doctrine, 138
    rejection, 136–137
Divine silence, 156
    indications, 162
Divine sorrow, understanding, 138
Draper, Paul, 27, 44, 133

E

Ekstrom, Laura Waddell, 72–73, 133
Enumerative induction, usage, 106
Epicurus, unanswered questions, 8

Epistemically forceful threatened consequence, 149
Epistemic humility, 97
Epistemic imminence, 149
    mitigation, 152–153
Eternal punishments, 151
Ethics, naturalistic fallacy, 30
Evidential arguments, 45
Evidential symmetry, 105–106
Evil
    absence, impact, 32–33, 78
    arguments, 97
    confusion, 117–119
    consistency, 80–81
    elimination, 77–78, 124
    evidence, 38
    evidential problem, 27–28
    evolution, 44, 45–50
    existence, 124
    extension, 125
    God creation, 81
    horrendous evil, 72, 124
    human free will, impact, 34
    Hume argument, 5
    illusion, 30
    inconsistency, 79–82
    inductive argument, 37
    interest, 24
    logical problem, 27
    moral evil, 58
    naming, 98
    necessity, 31–32
    overbalance/defeat, 126–127
    permission, 11, 14
        God's reason, 81, 99
    problems, 27, 29, 44, 56, 111
        response, 59
        return, 89
        solutions, 30–36
        split, 127
        treatment, 60
    quantity, 11–12
    soul-making, 92
Evil and the God of Love (Hick), 92
Evolution
    antecedent probability, 54
    defense, 46–47
    meaning, 46
Evolutionary naturalism, 51
Evolutionary theism, 52
Existence, prodigality, 96
Experience, religious character, 135
Explicit contradiction, proposition, 74
External insults, 6

F

False proposition, belief (justification), 42
Fascinans, 130

Feldman, Fred, 104
Felix culpa (blessed fault), 4, 11
First order evil, 33
First order good, 33
Frankfurt, Harry, 121, 137
Freedom
    causal determinism, incompatibility, 83
    morally significant freedom, 143–145
    preservation, 161
        theist explanation, 144
    prevention, 41
    senses, confusion, 35
    third order good, 34
    unpredictability, confusion, 82
Free human activity, impact, 82
Free Will, 34
    Defender, 81–82
        preliminary statement, 83
    defense, 57, 73, 81–84
        return, 89
    theodicies, 57–58, 81–82
    theory, paradox, 35
Friendly atheism, 43
Friendly atheists, 42

G

Gaon, Saadiah, 111, 121
General Relativity, theory, 99
Genetic thesis, 46
Global defeat, insufficiency, 126–128
Global goods, producer, 126
God
    absence, 146
    actions, limitations, 31
    antecedent/consequent will, scholastic distinction, 119
    architect, 94–95
    being, greatness, 129
    belief
        evidence, absence, 69
        objections, 157
        theological reason, 129
    character, examination, 133–134
    characterization, 95
    concept, 151, 158
    creative power, 94
    creative work, 93
    differences, 66
    emphasis, 60
    encounter, reasons, 158
    eternal power, 143
    evidence, 148
    existence, 87, 124, 157–159
        awareness, 146, 148
        issue, 135

God (*Cont.*)
    probabilifying demonstration/
        revelation, 147
    revelations, 150
experiences, 130
figures of speech, usage, 137
good, 127
goodness, 29, 124
    impact, 130
hiddenness, 140, 144, 159
    requirement, 145
infinite resourcefulness, 67
intimacy, opportunity, 140
love, 69
loving, 145–146
    relationship, 65–66
moral perfection, 65
nature, issue, 135
nearness/comfort, 134
nonexistence, 87
omnipotence, 29, 74, 78, 83
omniscience, 35, 78, 83
passibility, support, 137–138
personality, 161–164
pity, 138
pleasure-maximizer, 125
power
    limitation, 76
    nonlogical limitations, absence,
        83–84
preferences, 163–164
presence
    indication, 66
    theist sense, 135
rationality, implication, 47–48
relationship, flourishing, 67
responses, freedom/integrity
        (preservation), 160–161
silence, pain, 163
victory, 128–130
worship-worthiness, 65
God-and-Man, blessed head, 135
Gödel's theorem, 128
God, existence
    debates, 59–60
    impossibility, 57
    question, 62
    theist belief, 43
God-justifying goods, presence, 100
God of love, meeting, 113–114
God's children, 65
Good
    absence, 38–39
    Agnostic perspective, 100
    doubt, 99
    evil, coexistence, 31
    form (Platonism), 129

global scale, 126–127
necessity, 31–32
Goodness
    divine goodness, denial, 127
    insufficiency, 15
    libertarian freedom simpliciter,
        intrinsic goodness, 144
Goods
    God supply, 114
    total population, members
        (comprehension/
        understanding), 101
Gould, Stephen Jay, 45
Grand public theophanies, expectation,
        153
Great, absolute/relative term, 31–32

H
Happiness, basis, 24–25
Harmony, sense, 8
Hartshore, Charles, 136
Heart, desires, 111, 112–114
    notion, precision, 112
    person, flourishing, 120–121
    suffering, origin, 113
Heaven, confusion, 95
Heidelberg catechism, 130
Hick, John, 71, 92, 111–112
Hiddenness
    form, 67
    language, 62
Hitler, Adolf, 103
Holy Spirit, indwelling, 113
Horrendous evil, 72, 124
    category, defining, 125–126
    God's victory, 128–130
    overcoming, 130
    personal meaning, 129–130
    solutions
        impotence, 126–128
        reasons, 128
    whys, hows (contrast), 128–129
Horrors
    application, 127
    defeat, 129–130
    paradigmatic horrors, 126
Howard-Snyder, Daniel, 72, 97
Hull, John, 114
Human experience, commonness, 65
Human flourishing
    intrinsic value, 113
    measure, 112
    positive value, assignation, 115
    sufficiency, 114–115
Human freedom, prevention, 41
Human free will, impact, 34
Human life, improvement, 128

Human love, instances, 137
Human misery, feeling, 7
Human relationships, 164
Human responsibility, 59–60
Human suffering
    allowance, 112
    evil, evidence, 38
Hume, David, 4–5, 41, 94, 133

I
Identity-affecting, 110
Ignorance, varieties, 128–129
Imagination, loss, 96
Imitators, 145
Impassibilism, survival, 138
Inaccessibilism, 108, 109
Indifference, 105–106
    avoidance, 107
    divine indifference, 127
Indifferent atheism, 42
Indirect attack, 41
Inductive inference, usage, 106
Inept lover, 159
Intentions, betrayal, 8
Intervening, consequences, 102
Intervention
    expected value, 104
    prima facie rightness, 109
    unforeseeable consequences, 107
Irenaean tradition, 93

J
Jantzen, Grace M., 28, 56
Jesus, Messianic vocation, 126
Job
    adjudication, 119
    injustice, 133
    story, suggestions, 128–129
John of the Cross, 134

K
Kant, Immanuel, 80
King, Coretta Scott, 112, 113

L
Lazy sophism, 13
Learned, vulgar (agreement), 5
Leibniz, Gottfried, 4, 10, 71, 84
    Lapse, 89
L'Engle, Madeline, 162–163
Lenman, James, 103, 106
Levinas, Emmanuel, 28, 58
Libertarian freedom simpliciter, intrinsic
        goodness, 144
Life
    forms, existence, 50
    miseries, human complaints, 7

Logic
    laws, 76
    truth, 75
Logical arguments, 45
Logical necessity, 75
Love, 64
    properties, 63
Love of God, love of other persons
    (competition), 119
Loving Father, label, 65
Loving properties, conjunction, 64
Luther, Martin, 76

M

Mackie, J.J., 27, 29, 71, 73, 84
Man
    creation, two-stage conception,
        93–94
    enemy, 6
    finitely perfect being, 93
    God's creation, 93
    life, environment, 95–96
Mankind, moral progress, 58
Material object, knowledge (absence),
    41
McMullin, Ernan, 48
Medieval Christian tradition, history,
    113
Mill, John Stuart, 128
Mind, disorders, 7
Misery, first order evil, 33
Monotheisms, claim, 111
Moore, G.E., 41–42
    shift, application, 42
Moral Accessibilism, 109
Moral evil, 58
    creation, problem, 84
    permission, absence, 84
Moral good
    creation, problem, 84
    creatures, creation, 83
Morally significant freedom, 143–145
    intrinsic freedom, 145
Moral necessity, 16
Moral skepticism, 97
Moral Skepticism Objection, 98, 109
    premise, 107
    simple version, 98
Mother Teresa, 156
Murray, Michael J., 73, 142

N

Natural event, cause, 48
Naturalism, 46–47
    plausibility, 55
    probability, theism probability (ratio),
        54

Naturalistic fallacy, 30
Naturalistic science, success, 49
Natural necessity/possibility, 75
Natural selection, 52
Negative consequences, 152
Negligent father, 159
Neighbors, love
    importance, 116
    misunderstanding, 17
Nietzsche, Friedrich, 157
Non-horrendous evils, divine
    permission, 128
Nonintervention
    expected value, 104
    total consequences, 102–103
    unforeseeable consequences, 107
Non-zero probability, 150–151
No-self position, self-denial
    (incompatibility), 120

O

Objection. *See* Moral Skepticism
    Objection
    premise, rejection, 109
Objective Maximizing Act
    Consequentialism (OMAC),
        102–108
    endorsement, 102, 103
    expected value, 104
Objective Rossianism (OR), 108
Objector, troubles, 139–140
Obligatory/supererogatory actions,
    distinction, 153–154
Omelas, 23
    happiness, 4
Omnipotence, 29–30
    paradox, 31, 35
    sovereignty, analogy, 36
Omnipotent being
    limitations, absence, 124
    nonlogical limits, 76
Omnipotent/omniscience being,
    reasons, 51
Omniscient, wholly good (OG) being
    existence, 42
    impact, 38–39
On the Origin of Species (Darwin), 45, 49
Onto-theology, realist assumptions, 57
Operative attribute-analyses, accuracy,
    125
OR. *See* Objective Rossianism
Ora et labora (pray and work), 13
Ordinary logic, laws, 75
Other, presentation, 59
Others, self-centeredness, 113
Otto, Rudolf, 130, 134
Outcomes, identification, 105

P

Pain
    first order evil, 33
    increase, 9
    intellectual aspect, 24
    logical problem, 50–51
    pattern, meaning, 27–28
    pleasure
        relationship, 50–53
        systematic connection, 46
Paley, William, 51
Paradigmatic horrors, 126
Paradox of Omnipotence, 31, 35
Paradox of Sovereignty, 36
Partial evil, 30
Patermutus, 115
Perceived, God provisions, 153
Perfect person, defining, 45
Perpetual war, 6
Person
    experience, importance, 163
    silence, experience, 164
Personal horrors, 129
Personality disturbance, 138
Physical universe, closed system, 45
Plantinga, Alvin, 27, 48, 71, 73, 126
    suffering, 136
Platonism, 129
Pleasure, pattern (meaning), 27–28
Pleasure-maximizer (God), 125
Post-mythological era, 49
Pre-original position, 127
Prima facie rightness, 109
Private revelation, 153
Probabilistic imminence, 149
Prosyllogism, 11
Provine, William B., 45, 48
Psalm 47, 81, 137, 143
Psalmists, 112
Punishment
    reasons, 12–13, 15
    receiving, 151

Q

Quasi-logical rules, 76

R

Real, production, 14–15
Rea, Michael, 73, 156
Reasonable nonbelief, occurrence, 146
Reason-why
    inaccessibility, 128
    search, 126
Rebellion, defining, 22
Religion, philosophy (consequences), 70
Religious beliefs system, internal
    coherence, 125

Religious experience
    nature, 134–135
    suffering, 135–136
    understanding, 134
Representations, exaggeration, 9
Reproductive success, 51–52
    connection, 53
Requirement Ro/Rs, 109
Rowe, William, 27, 37, 133

S

Schellenberg, J.L., 28, 61, 73, 143
    arguments, 151–152
    critique, assessment, 150–154
    problem, 151
Second order good, 33
Secundum quid, 116–117
Self-centeredness, 113
Self-denial, 119–120
    Christian doctrine, 119
    no-self position, incompatibility, 120
Sensus divinitatus, 134
Seven Manners of Love, The (Beatrice of
    Nazareth), 138
Silence
    divine silence, 156
    interpretation, 162
Simpliciter, 116–117
Sin
    accessory (status), 13–14
    cause, 14–15
Skeptical theism, 98–99
Skeptical theist, defense, 72
SMAC. *See* Subjective Maximizing Act
    Consequentialism
Small, absolute/relative term, 31–32
Social intercourse, purpose, 116
Sons of glory, bringing, 94
Soul-making, 92
    account, 148
    impact, 147–148
    response, 147–148
        critique (Schellenberg), 145–147
    veil, 57–58, 71–72
Soul, testing, 111
Sovereignty, paradox, 36
Special creationism, 47–48
    theistic objections, problem, 48
Special creationists, arguments
    (weakness), 50
SR. *See* Subjective Rossianism

St. Aquinas, 116–117, 120
St. Augustine, 81, 116
Stern-minded attitude, 114–117,
    119–120
St. Paul, 93
    epistle, 143, 159
String Theory, 99
Stump, Eleonore, 72–73, 111, 134
Subjective Maximizing Act
    Consequentialism (SMAC),
    108–109
Subjective Rossianism (SR), 108–109
Suffering, 60
    allowance, 39
    evil, evidence, 38
    instances, prevention, 38–40
    occurrence, prevention, 38–40
    origin, 113
    prevention, 38–39
        total consequences, 102–103
    religious experience, 133, 135–136,
        140
    unwilling innocents, 112
Supernatural phenomena, delusion, 139
Suppositions, admission, 9
Supremely Valuable Object, 129
Surin, Ken, 58
Swinburne, Richard, 136
Symbolic, values, 58
Sympathetic identification, 129–130

T

Taliaferro, Charles, 136, 138
Teleology, elimination, 49
Temporal imminence, 149
Temporal punishments, 151
Teresa of Avila, work, 115–116
Theism
    evolutionary arguments, 46
    meaning, 44–45
    probability, ratio, 54
    rational defense, 40–42
    traditional theism, 70
Theist
    defining, 37
    direct/indirect attack, 41
    responses, 40–41
    self-contradiction, 73–79
    strategy, defense, 72
    viewpoint, 42–43
Theistic evolution, 45

Theistic religions, agreements, 158
Theodicy, 4, 57
    attack, 112
    Augustinian theodicy, 71
Theology and the Problem of Evil (Surin),
    58
Therese of Lisieux, 134, 138
Third order good, 34
Threatener, existence (certainty), 150
Threat imminence, 149
Threat-indifference, 149–150
Threat-induced desires, 149
Threat strength, 148–149
Tillich, Paul, 37
Traditional Christian view, 152
Traditional theism, 70
Transworld depravity, hypothesis, 71
Truth, Sojourner, 113
Tubman, Harriet, 113
Turks, crimes, 18

U

Unwilling innocents, sufferings, 112

V

Valuables, type, 129
Value-judgment, 94
Vanier, Jean, 113
Van Till, Howard J., 47, 48

W

Web of desire, 112–113
Will
    freedom, incoherence, 34
    supposition, 13
Wind in the Door, A (L'Engle), 162–163
Wolterstorff, Nicholas, 133, 134, 136
World
    actualization, 88
        impossibility, 89
    book, correspondence, 86
    creation, God (avoidance), 89
    examination, 87–88
    God's creation, 11
        power, 84–89
    moral good, presence (God creation),
        90–91
Worship, sense, 114

Z

Zoe, quality, 95